HOLMAN

Psalms & Proverbs

HOLMAN CHRISTIAN STANDARD BIBLE®

H
HOLMAN
BIBLE PUBLISHERS
NASHVILLE, TENNESSEE

Holman Christian Standard Bible® New Testaments available:

HCSB *UltraTrim New Testament*—Black bonded leather, 1-58640-009-6; Burgundy bonded leather, 1-58640-005-3; Paperback, 1-58640-004-5

HCSB *Experiencing the Word New Testament*—Burgundy bonded leather, 1-58640-008-8; Hardcover, 1-58640-007-X; Paperback, 1-58640-006-1

HCSB *Here's Hope New Testament*—Paperback, 1-58640-003-7

HCSB *Share Jesus Without Fear New Testament, Personal Evangelism Edition*—Black bonded leather, 1-58640-012-6

HCSB *Share Jesus Without Fear New Testament, TruthQuest™ Student Edition*—Black bonded leather, 1-58640-013-4

HCSB *Reader's Text Large Print Edition New Testament*—Paperback, 1-58640-019-3

Please visit us online at www.broadmanholman.com to view a complete list of available products and for additional information regarding the *Holman Christian Standard Bible®*.

ISBN 0-8400-4142-X
Printed in Canada

$\mathscr{I}$ntroduction

The Bible is God's inspired word, inerrant in the original manuscripts. It is the only means of knowing God's plan of salvation and His will for our lives. It is the only hope and answer for a rebellious, searching world. Bible translation, both a science and an art, is a bridge that brings God's word from the ancient world to the world today. Depending on God to accomplish this task, Holman Bible Publishers presents the *Holman Christian Standard Bible*®, a new English translation of God's word.

The Goals of This Translation

- to provide English-speaking people across the world with an accurate, readable Bible in contemporary English
- to equip serious Bible students with an accurate translation for personal study, private devotions, and memorization
- to give those who love God's word a text that is easy to read, visually attractive on the page, and appealing when heard
- to affirm the authority of the Scriptures as God's inerrant word and to champion its absolutes against social or cultural agendas that would compromise its accuracy.

The name, *Holman Christian Standard Bible*®, embodies these goals: *Holman* Bible Publishers presents a new *Bible* translation, for the *Christian* and English-speaking communities, which will set the *standard* in Bible translations for years to come.

Translation Philosophy

Bible translations generally follow one of three approaches to translating the original Hebrew, Aramaic, and Greek words into English:

1. <u>Formal Equivalence</u>: Often called "word for word" translation, formal equivalence seeks to represent each word of the original text with a corresponding word in the translation so that the reader can see word for word what the original human author wrote. The merit of this approach is that the Holy Spirit did inspire the very words of Scripture in the original manuscripts. A formal equivalent translation is good to the extent that its words accurately convey the meaning of the original words. However, a literal rendering can result in awkward English or in a misunderstanding of the author's intent.

2. <u>Dynamic Equivalence</u>: Often called "thought for thought" translation, dynamic equivalence seeks to translate the meaning of biblical words so the text makes the same impact on modern readers that the ancient text made on its original readers. Strengths of this approach include readability and understandability, especially in places where the original is difficult to render word for word. However, some serious questions can be asked about dynamic equivalence: How can a modern translator be certain of the original author's intent? Since meaning is

always conveyed by words, why not ensure accuracy by using words that are as close as possible in meaning to the original instead of words that just capture the idea? How can a modern person ever know the impact of the original text on its readers?

3. *Optimal Equivalence:* This approach seeks to combine the best features of both formal and dynamic equivalence. In the many places throughout Scripture where a word for word rendering is clearly understandable, a literal translation is used. In places where a literal rendering might be unclear, then a more dynamic translation is given. The HCSB® has chosen to use the balance and beauty of optimal equivalence for a fresh translation of God's word that is both faithful to the words God inspired and "user friendly" to modern readers.

History of the *Holman Christian Standard Bible*®

After several years of preliminary development, Holman Bible Publishers, the oldest Bible publisher in America, assembled an international, interdenominational team of 90 scholars, all of whom were committed to biblical inerrancy. This team completed the initial translation. Smaller teams of editors, stylists, and proofreaders then corrected and polished the translation. Outside consultants contributed valuable suggestions from their areas of expertise. An executive team then reviewed the final manuscripts.

Textual Base of the HCSB®

The textual base for the New Testament [NT] is the Nestle-Aland *Novum Testamentum Graece*, 27th edition, and the United Bible Societies' *Greek New Testament*, 4th corrected edition. The text for the Old Testament [OT] is the *Biblia Hebraica Stuttgartensia*, 5th edition.

Significant differences among Hebrew [Hb] and Aramaic [Aram] manuscripts of the OT, or among Greek [Gk] manuscripts of the NT are indicated in footnotes. In a few NT cases large square brackets indicate texts that are omitted in some ancient manuscripts. The HCSB® uses traditional verse divisions found in most Protestant Bibles in English.

Translation Features

In keeping with a long line of Bible publications, the *Holman Christian Standard Bible*® has retained a number of features found in traditional Bibles:

1. Traditional theological vocabulary (such as *justification, sanctification, redemption,* etc.) has been retained in the HCSB®, since such terms have no translation equivalent that adequately communicates their exact meaning.
2. Traditional spellings of names and places found in most Bibles have been used to make the HCSB® compatible with most Bible study tools.
3. To help readers easily locate the spoken words of the Lord Jesus Christ, some editions of the HCSB® will print the words of Christ in red letters.
4. Most nouns and pronouns that refer to any person of the Trinity are capitalized.
5. Descriptive headings, printed above each section of Scripture, help readers quickly identify the contents of that section.

6. Small lower corner brackets: ⌊ ⌋ indicate words supplied for clarity by the translators (but see discussion below, under <u>Agreement of Elements in Sentences</u>,
   about supplied words that are *not* bracketed).

Translation Style Issues

The Names of God

The HCSB® OT consistently translates the Hb names for God as follows:

HCSB® English:	Hb original:
God	*Elohim*
Lord	Yahweh or YHWH
Lord	*Adonai*
Lord God	*Adonai Yahweh*
Lord of Hosts	*Yahweh Sabaoth*
God Almighty	El Shaddai

The HCSB® uses *Yahweh*, the personal name of God in Hb, when a text emphasizes *Yahweh* as a name: His name is *Yahweh* (Ps 68:4).

Agreement of Elements in Sentences

The original text of the Bible does not always follow the standard rules of English grammar, especially in the agreement of subject and verb or agreement of person and number. In order to conform to standard usage, the HCSB® has often made these kinds of grammatical constructions agree in English and has not noted them using footnotes or lower corner brackets.

In addition, the Gk or Hb texts sometimes seem redundant or ambiguous by repeating nouns when we would substitute pronouns or by repeating pronouns when we would supply nouns for clarity and good style. The HCSB® sometimes changes a pronoun to its corresponding noun or a noun to its corresponding pronoun in the interests of clarity and good English style without noting this change with a footnote or lower corner brackets.

Special Formatting Features

The *Holman Christian Standard Bible*® has several distinctive formatting features:

1. OT passages quoted in the NT are set in boldface type. OT quotes less than two lines long are embedded in the Bible text. Quotes consisting of two or more lines are block indented.
2. In dialogue, a new paragraph is used for each new speaker as in most modern publications.
3. Many passages, such as 1 Co 13, have been formatted as Dynamic Prose (separate lines that are block indented like poetry) for ease in reading and comprehension.
4. A series of persons or items may be indented as a list. Examples are the genealogy of Christ (Mt 1:2-16), the 12 apostles (Mt 10:2-4), and the precious stones in the New Jerusalem (Rv 21:19-20).
5. A written inscription that was posted for people to read, such as the sign above Jesus on the cross (Mt 27:37), is placed inside a box and centered in the text.

6. Frequently used foreign, geographical, cultural, or ancient words are preceded by a superscripted bullet [•*Abba*] and listed in alphabetical order at the back of most editions under the heading HCSB Bullet Notes™.

Footnotes

Located at the bottom of the page, footnotes provide valuable information to help the reader understand the original biblical language or how it is translated in the HCSB®. The words of Scripture, quoted in a footnote, are always printed in *italics*.

OT Textual Notes

OT textual notes show important differences among Hb manuscripts and among ancient OT versions, such as the Septuagint (LXX) and the Vulgate (Vg). Some OT textual notes give only the alternate textual reading, but other OT textual notes list the manuscripts and versions that support a reading found in the HCSB® text and are followed by a semicolon, the alternative reading, and the manuscript evidence supporting that reading. For example, Ps 12:7 reads:

You will protect us[a] from this generation forever.

The textual footnote for this verse reads:

[a] **12:7** Some Hb mss, LXX; other Hb mss read *him*

The textual note in this example means that there are two different readings found in the Hb manuscripts: some manuscripts read *us* and others read *him*. The HCSB® translators decided to put the reading *us* in the text (which is also supported by the Septuagint [LXX]); the other reading *him* is placed in the footnote.

Occasionally, variations by scribal copyists in the Hb manuscript tradition will be noted as follows (in OT studies, these variations are referred to as *Kethiv/Qere* readings):

Alt Hb tradition(s) reads _____

A few times when there is uncertainty about what the original Hb text was, the following note is used:

Hb uncertain

Other Kinds of Footnotes

Lit _____	a literal rendering in English of the Hebrew, Aramaic, or Greek text
Or _____	an alternate English translation of the same Hebrew, Aramaic, or Greek text
Hb, Aram, Gk	the actual Hebrew, Aramaic, or Greek word is given using English letters
Hb obscure	in the OT, when the original Hebrew wording is difficult to translate
emend(ed) to_____	informs the reader that the original Hb text is so difficult to translate that in rare cases scholars have conjectured what the original text was in order to translate it.

Additional footnotes clarify the meaning of certain biblical texts or explain biblical history, persons, customs, places, activities, and weights and measures. Cross references are given for some parallel passages or passages with similar wording, and in the NT, for passages quoted from the OT.

Commonly Used Abbreviations in the HCSB®

A.D.	in the year of our Lord
alt	alternate
a.m.	from midnight until noon
Aram	Aramaic
B.C.	before Christ
c.	circa
chap	chapter
DSS	Dead Sea Scrolls
Eng	English
Gk	Greek
Hb	Hebrew
Lat	Latin
Lit	Literally
LXX	Septuagint—an ancient translation of the Old Testament into Greek
MT	Masoretic Text
NT	New Testament
ms(s)	manuscript(s)
OT	Old Testament
p.m.	from noon until midnight
pl	plural
Ps(s)	psalm(s)
Sam	Samaritan Pentateuch
sg	singular
syn.	synonym
Sym	Symmachus
Syr	Syriac
Tg	Targum
Theod	Theodotian
v., vv.	verse, verses
Vg	Vulgate—an ancient translation of the Bible into Latin
vol(s).	volume(s)

$\mathscr{P}$salms

BOOK I
PSALMS 1–41
PSALM 1
THE TWO WAYS

1   How happy is the man
    who does not follow the advice of the wicked,
    or take[a] the path of sinners,
    or join a group[b] of mockers!
2   Instead, his delight is in the LORD's
        instruction,
    and he meditates on it day and night.[c]
3   He is like a tree planted beside streams
        of water[d]
    that bears its fruit in season[e]
    and whose leaf does not wither.[f]
    Whatever he does prospers.
4   The wicked are not like this;
    instead, they are like husks that the wind blows
        away.
5   Therefore the wicked will not survive[g]
        the judgment,
    and sinners will not be in the community
        of the righteous.
6   For the LORD watches over the way
        of the righteous,
    but the way of the wicked leads to ruin.

PSALM 2
CORONATION OF THE SON

1   Why do the nations rebel[h]
    and the peoples plot in vain?

NOTES

a **2:2** Or *anointed one*
b **2:1-2** Ac 4:25-26
c **2:3** Lit *and throw their ropes from us*
d **2:3** Ps 149:8
e **2:4** Lit *who sits*
f **2:6** Or *king*
g **2:6** Ps 48:2; Jr 8:19
h **2:7** Or *me, 'You are My son*
i **2:7** Or *your*
j **2:7** Mt 3:17; Lk 3:22; Ac 13:33; Heb 1:5; 5:5
k **2:8** Or *your*
l **2:8** Or *your*
m **2:9** LXX, Syr, Tg read *shepherd*
n **2:9** Or *you*
o **2:9** Lit *a potter's vessel*
p **2:8-9** Rv 2:26-27; 12:5; 19:15
q **2:12** Lit *Kiss*
r **2:12** Or *son otherwise he*
s **2:12** Lit *perish way*
t **2:12** Or *his*
u **2:12** Or *him*
v **3:3** Ps 5:12; 28:7

WORD STUDY

Hebrew word:
goy [GOY]

HCSB translation:
nation

Focus passage:
Psalm 2:1,8

Goy refers to a group of people defined by political or territorial affiliation or by ethnicity (Gn 10:5). The OT uses *goy* in a variety of contexts, some referring to the nations that would descend from Abraham (Gn 17:4-6) or to the *nation* of Israel (Ex 19:6). *Goy* is most often used in reference to foreign *nations* outside Israel (Is 11:10,12), emphasizing the paganism of the *nations* that do not follow Israel's God (Dt 9:4,5). These idolatrous *nations* are hostile to God and His people (Lv 26:33,38). Traditional Bible translations often translate the plural form of this word (*goyim*) as *heathen* or *Gentiles*.

2 The kings of the earth take their stand
and the rulers conspire together
against the LORD and His Anointed One:[a] [b]
3 "Let us tear off their chains
and free ourselves from their restraints."[c] [d]
4 The One enthroned[e] in heaven laughs;
the Lord ridicules them.
5 Then He speaks to them in His anger
and terrifies them in His wrath:
6 "I have consecrated My King[f]
on Zion, My holy mountain."[g]
7 I will declare the LORD's decree:
He said to Me, "You are My Son;[h]
today I have become Your[i] Father.[j]
8 Ask of Me, and I will make the nations
Your[k] inheritance
and the ends of the earth Your[l] possession.
9 You will break[m] them with a rod of iron;
You[n] will shatter them like pottery."[o] [p]
10 So now, kings, be wise;
receive instruction, you judges of the earth.
11 Serve the LORD with reverential awe,
and rejoice with trembling.
12 Pay homage to[q] the Son, or He[r] will be angry,
and you will perish in your rebellion,[s]
for His[t] anger may ignite at any moment.
All those who take refuge in Him[u] are happy.

PSALM 3

CONFIDENCE IN TROUBLED TIMES

A psalm of David when he fled from his son Absalom.

1 LORD, how my foes increase!
There are many who attack me.
2 Many say about me,
"There is no help for him in God." •*Selah*
3 But You, LORD, are a shield around me;[v]
⌊You are⌋ my glory,
and the One who lifts up my head.
4 I cry aloud to the LORD,
and He answers me
from His holy mountain. •*Selah*

5 I lie down and sleep;
I wake again because the LORD
   sustains me.
6 I am not afraid of the thousands of people
who have taken their stand against me
   on every side.^a
7 Rise up, LORD!
Save me, my God!
You strike all my enemies on the cheek;
You break the teeth of the wicked.
8 Salvation belongs to the LORD;^b
may Your blessing be on Your people.   •*Selah*

^a **3:6** Ps 27:3
^b **3:8** Rv 7:10
^c **4:1** Or *God of my righteousness*
^d **4:1** Ps 25:17; 107:6,13
^e **4:4** Or *Tremble*
^f **4:4** Eph 4:26
^g **4:4** Ps 77:6; 119:55
^h **4:5** Or *Offer right sacrifices*; lit *Sacrifice sacrifices of righteousness*
ⁱ **4:6** Ps 80:3; Nm 6:26
^j **4:8** Ps 3:5; Dt 12:10; Jb 11:19

PSALM 4

A NIGHT PRAYER

For the choir director: with stringed instruments.
A Davidic psalm.

1 Answer me when I call,
O God who vindicates me.^c
You freed me from affliction;^d
be gracious to me and hear my prayer.
2 How long, exalted men, will my honor
   be insulted?
⌊How long⌋ will you love what is worthless
   and pursue a lie?   •*Selah*
3 Know that the LORD has set apart the faithful
   for Himself;
the LORD will hear when I call to Him.
4 Be angry^e and do not sin;^f
on your bed, reflect in your heart and be still.^g
                    •*Selah*
5 Offer sacrifices in righteousness^h
and trust in the LORD.
6 Many are saying, "Who can show us anything
   good?"
Look on us with favor, LORD.ⁱ
7 You have put more joy in my heart
than they have when their grain and new wine
   abound.
8 I will both lie down and sleep in peace,
for You alone, LORD, make me live
   in safety.^j

NOTES
a 5:6 Ps 55:23
b 5:8 Or *of those who lie in wait for me*
c 5:9 Lit *in his mouth*
d 5:9 Rm 3:13
e 5:12 Gn 15:1

PSALM 5

THE REFUGE OF THE RIGHTEOUS

For the choir director: with the flutes.
A Davidic psalm.

1 Listen to my words, LORD;
consider my sighing.
2 Pay attention to the sound of my cry,
my King and my God,
for I pray to You.
3 At daybreak, LORD, You hear my voice;
at daybreak I plead my case to You and watch
expectantly.
4 For You are not a God who delights
in wickedness;
evil cannot lodge with You.
5 The boastful cannot stand in Your presence;
You hate all evildoers.
6 You destroy those who tell lies;
the LORD abhors a man of bloodshed
and treachery.[a]
7 But I enter Your house by the abundance
of Your faithful love;
I bow down toward Your holy temple
in reverential awe of You.
8 LORD, lead me in Your righteousness,
because of my adversaries;[b]
make Your way straight before me.
9 For there is nothing reliable in what they say;[c]
destruction is within them;
their throat is an open grave;
they flatter with their tongues.[d]
10 Punish them, God;
let them fall by their own schemes.
Drive them out because of their many crimes,
for they rebel against You.
11 But let all who take refuge in You rejoice;
let them shout for joy forever.
May You shelter them,
and may those who love Your name boast
about You.
12 For You, LORD, bless the righteous one;
You surround him with favor
like a shield.[e]

PSALM 6

A PRAYER FOR MERCY

For the choir director: with stringed instruments, according to *Sheminith. A Davidic psalm.

1 LORD, do not rebuke me in Your anger;
do not discipline me in Your wrath.[a]

2 Be gracious to me, LORD, for I am weak;[b]
heal me, LORD, for my bones are shaking;

3 my whole being is shaken with terror.
And You, LORD—how long?

4 Turn, LORD! Rescue me;
save me because of Your faithful love.

5 For there is no remembrance of You in death;
who can thank You in *Sheol?[c]

6 I am weary from my groaning;
with my tears I dampen my pillow[d]
and drench my bed every night.

7 My eyes are swollen from grief;
they[e] grow old because of all my enemies.

8 Depart from me, all evildoers,
for the LORD has heard the sound of my weeping.

9 The LORD has heard my plea for help;
the LORD accepts my prayer.[f]

10 All my enemies will be ashamed and shake
with terror;
they will turn back and suddenly be disgraced.

PSALM 7

PRAYER FOR JUSTICE

A Shiggaion[g] of David, which he sang to the LORD concerning the words of Cush,[h] a Benjaminite.[i]

1 LORD my God, I seek refuge in You;
save me from all my pursuers and rescue me,

2 or they[j] will tear me like a lion,[k]
ripping me apart, with no one to rescue me.[l]

3 LORD my God, if I have done this,
if there is injustice on my hands,

4 if I have done harm to one at peace with me
or have plundered[m] my adversary
without cause,

NOTES

[a] 6:1 Ps 38:1
[b] 6:2 Or *sick*
[c] 6:4-5 Ps 30:8-10; 88:9-12
[d] 6:6 Lit *bed*
[e] 6:7 LXX, Aq, Sym, Jer read *I*
[f] 6:9 Ps 3:4; 4:3; 34:6
[g] Perhaps a passionate song with rapid changes of rhythm, or a dirge
[h] LXX, Aq, Sym, Theod, Jer read *of the Cushite*
[i] 2 Sm 18:21-33
[j] 7:2 Lit *he*
[k] 7:2 Ps 57:4; Is 38:13
[l] 7:2 Lit *ripping, and without a rescuer*
[m] 7:4 Or *me and have spared*

NOTES

a **7:6** LXX reads *awake, Lord my God*
b **7:6** Or *me; ordain*
c **7:7** MT reads *and return*
d **7:8** Lit *integrity on me*
e **7:8** Ps 26:1; 35:24; 43:1
f **7:9** Lit *examines hearts and kidneys*
g **7:9** Heb 4:12
h **7:10** Lit *upon*
i **7:12** Lit *He*
j **7:12** Lit *bent*; that is, bent the bow to string it
k **7:16** Ps 140:9-11; Est 9:25
l See Pss 81 and 84 superscriptions

5 may an enemy pursue and overtake me;
may he trample me to the ground
and leave my honor in the dust. •*Selah*

6 Rise up, LORD, in Your anger;
lift Yourself up against the fury of my adversaries;
awake for me;a You have ordainedb a judgment.

7 Let the assembly of peoples gather around You;
and take Your seatc on high over it.

8 The LORD judges the peoples;
vindicate me, LORD,
according to my righteousness and my integrity.d e

9 Let the evil of the wicked come to an end,
but establish the righteous.
The One who examines the thoughts
   and emotionsf
is a righteous God.g

10 My shield is withh God,
who saves the upright in heart.

11 God is a righteous judge,
and a God who executes justice every day.

12 If anyone does not repent, Godi will sharpen
   His sword;
He has strungj His bow and made it ready.

13 He has prepared His deadly weapons;
He tips His arrows with fire.

14 See, he is pregnant with evil,
conceives trouble, and gives birth to deceit.

15 He dug a pit and hollowed it out,
but fell into the hole he had made.

16 His trouble comes back on his own head,
and his violence falls on the top of his head.k

17 I will thank the LORD for His righteousness;
I will sing about the name of the LORD,
   the •Most High.

PSALM 8

GOD'S GLORY, MAN'S DIGNITY

For the choir director: on the •Gittith.l
A Davidic psalm.

1 O LORD, our Lord,
how magnificent is Your name
   throughout the earth!

6

You have covered the heavens
    with Your majesty.[a] [b]

2 Because of Your adversaries,
    You have established a stronghold[c]
from the mouths of children
    and nursing infants,[d]
to silence the enemy and the avenger.

3 When I observe Your heavens, the work
    of Your fingers,
the moon and the stars, which You set in place,

4 what is man, that You remember him,
the son of man, that You look after him?[e]

5 You made him little less than God[f] [g]
and crowned him with glory and honor.

6 You made him lord over the works
    of Your hands;
You put everything under his feet:[h] [i]

7 all the sheep and oxen,
as well as animals in the wild,

8 birds of the sky,
and fish of the sea
passing through the currents of the seas.

9 O LORD, our Lord,
how magnificent is Your name
    throughout the earth!

PSALM 9
CELEBRATION OF GOD'S JUSTICE

For the choir director: according to Muth-labben.[j]
A Davidic psalm.

1 I will thank the LORD with all my heart;
I will declare all Your wonderful works.

2 I will rejoice and boast about You;
I will sing about Your name, Most High.

3 When my enemies retreat,
they stumble and perish before You.

4 For You have upheld my just cause;[k]
You are seated on Your throne
    as a righteous judge.

5 You have rebuked the nations;
    You have destroyed the wicked;
You have erased their name forever and ever.

NOTES

[a] **8:1** Lit *earth, which has set Your splendor upon the heavens*

[b] **8:1** Ps 113:4; 148:13

[c] **8:2** LXX reads *established praise*

[d] **8:2** Mt 21:16

[e] **8:4** Jb 7:17-18

[f] **8:5** LXX reads *angels*

[g] **8:5** Or *gods*, or *a god*, or *heavenly beings*; Hb *Elohim*

[h] **8:6** Or *authority*

[i] **8:4-6** 1 Co 15:27; Eph 1:22; Heb 2:5-8

[j] Perhaps a musical term

[k] **9:4** Lit *my justice and my cause*

WORD STUDY

Hebrew word:
leb, lebab [LAYV, lay VAHV]

HCSB translation:
heart, mind

Focus passage:
Psalm 9:1;10:17;11:2

Leb(ab) refers literally to the body's blood-pumping organ (Ps 38:10) and to the chest region in general (Ex 28:29). Metaphorically, *leb* is the primary term used to describe the human inner self. In Hebrew thought *leb* is the agent responsible for the human mind, will, and emotions. As the seat of the intellect, it may express understanding (Dt 29:4) or remembrance (Dt 4:9). As the center of the will, it can exhibit desire or deliberation (Ps 20:4). As an emotional agent, it can experience feelings such as joy (Ps 4:7), agony (Ps 13:2), courage (2 Sm 17:10), or fear (Jos 2:11). *Leb* may also be used figuratively to refer to the human conscience (2 Sm 24:10). The Old Testament sometimes uses *leb* to speak of the intellectual, emotional, and volitional activity pertaining to God's heart. Due to the heart's inaccessibility, *leb* had another metaphorical use referring to the inaccessibility of an object (Ex 15:8).

NOTES
a **9:8** Ps 96:13; 98:9; Rv 19:11
b **9:10** Ps 91:14
c **9:12** Gn 9:5
d **9:12** Ps 12:5; Pr 22:22-23
e **9:14** Jerusalem
f **9:16** Or *justice, snaring*
g **9:16** LXX, Aq, Syr, Tg read *justice, the wicked is trapped*
h **9:17** Gn 3:19; Jb 17:16
i **9:18** Alt Hb tradition reads *humble*
j **10:1** A few Hb mss and LXX connect Pss 9–10. Together these 2 psalms form a partial •acrostic.

6 The enemy has come to eternal ruin;
You have uprooted the cities,
and the very memory of them has perished.

7 But the LORD sits enthroned forever;
He has established His throne for judgment.

8 He judges the world with righteousness;
He executes judgment on the peoples
with fairness.[a]

9 The LORD is a refuge for the oppressed,
a refuge in times of trouble.

10 Those who know Your name trust in You
because You have not abandoned those
who seek You, LORD.[b]

11 Sing to the LORD, who dwells in Zion;
proclaim His deeds among the peoples.

12 For the One who seeks an accounting
for bloodshed remembers them;[c]
He does not forget the cry of the afflicted.[d]

13 Be gracious to me, LORD;
consider my affliction at the hands of those
who hate me.
Lift me up from the gates of death,

14 so that I may declare all Your praises.
I will rejoice in Your salvation
within the gates of Daughter Zion.[e]

15 The nations have fallen into the pit they made;
their foot is caught in the net
they have concealed.

16 The LORD has revealed Himself;
He has executed justice,
striking down[f] the wicked[g] by the work
of their hands.   •*Higgaion.* •*Selah*

17 The wicked will return to •Sheol[h]—
all the nations that forget God.

18 For the oppressed will not always be forgotten;
the hope of the afflicted[i] will not perish forever.

19 Rise up, LORD! Do not let man prevail;
let the nations be judged in Your presence.

20 Put terror in them, LORD;
let the nations know they are only men.   •*Selah*

PSALM 10

1 LORD,[j] why do You stand so far away?
Why do You hide in times of trouble?

2 In arrogance the wicked relentlessly pursue
     the afflicted;
  let them be caught in the schemes
     they have devised.

3 For the wicked one boasts about
     his own cravings;
  the one who is greedy curses[a] and despises
     the LORD.

4 In all his scheming, the wicked arrogantly
     thinks:[b]
  "There is no accountability, ⌊since⌋ God does not
     exist."[c]

5 His ways are always secure;[d]
  Your lofty judgments are beyond his sight;
  he scoffs at all his adversaries.

6 He says to himself, "I will never be moved—
  from generation to generation
     without calamity."[e]

7 Cursing, deceit, and violence fill his mouth;
  trouble and malice are under his tongue.[f]

8 He waits in ambush near the villages;
  he kills the innocent in secret places;
  his eyes are on the lookout for the helpless.

9 He lurks in secret like a lion in a thicket.
  He lurks in order to seize the afflicted.
  He seizes the afflicted and drags him in his net.[g]

10 He crouches and bends down;
  the helpless fall because of his strength.

11 He says to himself, "God has forgotten;
  He hides His face and will never see."

12 Rise up, LORD God! Lift up Your hand.
  Do not forget the afflicted.

13 Why has the wicked despised God?
  He says to himself, "You will not demand
     an account."

14 But You Yourself have seen trouble and grief,
  observing it in order to take the matter
     into Your hands.
  The helpless entrusts himself to You;
  You are a helper of the fatherless.

15 Break the arm of the wicked and evil person;
  call his wickedness into account until nothing
     remains of it.[h]

16 The LORD is King forever and ever;[i]
  the nations will perish from His land.

[a] **10:3** Or *he blesses the greedy*
[b] **10:4** Lit *wicked according to the height of his nose*
[c] **10:4** Ps 10:11; 14:1; 53:1
[d] **10:5** Or *prosperous*
[e] **10:6** Ps 49:11
[f] **10:7** Rm 3:13-14
[g] **10:8-9** Ps 17:11-12
[h] **10:15** Lit *account You do not find*
[i] **10:16** Ps 29:10

NOTES

a 10:17 Other Hb mss, LXX, Syr read *afflicted*
b 10:18 Ps 68:5; Ex 22:22-24; Dt 10:18
c 11:1 LXX, Syr, Jer, Tg; Hb reads *to your mountain, bird*
d 11:2 Lit *their*
e 11:4 Lit *His eyelids examine*
f 11:6 Sym; Hb reads *rain snares, fire*; the difference between the 2 Hb words is 1 letter
g 11:6 Lit *be the portion of their cup*
h 11:6 Ezk 38:22; Rv 21:8
i 11:7 Ps 17:15; Jb 19:25-26
j 12:1 Mc 7:2

17 LORD, You have heard the desire of the humble;[a]
You will strengthen their hearts.
You will listen carefully,
18 doing justice for the fatherless and the oppressed,
so that men of the earth may terrify ⌊them⌋
no more.[b]

PSALM 11

REFUGE IN THE LORD

For the choir director. Davidic.

1 I have taken refuge in the LORD.
How can you say to me,
"Escape to the mountain like a bird![c]
2 For look, the wicked string the bow;
they put the[d] arrow on the bowstring
to shoot from the shadows at the upright
in heart.
3 When the foundations are destroyed,
what can the righteous do?"
4 The LORD is in His holy temple;
the LORD's throne is in heaven.
His eyes watch; He examines[e] •everyone.
5 The LORD examines the righteous
and the wicked.
He hates the lover of violence.
6 He will rain burning coals and sulfur[f]
on the wicked;
a scorching wind will be their portion.[g] [h]
7 For the LORD is righteous; He loves
righteous deeds.
The upright will see His face.[i]

PSALM 12

OPPRESSION BY THE WICKED

*For the choir director: according to •Sheminith.
A Davidic psalm.*

1 Help, LORD, for no faithful one remains;
the loyal have disappeared
from the •human race.[j]

2 They lie to one another;
they speak with flattering lips
    and deceptive hearts.
3 May the LORD cut off all flattering lips
and the tongue that speaks boastfully.
4 They say, "Through our tongues
    we have power;[a]
our lips are our own—who can be our master?"
5 "Because of the oppression of the afflicted
    and the groaning of the poor,
I will now rise up," says the LORD.
"I will put in a safe place the one who longs
    for it."
6 The words of the LORD are pure words,[b]
like silver refined in an earthen furnace,
purified seven times.
7 You, LORD, will guard us;[c]
You will protect us[d] from this generation
    forever.
8 The wicked wander[e] everywhere,
and what is worthless is exalted
    by the •human race.

PSALM 13

A PLEA FOR DELIVERANCE

For the choir director. A Davidic psalm.

1 LORD, how long will You continually forget me?
How long will You hide Your face from me?[f]
2 How long will I store up anxious concerns[g]
    within me,
agony in my mind every day?
How long will my enemy dominate me?
3 Consider me and answer, LORD, my God.
Restore brightness to my eyes; otherwise,
    I will sleep in death,
4 my enemy will say, "I have triumphed
    over him,"
and my foes will rejoice because I am defeated.[h]
5 But I have trusted in Your faithful love;
my heart will rejoice in Your deliverance.
6 I will sing to the LORD
because He has treated me generously.[i]

a **12:4** Lit *That say, "By our tongues we are strengthened*
b **12:6** Ps 18:30; 119:140; Pr 30:5
c **12:7** Some Hb mss, LXX, Jer; other Hb mss read *them*
d **12:7** Some Hb mss, LXX; other Hb mss read *him*
e **12:8** Lit *walk about*
f **13:1** Ps 89:46; Jb 13:24
g **13:2** Or *up counsels*
h **13:4** Lit *shaken*
i **13:6** Ps 116:7; 142:7

a **14:1** Ps 10:4; 53:1
b **14:3** Two Hb mss, some LXX mss add the material found in Rm 3:13-18
c **14:1-3** Rm 3:10-12
d **14:5** Or *There*
e **14:5** Lit *with the generation of the*
f **14:7** Or *let Jacob rejoice; let Israel be glad.*
g **15:1-2** Ps 24:3-5
h **15:4** Lit *in his eyes the rejected is despised*
i **15:4** Lv 5:4; 27:2; Dt 23:21-23

PSALM 14

A PORTRAIT OF SINNERS

For the choir director. Davidic.

1 The fool says in his heart, "God does not exist."ᵃ
They are corrupt; their actions are revolting.
There is no one who does good.
2 The LORD looks down from heaven
on the •human race
to see if there is one who is wise, one who seeks
God.
3 All have turned away; they have all become
corrupt.
There is no one who does good,
not even one.ᵇ ᶜ
4 Will evildoers never understand?
They consume my people as they consume bread;
they do not call on the LORD.
5 Thenᵈ they will be filled with terror,
for God is with those who areᵉ righteous.
6 You ⌊sinners⌋ frustrate the plans of the afflicted,
but the LORD is his refuge.
7 Oh, that Israel's deliverance would come
from Zion!
When the LORD restores His captive people,
Jacob will rejoice; Israel will be glad.ᶠ

PSALM 15

A DESCRIPTION OF THE GODLY

A Davidic psalm.

1 LORD, who can dwell in Your tent?
Who can live on Your holy mountain?
2 The one who lives honestly, practices
righteousness,
and acknowledges the truth in his heartᵍ—
3 who does not slander with his tongue,
who does not harm his friend
or discredit his neighbor,
4 who despises the one rejected by the LORD,ʰ
but honors those who •fear the LORD,
who keeps his word whatever the cost,ⁱ

5 who does not lend his money at interest
   or take a bribe against the innocent—
   the one who does these things will never
       be moved.

PSALM 16

CONFIDENCE IN THE LORD

A Davidic •Miktam.

1 Protect me, God, for I take refuge in You.
2 I[a] said to the LORD, "You are my Lord,
   I have no good besides You." [b]
3 As for the holy people who are in the land,
   they are the noble ones in whom is all
       my delight.
4 The sorrows of those who take another ⌊god⌋
       for themselves multiply;[c]
   I will not pour out their drink offerings
       of blood,[d]
   and I will not speak their names with my lips.
5 LORD, You are my portion[e] and my cup
       ⌊of blessing⌋;
   You hold my future.
6 The boundary lines have fallen for me
       in pleasant places;
   indeed, I have a beautiful inheritance.
7 I will praise the LORD who counsels me—
   even at night my conscience instructs me.
8 I keep the LORD in mind[f] always.
   Because He is at my right hand, I will not
       be defeated.
9 Therefore my heart is glad, and my spirit[g]
       rejoices;
   my body also rests securely.
10 For You will not abandon me to •Sheol;
   You will not allow Your Faithful One to see
       the •Pit. [h] [i]
11 You reveal the path of life to me;
   in Your presence is abundant joy;
   in Your right hand are eternal pleasures.[j]

NOTES

[a] **16:2** Some Hb mss, LXX, Syr, Jer; other Hb mss read *You*
[b] **16:2** Or *"Lord, my good; there is none besides You."*
[c] **16:4** Jr 2:11
[d] **16:4** Ps 106:37-38
[e] **16:5** Or *allotted portion*
[f] **16:8** Lit *front of me*
[g] **16:9** LXX reads *tongue*
[h] **16:10** LXX reads *see decay*
[i] **16:10** Ac 2:27; 13:35
[j] **16:8-11** Ac 2:25-28

a **17:3** LXX, Aq, Sym, Syr, Jer
read *found no unrighteousness*
b **17:3** Ps 66:10; Jb 23:10; Zch
13:9
c **17:3** Or *[evil]; my mouth will
not sin*
d **17:4** *God's law*
e **17:7** Or *love, You who save
with Your right hand those
seeking refuge from adversaries*
f **17:8** Lit *as the pupil, the
daughter of the eye*
g **17:8** Ps 57:1; 91:1,4; Ru 2:12
h **17:9** Lit *from the presence of*
i **17:9** Or *who plunder me*
j **17:10** Lit *have closed up their
fat*
k **17:11** LXX
l **17:11** Lit *They set their eyes*
m **17:12** Lit *He is*
n **17:11-12** Ps 10:8-9

PSALM 17

A PRAYER FOR PROTECTION

A Davidic prayer.

1 LORD, hear a just cause;
pay attention to my cry;
listen to my prayer—
from lips free of deceit.

2 Let my vindication come from You,
⌊for⌋ You see what is right.

3 You have tested my heart;
You have visited by night;
You have tried me and found nothing ⌊evil⌋;ᵃ ᵇ
I have determined that my mouth will not sin.ᶜ

4 Concerning what people do: by the word
of Your lipsᵈ
I have avoided the ways of the violent.

5 My steps are on Your paths;
my feet have not slipped.

6 I call on You, God, because You will answer me;
listen closely to me; hear what I say.

7 Display the wonders of Your faithful love,
Savior of all who seek refuge
from those who rebel against Your right hand.ᵉ

8 Guard me as the apple of Your eye;ᶠ
hide me in the shadow of Your wingsᵍ

9 fromʰ the wicked who treat me violently,ⁱ
my deadly enemies who surround me.

10 They have become hardened;ʲ
their mouths speak arrogantly.

11 They advance against me; now they surround me.ᵏ
They are determinedˡ to throw ⌊me⌋
to the ground.

12 They areᵐ like a lion eager to tear,
like a young lion lurking in ambush.ⁿ

13 Rise up, LORD!
Confront him; bring him down.
With Your sword, save me from the wicked.

14 With Your hand, LORD, ⌊save me⌋ from men,
from men of the world, whose portion is
in this life:
You fill their bellies with what You have in store,
their sons are satisfied,
and they leave their surplus to their children.

15 But I will see Your face in righteousness;^a
when I awake, I will be satisfied
   with Your presence.^b

^a **17:15** Jb 19:25-26; Mt 5:8; 1 Co 13:12
^b **17:15** Lit *form*
^c 2 Sm 22:1-51
^d **18:2** 1 Sm 2:1,10; Lk 1:69
^e **18:8** Or *ablaze from Him*

PSALM 18

PRAISE FOR DELIVERANCE

*For the choir director. Of the servant of the LORD,
David, who spoke the words of this song to the LORD
on the day the LORD rescued him from the hand of all
his enemies and from the hand of Saul.^c He said:*

1 I love You, LORD, my strength.
2 The LORD is my rock, my fortress,
   and my deliverer,
my God, my mountain where I seek refuge,
my shield and the •horn of my salvation,^d
   my stronghold.
3 I called to the LORD, who is worthy of praise,
and I was saved from my enemies.
4 The ropes of death were wrapped
   around me;
the torrents of destruction terrified me.
5 The ropes of •Sheol entangled me;
the snares of death stared me in the face.
6 I called to the LORD in my distress,
and I cried to my God for help.
From His temple He heard my voice,
and my cry to Him reached His ears.
7 Then the earth shook and trembled;
the foundations of the mountains quaked;
they shook because He burned with anger.
8 Smoke rose from His nostrils,
and consuming fire ⌊came⌋ from His mouth;
coals were set ablaze by it.^e
9 He parted the heavens and came down,
a dark cloud beneath His feet.
10 He rode on a cherub and flew,
soaring on the wings of the wind.
11 He made darkness His hiding place,
dark storm clouds His canopy around Him.
12 From the radiance of His presence,
His clouds swept onward with hail
   and blazing coals.

NOTES

^a **18:13** Some Hb mss, LXX, Tg, Jer; other Hb mss read *in*
^b **18:13** Other Hb mss read *voice, with hail and fiery coals*
^c **18:14** Or *multiplied*
^d **18:21-22** Lit *wickedness, all His ordinances have been in front of me*
^e **18:29** Or *ridge*

13 The LORD thundered from[a] heaven;
the Most High projected His voice.[b]

14 He shot His arrows and scattered them;
He hurled[c] lightning bolts and routed them.

15 The depths of the sea became visible,
the foundations of the world were exposed,
at Your rebuke, LORD,
at the blast of the breath of Your nostrils.

16 He reached down from on high and took hold
of me;
He pulled me out of deep water.

17 He rescued me from my powerful enemy
and from those who hated me, for they were
too strong for me.

18 They confronted me in the day of my distress,
but the LORD was my support.

19 He brought me out to a wide-open place;
He rescued me because He delighted in me.

20 The LORD rewarded me according to
my righteousness;
He repaid me according to the cleanness
of my hands.

21 For I have kept the ways of the LORD
and have not turned from my God
to wickedness.

22 Indeed, I have kept all His ordinances in mind[d]
and have not disregarded His statutes.

23 I was blameless toward Him
and kept myself from sinning.

24 So the LORD repaid me according to
my righteousness,
according to the cleanness of my hands
in His sight.

25 With the faithful You prove Yourself faithful;
with the blameless man You prove Yourself
blameless;

26 with the pure You prove Yourself pure,
but with the crooked You prove Yourself
shrewd.

27 For You rescue an afflicted people,
but You humble those with haughty eyes.

28 LORD, You light my lamp;
my God illuminates my darkness.

29 With You I can attack a barrier,[e]
and with my God I can leap a wall.

NOTES
ᵃ **18:33** Or *on my high places*
ᵇ **18:40** Or *You gave me the necks of my enemies*
ᶜ **18:42** Some Hb mss, LXX, Syr, Tg; other Hb mss read *I poured them out*
ᵈ **18:44** Lit *At the hearing of the ear*

30 God—His way is perfect;
the word of the LORD is pure.
He is a shield to all who take refuge in Him.

31 For who is God besides the LORD?
And who is a rock? Only our God.

32 God—He clothes me with strength
and makes my way perfect.

33 He makes my feet like the feet of a deer
and sets me securely on the heights.ᵃ

34 He trains my hands for war;
my arms can bend a bow of bronze.

35 You have given me the shield
of Your salvation;
Your right hand upholds me,
and Your humility exalts me.

36 You widen ⌊a place⌋ beneath me for my steps,
and my ankles do not give way.

37 I pursue my enemies and overtake them;
I do not turn back until they are wiped out.

38 I crush them, and they cannot get up;
they fall beneath my feet.

39 You have clothed me with strength for battle;
You subdue my adversaries beneath me.

40 You have made my enemies retreat before me;ᵇ
I annihilate those who hate me.

41 They cry for help, but there is no one to save
⌊them⌋—
to the LORD, but He does not answer them.

42 I pulverize them like dust before the wind;
I trample themᶜ like mud in the streets.

43 You have freed me from the feuds
among the people;
You have appointed me the head of nations;
a people I had not known serve me.

44 As soon as they hear,ᵈ they obey me;
foreigners submit to me grudgingly.

45 Foreigners lose heart
and come trembling from their fortifications.

46 The LORD lives—may my rock be praised!
The God of my salvation is exalted.

47 God—He gives me vengeance
and subdues peoples under me.

48 He frees me from my enemies.
You exalt me above my adversaries;
You rescue me from the violent man.

a **19:1** Or *expanse*
b **19:1** Gn 1:6-8; Dn 12:3
c **19:2** Or *Day to day pours out speech, and night to night communicates knowledge*
d **19:4** LXX, Sym, Syr, Vg; Hb reads *line*
e **19:4** Rm 10:18
f **19:4** Lit *In them*
g **19:5** Lit *his*
h **19:6** Lit *its circuit is*
i **19:8** 1 Sm 14:27-29

49   Therefore I will praise You, LORD,
       among the nations;
     I will sing about Your name.
50   He gives great victories to His king;
     He shows loyalty to His anointed,
     to David and his descendants forever.

PSALM 19

THE WITNESS OF CREATION AND SCRIPTURE

For the choir director. A Davidic psalm.

1   The heavens declare the glory of God,
    and the sky[a] [b] proclaims the work of His hands.
2   Day after day they pour out speech;
    night after night they communicate knowledge.[c]
3   There is no speech; there are no words;
    their voice is not heard.
4   Their message[d] has gone out to all the earth,
    and their words to the ends
       of the inhabited world.[e]
    In the heavens[f] He has pitched a tent
       for the sun.
5   It is like a groom coming from
       the[g] bridal chamber;
    it rejoices like an athlete running a course.
6   It rises from one end of the heavens
    and circles[h] to their other end;
    nothing is hidden from its heat.
7   The instruction of the LORD is perfect, reviving
       the soul;
    the testimony of the LORD is trustworthy,
       making the inexperienced wise.
8   The precepts of the LORD are right, making
       the heart glad;
    the commandment of the LORD is radiant,
       making the eyes light up.[i]
9   The •fear of the LORD is pure, enduring forever;
    the ordinances of the LORD are reliable
       and altogether righteous.
10 They are more desirable than gold—
       than an abundance of pure gold;
    and sweeter than honey—than honey dripping
       from the comb.

NOTES

ᵃ **20:6** Other Hb mss, Aq, Sym, Jer, Syr read *with the victorious might of*

ᵇ **20:9** Or LORD, *save. May the king*

11 In addition, Your servant is warned by them;
there is great reward in keeping them.

12 Who perceives his unintentional sins?
Cleanse me from my hidden faults.

13 Moreover, keep Your servant from willful sins;
do not let them rule over me.
Then I will be innocent,
and cleansed from blatant rebellion.

14 May the words of my mouth and the meditation
of my heart
be acceptable to You,
O LORD, my rock and my Redeemer.

PSALM 20

DELIVERANCE IN BATTLE

For the choir director. A Davidic psalm.

1 May the LORD answer you in a day of trouble;
may the name of Jacob's God protect you.

2 May He send you help from the sanctuary
and sustain you from Zion.

3 May He remember all your offerings
and accept your •burnt offering.   •*Selah*

4 May He give you what your heart desires
and fulfill your whole purpose.

5 Let us shout for joy at your victory
and lift the banner in the name of our God.
May the LORD fulfill all your requests.

6 Now I know that the LORD gives victory
to His anointed;
He will answer him from His holy heaven
with miraculous victories fromᵃ His right hand.

7 Some take pride in a chariot, and others
in horses,
but we take pride in the name of the LORD
our God.

8 They collapse and fall,
but we rise and stand firm.

9 LORD, give victory to the king!
May Heᵇ answer us on the day that we call.

19

NOTES

a **21:11** Lit *they stretch out evil against*

b **21:12** Lit *aim with your bowstrings*

c Perhaps a musical term

d **22:1** Mt 27:46; Mk 15:34

e **22:1** Or *My words of groaning are so far from delivering me* (as a statement)

WORD STUDY

Hebrew word:
'elyon [ehl YOHN]

HCSB translation:
Most High

Focus passage:
Psalm 21:7

'Elyon is always preceded by *'El*, the general name for God. *'El 'elyon* stresses God's supremacy over all creation. In the OT, *Most High* usually appears in poetic texts but occurs in narrative passages in Genesis and Daniel. As the supreme being of the universe, the *Most High* is above all other heavenly beings (Ps 97:9), reigns as the great King over the earth (Ps 47:3), and sets the boundaries of the nations (Dt 32:8). He establishes righteousness (Ps 7:17), judging both the nations (Ps 46:5) and His own people (Ps 82:6). The *Most High* is the Redeemer of His people (Ps 78:35), lives among them in Jerusalem (Ps 46:4), and is a refuge for them (Ps 91:9).

20

PSALM 21

THE KING'S VICTORY

For the choir director. A Davidic psalm.

1 LORD, the king finds joy in Your strength.
  How greatly he rejoices in Your victory!

2 You have given him his heart's desire
  and have not denied the request of his lips. •*Selah*

3 For You meet him with rich blessings;
  You place a crown of pure gold on his head.

4 He asked You for life, and You gave it to him—
  length of days forever and ever.

5 His glory is great through Your victory;
  You confer majesty and splendor on him.

6 You give him blessings forever;
  You cheer him with joy in Your presence.

7 For the king relies on the LORD;
  through the faithful love of the •Most High he is not shaken.

8 Your hand will capture all your enemies;
  your right hand will seize those who hate you.

9 You will make them ⌊burn⌋ like a fiery furnace when you appear;
  the LORD will engulf them in His wrath,
  and fire will devour them.

10 You will wipe their descendants from the earth
  and their offspring from the •human race.

11 Though they intend to harm[a] you
  and devise a wicked plan, they will not prevail.

12 Instead, you will put them to flight
  when you aim your bow[b] at their faces.

13 Be exalted, LORD, in Your strength;
  we will sing and praise Your might.

PSALM 22

FROM SUFFERING TO PRAISE

For the choir director: according to "The Deer of the Dawn."[c] A Davidic psalm.

1 My God, my God, why have You forsaken me?[d]
  ⌊Why are You⌋ so far from my deliverance
  and from my words of groaning?[e]

2   My God, I cry by day, but You do not answer,
    by night, yet I have no rest.
3   But You are holy,
    enthroned on the praises of Israel.
4   Our fathers trusted in You;
    they trusted, and You rescued them.
5   They cried to You and were set free;
    they trusted in You and were not disgraced.
6   But I am a worm and not a man,
    scorned by men and despised by people.
7   Everyone who sees me mocks me;
    they sneer[a] and shake their heads:
8   "He relies on[b] the LORD; let Him rescue him;
    let the LORD[c] deliver him, since He takes
        pleasure in him."[d]
9   You took me from the womb,
    making me secure while at my mother's breast.
10 I was given over to You at birth;[e]
    You have been my God
        from my mother's womb.
11 Do not be far from me, because distress
        is near
    and there is no one to help.
12 Many bulls surround me;
    strong ones of Bashan encircle me.
13 They open their mouths against me—
    lions, mauling and roaring.
14 I am poured out like water,
    and all my bones are disjointed;
    my heart is like wax,
        melting within me.
15 My strength is dried up like baked clay;
    my tongue sticks to the roof of my mouth.
    You put me into the dust of death.
16 For dogs have surrounded me;
    a gang of evildoers has closed in on me;
    they pierced[f] my hands and my feet.[g]
17 I can count all my bones;
    people[h] look and stare at me.
18 They divided my garments among themselves,
    and they cast lots for my clothing.[i]
19 But You, LORD, don't be far away;
    my strength, come quickly to help me.
20 Deliver my life from the sword,
    my very life[j] from the power of the dog.

NOTES

a **22:7** Lit *separate with the lip*
b **22:8** Or *Rely on*
c **22:8** Lit *let Him*
d **22:8** Mt 27:43
e **22:10** Lit *was cast on You from the womb*
f **22:16** Some Hb mss, LXX, Syr; other Hb mss read *me; like a lion*
g **22:16** Jn 20:25
h **22:17** Lit *they*
i **22:18** Mt 27:35; Lk 23:34; Jn 19:24
j **22:20** Lit *my only one*

21

NOTES
a 22:21 Lit *answered*
b 22:22 Heb 2:12
c 22:25 Lit *my praise*
d 22:25 Lit *Him*
e 22:26 Or *poor*, or *afflicted*

21 Save me from the mouth of the lion!
You have rescued[a] me from the horns
    of the wild oxen.

22 I will proclaim Your name to my brothers;
I will praise You in the congregation.[b]

23 You who •fear the LORD, praise Him!
All you descendants of Jacob, honor Him!
All you descendants of Israel, revere Him!

24 For He has not despised or detested the torment
    of the afflicted.
He did not hide His face from him,
but listened when he cried to Him for help.

25 I will give praise[c] in the great congregation
    because of You;
I will fulfill my vows before those who •fear You.[d]

26 The humble[e] will eat and be satisfied;
those who seek the LORD will praise Him.
May your hearts live forever!

27 All the ends of the earth will remember and turn
    to the LORD.
All the families of the nations will bow down
    before You,

28 for kingship belongs to the LORD;
He rules over the nations.

29 All who prosper on earth will eat
    and bow down;
all those who go down to the dust
will kneel before Him—
even the one who cannot preserve his life.

30 Descendants will serve Him;
the next generation will be told about the Lord.

31 They will come and tell a people yet to be born
about His righteousness—
what He has done.

PSALM 23

THE GOOD SHEPHERD

A Davidic psalm.

1 The LORD is my shepherd;
there is nothing I lack.

2 He lets me lie down in green pastures;
He leads me beside quiet waters.

3   He renews my life;
    He leads me along the right paths[a]
        for His name's sake.
4   Even when I go through the darkest valley,[b]
    I am not afraid of ⌊any⌋ danger,
    for You are with me;
    Your rod and Your staff[c]—they give me comfort.
5   You prepare a table before me
    in full view of my enemies;
    You anoint my head with oil;
    my cup is full.
6   Only goodness and faithful love will pursue me
        all the days of my life,
    and I will dwell in[d] the house of the LORD
        as long as I live.[e] [f]

[a] **23:3** Or *me in paths of righteousness*
[b] **23:4** Or *the valley of the shadow of death*
[c] **23:4** A shepherd's rod and crook
[d] **23:6** LXX, Sym, Syr, Tg, Vg, Jer; Hb reads *will return to*
[e] **23:6** Lit LORD *for length of days*; traditionally LORD *forever*
[f] **23:6** Ps 27:4
[g] **24:3** Is 2:2-3
[h] **24:4** Or *not lifted up his soul*
[i] **24:6** Some Hb mss, LXX, Syr; other Hb mss read *seek Your face, Jacob*

PSALM 24

THE KING OF GLORY

A Davidic psalm.

1   The earth and everything in it,
    the world and its inhabitants, belong
        to the LORD;
2   for He laid its foundation on the seas
    and established it on the rivers.
3   Who may ascend the mountain of the LORD?[g]
    Who may stand in His holy place?
4   The one who has clean hands and a pure heart,
    who has not set his mind[h] on what is false,
    and who has not sworn deceitfully.
5   He will receive blessing from the LORD,
    and righteousness from the God of his salvation.
6   Such is the generation of those who seek Him,
    who seek the face of the God of Jacob.[i]   •*Selah*
7   Lift up your heads, O gates!
    Rise up, O ancient doors!
    Then the King of glory will come in.
8   Who is this King of glory?
    The LORD, strong and mighty,
    the LORD, mighty in battle.
9   Lift up your heads, O gates!
    Rise up, O ancient doors!
    Then the King of glory will come in.

WORD STUDY

Hebrew word:
kabod [kah VOHD]

HCSB translation:
glory, weight, honor, majesty

Focus passage:
Psalm 24:7-10

The noun *kabod* expresses the concept of *heaviness, weightiness,* or *impressiveness. Kabod* can refer to a large number or quantity (Is 22:24), as well as to great wealth (Gn 31:1). It may refer to the visible *glory, majesty,* or *splendor* of an object (Jr 14:21). Since the *splendor* of a king or country is measured by visible factors such as military/political might and economic prosperity (Is 8:7), Israel's future *glory* is measured by the blessed status of the land, people, and temple during Yahweh's reign (Is 11:10). *Kabod* may also refer to the *dignity, respect,* or *honor* due a person (Ec 6:2). Worshipers give *kabod* (*honor, respect*) to Yahweh (Mal 1:6), and they reverence God's *majesty* (Ps 145:5). Physical manifestations of Yahweh's *glory* are prominent in the account of Israel's wilderness wanderings (Ex 24:17) and in the book of Ezekiel (Ez 1:28).

NOTES

a **25:1** The lines of this poem form an •acrostic.

b **25:1** Or *To You, LORD, I lift up my soul*

c **25:6** Or *everlasting*

d **25:13** Or *earth*

WORD STUDY

Hebrew word:
zakar [zah KAHR]

HCSB translation:
remember

Focus passage:
Psalm 25:6-7

Zakar is frequently used in reference to God. God *remembers* His covenants (Gn 9:15), His attributes (Ps 25:6), humanity (Ps 8:4), individuals (Gn 8:1), His covenant people (Ps 115:12), and human actions (Hs 7:2). When Scripture says God *remembers*, it means that He acts, rather than that He recalls something previously forgotten. An appeal for God to *remember* the worshiper is an appeal for God to act on the worshiper's behalf. When the subject of *zakar* is human, *remembering* involves recalling and reflecting on God's character, covenant, and saving acts. This kind of *remembrance* was not intended to be merely a mental exercise but was to be practically applied to present circumstances, often with a view to effecting a change in behavior or attitude (Is 47:7). For Israel, *remembering* was closely tied to the act of obedience (Nm 15:39).

---

10 Who is He, this King of glory?
The LORD of •Hosts,
He is the King of glory.   •Selah

PSALM 25

DEPENDENCE ON THE LORD

Davidic.

1 LORD,[a] I turn my hope to You.[b]

2 My God, I trust in You.
Do not let me be disgraced;
do not let my enemies gloat over me.

3 Not one person who waits for You will be disgraced;
those who act treacherously without cause will be disgraced.

4 Make Your ways known to me, LORD;
teach me Your paths.

5 Guide me in Your truth and teach me,
for You are the God of my salvation;
I wait for You all day long.

6 Remember, LORD, Your compassion and Your faithful love,
for they ⌊have existed⌋ from antiquity.[c]

7 Do not remember the sins of my youth or my acts of rebellion;
in keeping with Your faithful love, remember me
because of Your goodness, LORD.

8 The LORD is good and upright;
therefore He shows sinners the way.

9 He leads the humble in what is right
and teaches them His way.

10 All the LORD's ways ⌊show⌋ faithful love and truth
to those who keep His covenant and decrees.

11 Out of regard for Your name, LORD,
forgive my sin, for it is great.

12 Who is the person who •fears the LORD?
He will show him the way he should choose.

13 He will live a good life,
and his descendants will inherit the land.[d]

14 The secret counsel of the LORD is for those
   who •fear Him,
   and He reveals His covenant to them.
15 My eyes are always on the LORD,
   for He will pull my feet out of the net.
16 Turn to me and be gracious to me,
   for I am alone and afflicted.
17 The distresses of my heart increase;[a]
   bring me out of my sufferings.
18 Consider my affliction and trouble,
   and take away all my sins.
19 Consider my enemies; they are numerous,
   and they hate me violently.
20 Guard me and deliver me;
   do not let me be put to shame, for I take refuge
   in You.
21 May integrity and uprightness keep me,
   for I wait for You.
22 Redeem Israel, O God, from all its distresses.

PSALM 26

PRAYER FOR VINDICATION

Davidic.

1 Vindicate me, LORD,
   because I have lived with integrity
   and have trusted in the LORD without wavering.
2 Test me, LORD, and try me;
   examine my heart and mind.
3 For Your faithful love is before my eyes,
   and I live by Your truth.
4 I do not sit with the worthless
   or associate with hypocrites.
5 I hate a crowd of evildoers,
   and I do not sit with the wicked.
6 I wash my hands[b] in innocence
   and go around Your altar, LORD,
7 raising my voice in thanksgiving
   and telling about Your wonderful works.
8 LORD, I love the house where You dwell,
   the place where Your glory resides.
9 Do not destroy me along with sinners,
   or my life along with men of bloodshed

NOTES

[a] **25:17** Or *Relieve the distresses of my heart*
[b] **26:6** A ritual or ceremonial washing to express innocence

10 in whose hands are evil schemes,
and whose right hands are filled with bribes.

11 But I live with integrity;
redeem me and be gracious to me.

12 My foot stands on level ground;
I will praise the LORD in the assemblies.

PSALM 27
MY STRONGHOLD

Davidic.

1 The LORD is my light and my salvation—
whom should I fear?
The LORD is the stronghold of my life—
of whom should I be afraid?

2 When evildoers came against me to devour
my flesh,
my foes and my enemies stumbled and fell.

3 Though an army deploy against me,
my heart is not afraid;
though war break out against me,
still I am confident.

4 I have asked one thing from the LORD; it is what
I desire:
to dwell in the house of the LORD all the days
of my life,ᵃ
gazing on the beauty of the LORD
and seeking ⌊Him⌋ in His temple.

5 For He will conceal me in His shelter in the day
of adversity;
He will hide me under the cover of His tent;
He will set me high on a rock.

6 Then my head will be high above my enemies
around me;
I will offer sacrifices in His tent with shouts
of joy.
I will sing and make music to the LORD.

7 LORD, hear my voice when I call;
be gracious to me and answer me.

8 In Your behalf my heart says, "Seek My face."
LORD, I will seek Your face.

9 Do not hide Your face from me;
do not turn Your servant away in anger.

You have been my help;
do not leave me or abandon me,
O God of my salvation.

10 Even if my father and mother abandon me,
the LORD cares for me.

11 Because of my adversaries,
show me Your way, LORD,
and lead me on a level path.

12 Do not give me over to the will of my foes,
for false witnesses rise up against me, breathing
violence.

13 I am certain that I will see the LORD's goodness
in the land of the living.

14 Wait for the LORD;
be courageous and let your heart be strong.
Wait for the LORD.

PSALM 28

MY STRENGTH

Davidic.

1 LORD, I call to You;
my rock, do not be deaf to me.
If You remain silent to me,
I will be like those going down to the •Pit.

2 Listen to the sound of my pleading when I cry
to You for help,
when I lift up my hands toward
Your holy sanctuary.

3 Do not drag me away with the wicked,
with the evildoers,
who speak in friendly ways with their neighbors,
while malice is in their hearts.^a

4 Repay them according to what they have done—
according to the evil of their deeds.
Repay them according to the work of their hands;
give them back what they deserve.

5 Because they do not consider what the LORD
has done
or the work of His hands,
He will tear them down and not rebuild them.

6 May the LORD be praised,
for He has heard the sound of my pleading.

NOTES

^a **28:8** Some Hb mss, LXX, Syr; other Hb mss read *strength for them*

^b **29:1** Or *you angels*, or *you sons of the mighty*; lit LORD *sons of [the] gods*

^c **29:2** Or *attire*, or *appearance*

^d **29:6** Mount Hermon; Dt 3:9

^e **29:9** Or *the oaks shake*

7 The LORD is my strength and my shield;
   my heart trusts in Him, and I am helped.
   Therefore my heart rejoices,
   and I praise Him with my song.

8 The LORD is the strength of His people;[a]
   He is a stronghold of salvation for His anointed.

9 Save Your people, bless Your possession,
   shepherd them, and carry them forever.

PSALM 29
THE VOICE OF THE LORD

A Davidic psalm.

1 Give the LORD—you heavenly beings[b]—
   give the LORD glory and strength.

2 Give the LORD the glory due His name;
   worship the LORD in holy splendor.[c]

3 The voice of the LORD is above the waters.
   The God of glory thunders—
   the LORD, above vast waters,

4 the voice of the LORD in power,
   the voice of the LORD in splendor.

5 The voice of the LORD breaks the cedars;
   the LORD shatters the cedars of Lebanon.

6 He makes Lebanon skip like a calf,
   and Sirion,[d] like a young wild ox.

7 The voice of the LORD flashes flames of fire.

8 The voice of the LORD shakes the wilderness;
   the LORD shakes the wilderness of Kadesh.

9 The voice of the LORD makes the deer give birth[e]
   and strips the woodlands bare.
   In His temple all cry, "Glory!"

10 The LORD sat enthroned at the flood;
   the LORD sits enthroned, King forever.

11 The LORD gives His people strength;
   the LORD blesses His people with peace.

PSALM 30
JOY IN THE MORNING

A psalm; a dedication song for the house. Davidic.

1 I will exalt You, LORD, because You have lifted
   me up

NOTES

and have not allowed my enemies to triumph
over me.

2 O LORD my God,
I cried to You for help, and You healed me.

3 O LORD, You brought me up from •Sheol;
You spared me from among those going down[a]
to the •Pit.

4 Sing to the LORD, you His faithful ones,
and praise His holy name.

5 For His anger lasts only a moment,
but His favor, a lifetime.
Weeping may spend the night,
but there is joy in the morning.

6 When I was secure, I said,
"I will never be shaken."

7 LORD, when You showed Your favor,
You made me stand like a strong mountain;
when You hid Your face, I was terrified.

8 LORD, I called to You;
I sought favor from my Lord:

9 "What gain is there in my death,
in my descending to the •Pit?
Will the dust praise You?
Will it proclaim Your truth?

10 LORD, listen and be gracious to me;
LORD, be my helper."

11 You turned my lament into dancing;
You removed my •sackcloth and clothed me
with gladness,

12 so that I can sing to You and not be silent.
LORD my God, I will praise You forever.

PSALM 31

A PLEA FOR PROTECTION

For the choir director. A Davidic psalm.

1 LORD, I seek refuge in You;
let me never be disgraced.
Save me by Your righteousness.

2 Listen closely to me; rescue me quickly.
Be a rock of refuge for me,
a mountain fortress to save me.

3 For You are my rock and my fortress;[b]
You lead and guide me because of Your name.[c]

a 30:3 Some Hb mss, LXX, Theod, Orig, Syr; other Hb mss, Aq, Sym, Tg, Jer read *from going down*
b 31:3 Ps 18:2
c 31:3 Ps 23:3

NOTES

a 31:4 Ps 25:15
b 31:5 Lk 23:46
c 31:5 Or *You have redeemed*, or *You will redeem*, or *spirit. Redeem*
d 31:6 One Hb ms, LXX, Syr, Vg, Jer read *You*
e 31:9 Lit *my soul and my belly*
f 31:10 LXX, Syr, Sym read *affliction*
g 31:17 LXX reads *brought down*
h 31:17 Or *them perish* or *wail*
i 31:17 Ps 94:17; 115:17

4 You will free me from the net[a] that is secretly set
    for me,
for You are my refuge.

5 Into Your hand I entrust my spirit;[b]
You redeem[c] me, LORD, God of truth.

6 I[d] hate those who are devoted
    to worthless idols,
but I trust in the LORD.

7 I will rejoice and be glad in Your faithful love
because You have seen my affliction.
You have known the troubles of my life

8 and have not handed me over to the enemy.
You have set my feet in a spacious place.

9 Be gracious to me, LORD, because I am
    in distress;
my eyes are worn out from angry sorrow—
my whole being[e] as well.

10 Indeed, my life is consumed with grief,
and my years with groaning;
my strength has failed because of my sinfulness,[f]
and my bones waste away.

11 I am ridiculed by all my adversaries
and even by my neighbors.
I am an object of dread to my acquaintances;
those who see me in the street run from me.

12 I am forgotten: gone from memory
like a dead person—like broken pottery.

13 I have heard the gossip of many;
terror is on every side.
When they conspired against me,
they plotted to take my life.

14 But I trust in You, LORD;
I say, "You are my God."

15 The course of my life is in Your power;
deliver me from the power of my enemies
    and from my persecutors.

16 Show Your favor to Your servant;
save me by Your faithful love.

17 LORD, do not let me be disgraced when I call
    on You.
Let the wicked be disgraced;
let them be silent[g] [h] in •Sheol.[i]

18 Let lying lips be quieted;
they speak arrogantly against the righteous
    with pride and contempt.

NOTES
a **31:20** Lit *canopy*
b **31:21** Or *a fortified city*
c **32:3** Probably a reference to a refusal to confess sin
d **32:4** Hb obscure

19 How great is Your goodness
that You have stored up for those
who •fear You,
and accomplished in the sight
of •everyone
for those who take refuge in You.

20 You hide them in the protection
of Your presence;
You conceal them in a shelter[a]
from the schemes of men,
from quarrelsome tongues.

21 May the LORD be praised,
for He has wonderfully shown His faithful love
to me
in a city under siege.[b]

22 In my alarm I had said,
"I am cut off from Your sight."
But You heard the sound of my pleading
when I cried to You for help.

23 Love the LORD, all His faithful ones.
The LORD protects the loyal,
but fully repays the arrogant.

24 Be strong and courageous,
all you who hope in the LORD.

PSALM 32

THE JOY OF FORGIVENESS

Davidic. A •Maskil.

1 How happy is the one whose transgression
is forgiven,
whose sin is covered!

2 How happy is the man whom the LORD
does not charge with sin,
and in whose spirit is no deceit!

3 When I kept silent,[c] my bones became brittle
from my groaning all day long.

4 For day and night Your hand was heavy
on me;
my strength was drained[d]
as in the summer's heat.   •Selah

5 Then I acknowledged my sin to You
and did not conceal my iniquity.

NOTES

a 32:6 Lit *time of finding*
b 33:7 LXX, Tg, Syr, Vg, Jer read *sea as in a bottle*

I said, "I will confess my transgressions
  to the LORD,"
and You took away the guilt of my sin.   •*Selah*

6 Therefore let everyone who is faithful pray
    to You
  at a time that You may be found.[a]
  When great floodwaters come,
  they will not reach him.

7 You are my hiding place;
  You protect me from trouble.
  You surround me with joyful shouts
    of deliverance.   •*Selah*

8 I will instruct you and show you the way to go;
  with My eye on you, I will give counsel.

9 Do not be like a horse or mule,
    without understanding,
  that must be controlled with bit and bridle,
  or else it will not come near you.

10 Many pains come to the wicked,
  but the one who trusts in the LORD
  will have faithful love surrounding him.

11 Be glad in the LORD and rejoice,
    you righteous ones;
  shout for joy, all you upright in heart.

PSALM 33

PRAISE TO THE CREATOR

1 Rejoice in the LORD, O you righteous ones;
  praise from the upright is beautiful.

2 Praise the LORD with the lyre;
  make music to Him with a ten-stringed harp.

3 Sing a new song to Him;
  play skillfully on the strings, with a joyful shout.

4 For the word of the LORD is right,
  and all His work is trustworthy.

5 He loves righteousness and justice;
  the earth is full of the LORD's unfailing love.

6 The heavens were made by the word
    of the LORD,
  and all the stars, by the breath of His mouth.

7 He gathers the waters of the sea into a heap;[b]
  He puts the depths into storehouses.

8 Let the whole earth tremble before the LORD;

let all the inhabitants of the world stand in awe
    of Him.

9   For He spoke, and it came into being;
    He commanded, and it came into existence.

10 The LORD frustrates the counsel of the nations;
    He thwarts the plans of the peoples.

11 The counsel of the LORD stands forever,
    the plans of His heart from generation
        to generation.

12 Happy is the nation whose God is the LORD—
    the people He has chosen to be
        His own possession!

13 The LORD looks down from heaven;
    He observes everyone.

14 He gazes on all the inhabitants of the earth
    from His dwelling place.

15 He alone crafts their hearts;
    He considers all their works.

16 A king is not saved by a large army;
    a warrior will not be delivered by great strength.

17 The horse is a false hope for safety;
    it provides no escape by its great power.

18 Now the eye of the LORD is on those who •fear
    Him—
    those who depend on His faithful love

19 to deliver their souls from death
    and to keep them alive in famine.

20 We wait for the LORD;
    He is our help and shield.

21 For our hearts rejoice in Him,
    because we trust in His holy name.

22 May Your faithful love rest on us, LORD,
    for we hope in You.

PSALM 34

THE LORD DELIVERS THE RIGHTEOUS

*Concerning David, when he pretended to be insane in
the presence of Abimelech,* [a] [b] *who drove him out, and
he departed.*

1   I[c] will praise the LORD at all times;
    His praise will always be on my lips.

2   I will boast in the LORD;
    the humble will hear and be glad.

NOTES

[a] A reference to Achish, king of
   Gath
[b] 1 Sm 21:10-15
[c] **34:1** The lines of this poem
   form an •acrostic.

NOTES

a **34:5** Some Hb mss, LXX, Aq, Syr, Jer read *Look to Him and be*

b **34:10** LXX, Syr, Vg read *The rich*

c **34:12-16** 1 Pt 3:10-12

d **34:17** Lit *They*

e **34:20** Jn 19:36

3 Proclaim with me the LORD's greatness;
let us exalt His name together.

4 I sought the LORD, and He answered me
and delivered me from all my fears.

5 Those who look to Him are[a] radiant with joy;
their faces will never be ashamed.

6 This poor man cried, and the LORD heard ⌊him⌋
and saved him from all his troubles.

7 The angel of the LORD encamps
around those who •fear Him, and rescues them.

8 Taste and see that the LORD is good.
How happy is the man who takes refuge in Him!

9 •Fear the LORD, you His saints,
for those who fear Him lack nothing.

10 Young lions[b] lack food and go hungry,
but those who seek the LORD will not lack any
good thing.

11 Come, children, listen to me;
I will teach you the •fear of the LORD.

12 Who is the man who delights in life,
loving a long life to enjoy what is good?

13 Keep your tongue from evil
and your lips from deceitful speech.

14 Turn away from evil and do good;
seek peace and pursue it.

15 The eyes of the LORD are on the righteous,
and His ears are open to their cry for help.

16 The face of the LORD is set against those who do
evil,[c]
to erase all memory of them from the earth.

17 The righteous[d] cry out, and the LORD hears,
and delivers them from all their troubles.

18 The LORD is near the brokenhearted;
He saves those crushed in spirit.

19 Many adversities come to the one who is
righteous,
but the LORD delivers him from them all.

20 He protects all his bones;
not one of them is broken.[e]

21 Evil brings death to the sinner,
and those who hate the righteous
will be punished.

22 The LORD redeems the life of His servants,
and all who take refuge in Him will not
be punished.

PSALM 35

PRAYER FOR VICTORY

Davidic.

1   Oppose my opponents, LORD;
    fight those who fight me.

2   Take Your shields—large and small—
    and come to my aid.

3   Draw the spear and javelin
     against my pursuers,
    and assure me: "I am your deliverance."

4   Let those who seek to kill me
    be disgraced and humiliated;
    let those who plan to harm me
    be turned back and ashamed.

5   Let them be like husks in the wind,
    with the angel of the LORD driving them away.

6   Let their way be dark and slippery,
    with the angel of the LORD pursuing them.

7   They hid their net for me without cause;
    they dug a pit for me without cause.

8   Let ruin come on him unexpectedly,
    and let the net that he hid ensnare him;
    let him fall into it—to his ruin.

9   Then I will rejoice in the LORD;
    I will delight in His deliverance.

10   My very bones will say,
    "LORD, who is like You,
    rescuing the poor from one too strong
     for him,
    the poor or the needy from one who robs
     him?"

11   Malicious witnesses come forward;
    they question me about things I do not know.

12   They repay me evil for good,
    making me desolate.

13   Yet when they were sick,
    my clothing was •sackcloth;
    I humbled myself with fasting,
    and my prayer was genuine.[a]

14   I went about ⌊grieving⌋ as if for my friend
     or brother;
    I was bowed down with grief, like one mourning
     a mother.

NOTES

[a] **35:13** Lit *prayer returned to my chest*

35

NOTES

[a] **35:16** Hb obscure
[b] **35:17** Lit *my only one*
[c] **35:20** Lit *but devise deceitful words*
[d] **35:21** Lit *Our eyes saw!*

15 But when I stumbled, they gathered in glee;
they gathered against me.
Assailants I did not know
tore at me and did not stop.

16 With godless mockery[a]
they gnashed their teeth at me.

17 Lord, how long will You look on?
Rescue my life from their ravages,
my very life[b] from the young lions.

18 I will praise You in the great congregation;
I will exalt You among many people.

19 Do not let my deceitful enemies rejoice
over me;
do not let those who hate me without cause
look at me maliciously.

20 For they do not speak in friendly ways,
but contrive deceitful schemes[c]
against those who live peacefully in the land.

21 They open their mouths wide against me
and say,
"Aha, aha! We saw it!"[d]

22 You saw it, LORD; do not be silent.
Lord, do not be far from me.

23 Wake up and rise to my defense,
to my cause, my God and my Lord!

24 Vindicate me, LORD, my God,
in keeping with Your righteousness,
and do not let them rejoice over me.

25 Do not let them say in their hearts,
"Aha! Just what we wanted."
Do not let them say,
"We have swallowed him up!"

26 Let those who rejoice at my misfortune
be disgraced and humiliated;
let those who exalt themselves over me
be clothed with shame and reproach.

27 Let those who want my vindication
shout for joy and be glad;
let them continually say,
"The LORD be exalted,
who wants His servant's well-being."

28 And my tongue will proclaim
Your righteousness,
Your praise all day long.

PSALM 36

HUMAN WICKEDNESS AND GOD'S LOVE

*For the choir director. [A psalm] of David,
the LORD's servant.*

1 An oracle[a] within my[b] heart concerning
  the transgression of the wicked:
  There is no dread of God before his eyes,[c]

2 for in his own eyes he flatters himself [too much]
  to discover and hate his sin.

3 The words of his mouth are malicious
  and deceptive;
  he has stopped acting wisely and doing good.

4 Even on his bed he makes malicious plans.
  He sets himself on a path that is not good
  and does not reject evil.

5 LORD, Your faithful love [reaches] to heaven,
  Your faithfulness to the skies.

6 Your righteousness is like the highest mountain;
  Your judgments, like the deepest sea.
  LORD, You preserve man and beast.

7 God, Your faithful love is so valuable
  that •people take refuge in the shadow
  of Your wings.

8 They are filled from the abundance of Your house;
  You let them drink from Your refreshing stream,

9 for with You is life's fountain.
  In Your light we will see light.

10 Spread Your faithful love over those who know
   You,
   and Your righteousness over the upright in heart.

11 Do not let the foot of the arrogant come near me
   or the hand of the wicked drive me away.

12 There the evildoers fall;
   they have been thrown down and cannot rise.

PSALM 37

INSTRUCTION IN WISDOM

Davidic.

1 Do[d] not be agitated by evildoers;
  do not envy those who do wrong.

NOTES

a **36:1** A term found in the
Prophets to indicate the Lord's
revelation or utterance to them

b **36:1** Some Hb mss; other Hb
mss, LXX, Syr, Jer, Vg read *his*

c **36:1** Rm 3:18

d **37:1** The lines of this poem
form an •acrostic.

WORD STUDY

Hebrew word:
'awen [ah VEHN]

HCSB translation:
evil, malicious, disaster, sorrow

Focus passage:
Psalm 36:3,4,12

'Awen occurs in the OT almost
exclusively in poetic texts and is
most often used to describe evil
acts performed by others. It may
refer to various forms of sin or
injustice, including slander (Ps
10:7), oppression (Ps 14:4), and
idolatry (1 Sm 15:23). The term
"*evildoers*" describes those who
commit such evil acts. *'Awen* may
refer not only to evil deeds, but
also to their consequences such as
disaster (Ps 55:3), or *sorrow* (Ps
90:10). The word is occasionally
translated "deception" or "empti-
ness" to emphasize the fleeting
nature of something (Is 41:29).
'Awen also appears in the place
"Beth-awen," perhaps a deroga-
tory term for the town of Bethel
(Jos 7:2).

Notes

a 37:3 Or *and cultivate faithfulness*
b 37:9 Or *earth*
c 37:11 Or *earth*
d 37:11 Mt 5:5
e 37:13 Ps 2:4; 59:8; Hab 1:10
f 37:14 Lit *their*
g 37:17 Or *power*

2 For they wither quickly like grass
and wilt like tender green plants.

3 Trust in the LORD and do good;
dwell in the land and live securely.[a]

4 Take delight in the LORD,
and He will give you your heart's desires.

5 Commit your way to the LORD;
trust in Him, and He will act,

6 making your righteousness shine
like the dawn,
your justice like the noonday.

7 Be silent before the LORD and wait expectantly
for Him;
do not be agitated by one who prospers
in his way,
by the man who carries out evil plans.

8 Refrain from anger and give up ⌊your⌋ rage;
do not be agitated—it can only bring harm.

9 For evildoers will be destroyed,
but those who hope in the LORD will inherit
the land.[b]

10 A little while, and the wicked will be no more;
though you look for him, he will not be there.

11 But the humble will inherit the land[c] [d]
and will enjoy abundant prosperity.

12 The wicked schemes against the righteous
and gnashes his teeth at him.

13 The Lord laughs at him[e]
because He sees that his day is coming.

14 The wicked have drawn the sword and strung
the[f] bow
to bring down the afflicted and needy
and to slaughter those whose way is upright.

15 Their swords will enter their own hearts,
and their bows will be broken.

16 Better the little that the righteous man has
than the abundance of many wicked people.

17 For the arms[g] of the wicked will be broken,
but the LORD supports the righteous.

18 The LORD watches over the blameless
all their days,
and their inheritance will last forever.

19 They will not be disgraced in times
of adversity;
they will be satisfied in days of hunger.

20 But the wicked will perish;
the LORD's enemies, like the glory
of the pastures, will fade away—
they will fade away like smoke.

21 The wicked borrows and does not repay,
but the righteous is gracious and giving.

22 Those who are blessed by Him will inherit
the land,[a]
but those cursed by Him will be destroyed.

23 A man's steps are established by the LORD,
and He takes pleasure in his way.

24 Though he falls, he will not be overwhelmed,
because the LORD holds his hand.[b]

25 I have been young and now I am old,
yet I have not seen the righteous abandoned
or his children begging bread.

26 He is always generous, always lending,
and his children are a blessing.

27 Depart from evil and do good,
and dwell there[c] forever.

28 For the LORD loves justice
and will not abandon His faithful ones.
They are kept safe forever,
but the children of the wicked will be destroyed.

29 The righteous will inherit the land[d]
and dwell in it permanently.

30 The mouth of the righteous utters wisdom;
his tongue speaks what is just.

31 The instruction of his God is in his heart;
his steps do not falter.

32 The wicked lies in wait for the righteous
and seeks to kill him;

33 the LORD will not leave him in his hand[e]
or allow him to be condemned
when he is judged.

34 Wait for the LORD and keep His way,
and He will exalt you to inherit the land.
You will watch when the wicked are destroyed.

35 I have seen a wicked, violent man
well-rooted[f] like a flourishing native tree.[g]

36 Then I passed by and[h] noticed he was gone;
I searched for him, but he could not be found.

37 Watch the blameless and observe
the upright,
for the man of peace will have a future.[i]

NOTES

a **37:22** Or *earth*
b **37:24** Or *LORD supports with His hand*
c **37:27** Dwell in the land
d **37:29** Or *earth*
e **37:33** Or *power*
f **37:35** Hb obscure
g **37:35** LXX reads *man, lifting himself up like the cedars of Lebanon*
h **37:36** DSS, LXX, Syr, Vg, Jer; MT reads *Then he passed away, and I*
i **37:37** Or *posterity*

NOTES

a **37:38** Or *posterity*
b **38:1** Ps 6:1
c **38:9** Lit *is in front of*
d **38:10** Or *and the light of my eyes—even that is not with me*

38　But transgressors will all be eliminated;
the future[a] of the wicked will be destroyed.

39　The salvation of the righteous is from the LORD,
their refuge in a time of distress.

40　The LORD helps and delivers them;
He will deliver them from the wicked
　　and will save them
because they take refuge in Him.

PSALM 38

PRAYER OF A SUFFERING SINNER

A Davidic psalm for remembrance.

1　O LORD, do not punish me in Your anger
or discipline me in Your wrath.[b]

2　For Your arrows have sunk into me,
and Your hand has pressed down on me.

3　There is no soundness in my body because of
　　Your indignation;
there is no health in my bones because of my sin.

4　For my sins have flooded over my head;
they are a burden too heavy for me to bear.

5　My wounds are foul and festering
because of my foolishness.

6　I am bent over and brought low;
all day long I go around in mourning.

7　For my loins are full of burning pain,
and there is no health in my body.

8　I am faint and severely crushed;
I groan because of the anguish of my heart.

9　Lord, my every desire is known to[c] You;
my sighing is not hidden from You.

10　My heart races, my strength leaves me,
and even the light of my eyes has faded.[d]

11　My loved ones and friends stand back
　　from my affliction,
and my relatives stand at a distance.

12　Those who seek my life set traps,
and those who want to harm me threaten
　　to destroy me;
they plot treachery all day long.

13　I am like a deaf person; I do not hear.
I am like a speechless person who does not open
　　his mouth.

14 I am like a man who does not hear
and has no arguments in his mouth.
15 I hope in You, LORD;
You will answer, Lord my God.
16 For I said, "Don't let them rejoice over me—
those who are arrogant toward me
when I stumble."
17 For I am about to fall,
and my pain is constantly with me.
18 So I confess my guilt;
I am anxious because of my sin.
19 But my enemies are vigorous and powerful;[a]
many hate me for no reason.
20 Those who repay evil for good
attack me for pursuing good.
21 LORD, do not abandon me;
my God, do not be far from me.
22 Hurry to help me,
O Lord, my Savior.

PSALM 39

THE FLEETING NATURE OF LIFE

For the choir director, for Jeduthun.[b]
A Davidic psalm.

1 I said, "I will guard my ways
so that I may not sin with my tongue;
I will guard my mouth with a muzzle
as long as the wicked are in my presence."
2 I was speechless and quiet;
I kept silent, even from ⌊speaking⌋ good,
and my pain intensified.
3 My heart grew hot within me;
as I mused, a fire burned.
I spoke with my tongue:
4 "LORD, reveal to me the end of my life
and the number of my days.
Let me know how transitory I am.[c]
5 You, indeed, have made my days short in length,
and my life span as nothing in Your sight.
Yes, every mortal man is only a vapor. •*Selah*
6 Certainly, man walks about like a mere shadow.
Indeed, they frantically rush around in vain,

NOTES
[a] **38:19** Or *numerous*
[b] 1 Ch 25:1-6
[c] **39:4** Ps 90:12

NOTES
a 40:2 Or *watery*

gathering possessions without knowing
who will get them.

7 "Now, Lord, what do I wait for?
My hope is in You.

8 Deliver me from all my transgressions;
do not make me the taunt of fools.

9 I am speechless; I do not open my mouth
because of what You have done.

10 Remove Your torment from me;
I fade away because of the force of Your hand.

11 You discipline a man with punishment for sin,
consuming like a moth what is precious to him;
every man is a mere vapor.   •*Selah*

12 "Hear my prayer, LORD,
and listen to my cry for help;
do not be silent at my tears.
For I am a foreigner residing with You,
a sojourner like all my fathers.

13 Turn Your angry gaze from me so that I may be
cheered up
before I die and am gone."

PSALM 40

THANKSGIVING AND A CRY FOR HELP

For the choir director. A Davidic psalm.

1 I waited patiently for the LORD,
and He turned to me and heard my cry for help.

2 He brought me up from a desolate a pit,
out of the muddy clay,
and set my feet on a rock,
making my steps secure.

3 He put a new song in my mouth,
a hymn of praise to our God.
Many will see and fear,
and put their trust in the LORD.

4 How happy is the man
who has put his trust in the LORD
and has not turned to the proud
or to those who run after lies!

5 LORD my God, You have done many things—
Your wonderful works and Your plans for us;
none can compare with You.
If I were to report and speak ⌊of them⌋,

they are more than can be told.

6 You do not delight in sacrifice and offering;
You open my ears to listen.[a]
You do not ask for a whole •burnt offering
or a •sin offering.

7 Then I said, "See, I have come;
it is written about me in the volume of the scroll.

8 I delight to do Your will, my God;
Your instruction resides within me."[b] [c]

9 I proclaim righteousness in the great assembly;
see, I do not keep my mouth closed[d]—
as You know, LORD.

10 I did not hide Your righteousness in my heart;
I spoke about Your faithfulness and salvation;
I did not conceal Your constant love and truth
from the great assembly.

11 LORD, do not withhold Your compassion from me;
Your constant love and truth will always guard me.

12 For troubles without number have surrounded me;
my sins have overtaken me; I am unable to see.
They are more than the hairs of my head,
and my courage leaves me.

13 LORD, be pleased to deliver me;
hurry to help me, LORD.

14 Let those who seek to take my life
be disgraced and confounded.
Let those who wish my harm
be driven back and humiliated.

15 Let those who say to me, "Aha, aha!"
be horrified because of their shame.

16 Let all who seek You rejoice and be glad in You;
let those who love Your salvation continually say,
"Great is the LORD!"

17 Though I am afflicted and needy,
the Lord thinks of me.
You are my help and my deliverer;
my God, do not delay.[e]

PSALM 41

VICTORY IN SPITE OF BETRAYAL

For the choir director. A Davidic psalm.

1 Happy is one who cares for the poor;
the LORD will save him in a day of adversity.

NOTES

a **41:9** Lit *Even a man of my peace*

b **41:9** Jn 13:18

c 1 Ch 9:19

d **42:2** Ps 84:7; Ex 23:17

WORD STUDY

Hebrew word:
maskil [mas KEEL]

HCSB translation:
Maskil

Focus passage:
Psalm 42 superscript

Maskil appears in the superscriptions of 13 psalms. The term refers to a specific type of psalm and always occurs in relation to an individual or group. No single explanation of *Maskil's* meaning adequately fits every psalm in which it appears. It is often translated as *psalm, hymn, psalm of praise,* or *skillful psalm.* Attempts at a fuller explanation of *Maskil's* meaning include "memory passage," "didactic poem," "artfully molded song," "wisdom song performed to music," and "contemplative poem." *Maskil*, a form of the verb *sakal* (*to be insightful, clever, prudent, wise*), indicates the act of instructing. As a noun, *maskil* refers to a person with insight or intelligence, usually in relation to practical wisdom (Ps 14:2), but sometimes in reference to intellectual skill (Dn 11:33). Based on this background, a *Maskil* may have been a psalm noted for its instructive value or musical difficulty.

2 The LORD will keep him and preserve him;
he will be blessed in the land.
You will not give him over to the desire
of his enemies.

3 The LORD will sustain him on his sickbed;
You will heal him on the bed where he lies.

4 I said, "LORD, be gracious to me;
heal me, for I have sinned against You."

5 My enemies speak maliciously about me:
"When will he die and be forgotten?"

6 When one ⌊of them⌋ comes to visit, he speaks deceitfully;
he stores up evil in his heart;
he goes out and talks.

7 All who hate me whisper together about me;
they plan to harm me.

8 "Lethal poison has been poured into him,
and he won't rise again from where he lies!"

9 Even my friend[a] in whom I trusted,
one who ate my bread,
has lifted up his heel against me.[b]

10 But You, LORD, be gracious to me and raise me up;
then I will repay them.

11 By this I know that You delight in me:
my enemy does not shout in triumph over me.

12 You supported me because of my integrity
and set me in Your presence forever.

13 May the LORD, the God of Israel, be praised
from everlasting to everlasting.
Amen and amen.

BOOK II
(PSALMS 42–72)
PSALM 42
LONGING FOR GOD

*For the choir director. A *Maskil of the sons of Korah.*[c]

1 As a deer longs for streams of water,
so I long for You, God.

2 I thirst for God, the living God.
When can I come and appear before God?[d]

3   My tears have been my food day and night,
     while all day long people say to me,
     "Where is your God?"

4   I remember this as I pour out my heart:
     how I walked with many,
     leading the festive procession to the house
          of God,
     with joyful and thankful shouts.

5   Why am I so depressed?
     Why this turmoil within me?
     Hope in God, for I will still praise Him,
     my Savior and my God.

6   I[a] am deeply depressed;
     therefore I remember You from the land
          of Jordan
     and the peaks of Hermon,
     from Mount Mizar.

7   Deep calls to deep in the roar of Your waterfalls;
     all Your breakers and Your billows have swept
          over me.[b]

8   The LORD will send His faithful love by day;
     His song will be with me in the night—
     a prayer to the God of my life.

9   I will say to God, my rock,[c]
     "Why have You forgotten me?
     Why must I go about in sorrow
     because of the enemy's oppression?"

10   My adversaries taunt me,
     as if crushing my bones,
     while all day long they say to me,
     "Where is your God?"

11   Why am I so depressed?
     Why this turmoil within me?
     Hope in God, for I will still praise Him,
     my Savior and my God.

PSALM 43[d]

1   Vindicate me, God, and defend my cause
     against an ungodly nation;
     rescue me from the deceitful and unjust man.

2   For You are the God of my refuge.
     Why have You rejected me?
     Why must I go about in sorrow
     because of the enemy's oppression?

^a 1 Ch 9:19
^b 44:4 LXX, Syr, Aq; MT reads
King, God; ordain

3 Send Your light and Your truth; let them lead me.
Let them bring me to Your holy mountain,
to Your dwelling place.

4 Then I will come to the altar of God,
to God, my greatest joy.
I will praise You with the lyre,
O God, my God.

5 Why am I so depressed?
Why this turmoil within me?
Hope in God, for I will still praise Him,
my Savior and my God.

PSALM 44

ISRAEL'S COMPLAINT

For the choir director. A •Maskil of the sons of Korah.^a

1 God, we have heard with our ears—
our forefathers have told us—
the work You accomplished in their days,
in days long ago:

2 to plant them, You drove out the nations
with Your hand;
to settle them, You crushed the peoples.

3 For they did not take the land
by their sword—
their arm did not bring them victory—
but by Your right hand, Your arm, and the light
of Your face,
for You were pleased with them.

4 You are my King, My God,
who ordains^b victories for Jacob.

5 Through You we drive back our foes;
through Your name we trample our enemies.

6 For I do not trust in my bow,
and my sword does not bring me victory.

7 But You give us victory over our foes
and let those who hate us be disgraced.

8 We boast in God all day long;
we will praise Your name forever.   •*Selah*

9 But You have rejected and humiliated us;
You do not march out with our armies.

10 You make us retreat from the foe,
and those who hate us have taken plunder
for themselves.

11 You hand us over to be eaten like sheep
and scatter us among the nations.
12 You sell Your people for nothing;
You make no profit from selling them.
13 You make us an object of reproach
   to our neighbors,
a source of mockery and ridicule to those
   around us.
14 You make us a joke among the nations,
a laughingstock[a] among the peoples.
15 My disgrace is before me all day long,
and shame has covered my face,
16 because of the voice of the scorner and reviler,
because of the enemy and avenger.
17 All this has happened to us, but we have not
   forgotten You
or betrayed Your covenant.
18 Our hearts have not turned back;
our steps have not strayed from Your path.
19 But You have crushed us in a haunt of jackals
and have covered us with deepest darkness.
20 If we had forgotten the name of our God
and spread out our hands to a foreign god,
21 wouldn't God have found this out,
since He knows the secrets of the heart?
22 Because of You we are slain all day long;
we are counted as sheep to be slaughtered.[b]
23 Wake up, LORD! Why are You sleeping?
Get up! Don't reject us forever!
24 Why do You hide Yourself
and forget our affliction and oppression?
25 For we have sunk down to the dust;
our bodies cling to the ground.
26 Rise up! Help us!
Redeem us because of Your faithful love.

NOTES
[a] **44:14** Lit *shaking of the head*
[b] **44:22** Rm 8:36
[c] Apparently a hymn tune; compare Pss 60; 69; 80
[d] 1 Ch 9:19

PSALM 45

A ROYAL WEDDING SONG

For the choir director: according to "The Lilies."[c]
A ·Maskil of the sons of Korah.[d] *A love song.*

1 My heart is moved by a noble theme
as I recite my verses to the king;
my tongue is the pen of a skillful writer.

2 You are the most handsome of •men;
grace flows from your lips.
Therefore God has blessed you forever.

3 Mighty warrior, strap your sword at your side.
In your majesty and splendor—

4 in your splendor ride triumphantly
in the cause of truth, humility, and justice.
May your right hand show your awe-inspiring
deeds.

5 Your arrows pierce the hearts
of the king's enemies;
the peoples fall under you.

6 Your throne, God, is forever and ever;
the scepter of Your kingdom is a scepter
of justice.

7 You love righteousness and hate wickedness;
therefore God, your God, has anointed you,
more than your companions, with the oil
of joy.a

8 Myrrh, aloes, and cassia ⌊perfume⌋ all
your garments;
from ivory palaces harps bring you joy.

9 Kings' daughters are among
your honored women;
the queen, adorned with gold from Ophir,b
stands at your right hand.

10 Listen, daughter, pay attention and consider:
forget your people and your father's house,

11 and the king will desire your beauty.
Bow down to him, for he is your lord.

12 The daughter of Tyre, the wealthy people,
will seek your favor with gifts.

13 In ⌊her chamber⌋, the royal daughter is all
glorious,
her clothing embroidered with gold.

14 In colorful garments she is led to the king;
after her, the virgins, her companions,
are brought to you.

15 They are led in with gladness and rejoicing;
they enter the king's palace.

16 Your sons will succeed your ancestors;
you will make them princes
throughout the land.

17 I will cause your name to be remembered for all
generations;

therefore the peoples will praise you forever
and ever.

PSALM 46
GOD OUR REFUGE

*For the choir director. A song of the sons of Korah.
According to Alamoth.*^a

1 God is our refuge and strength,
a helper who is always found in times of trouble.

2 Therefore we will not be afraid,
though the earth trembles
and the mountains topple into the depths
of the seas,

3 though its waters roar and foam
and the mountains quake with its turmoil.•*Selah*

4 ⌊There is⌋ a river—its streams delight the city
of God,
the holy dwelling place of the •Most High.

5 God is within her; she will not be toppled.
God will help her when the morning dawns.

6 Nations rage, kingdoms topple;
the earth melts when He lifts His voice.

7 The LORD of •Hosts is with us;
the God of Jacob is our stronghold.   •*Selah*

8 Come, see the works of the LORD,
who brings devastation on the earth.

9 He makes wars cease throughout the earth.
He shatters bows and cuts spears to pieces;
He burns up the chariots.^{b c}

10 "Stop ⌊your fighting⌋—and know that I am God,
exalted among the nations, exalted on the earth."

11 The LORD of •Hosts is with us;
the God of Jacob is our stronghold.   •*Selah*

PSALM 47
GOD OUR KING

For the choir director. A psalm of the sons of Korah.

1 Clap your hands, all you peoples;
shout to God with a jubilant cry.

NOTES

^a This notation may refer to a
high pitch, perhaps a tune sung
by soprano voices; the Hb
word means "young women."

^b **46:9** Other Hb mss, LXX, Tg
read *shields*

^c **46:9** Lit *chariots with fire*

WORD STUDY

Hebrew word:
selah [see LAH]

HCSB translation:
Selah

Focus passage:
Psalm 46:3,7,11

Selah is an expression found only
in Psalms and Habakkuk. There
are three popular theories of
Selah's meaning and function. The
first proposes that *Selah* comes
from *salal* (*to lift up, exalt*).
According to this view, *Selah*
might be a call for worshipers to
lift their eyes to heaven and repeat
the psalm, or to raise their voices
and repeat a refrain, or for musicians to lift their instruments and
perform a musical interlude during a liturgical pause. The second
theory suggests that *Selah* was
read and pronounced as *nesah*
(*forever*) and represented a call for
worshipers to respond with a
praise refrain. The third theory
suggests that *Selah* is related to the
root *sl* (*to bow, pray*) and is a call
for worshipers to bow down in
prayer.

NOTES
^a 47:4 Nah 2:2
^b 47:7 Hb *a* •*Maskil*
^c 47:9 Lit *shields*

2 For the LORD •Most High is awe-inspiring,
a great King over all the earth.

3 He subdues peoples under us
and nations under our feet.

4 He chooses for us our inheritance—
the pride of Jacob,[a] whom He loves.   •*Selah*

5 God ascends amid shouts of joy,
the LORD, amid the sound of trumpets.

6 Sing praise to God, sing praise;
sing praise to our King, sing praise!

7 Sing a song of instruction,[b]
for God is King of all the earth.

8 God reigns over the nations;
God is seated on His holy throne.

9 The nobles of the peoples have assembled
⌊with⌋ the people of the God of Abraham.
For the leaders[c] of the earth belong to God;
He is greatly exalted.

PSALM 48

ZION EXALTED

A song. A psalm of the sons of Korah.

1 The LORD is great and is highly praised
in the city of our God.
His holy mountain, 2 rising splendidly,
is the joy of the whole earth.
Mount Zion on the slopes of the north
is the city of the great King.

3 God is known as a stronghold
in its citadels.

4 Look! The kings assembled;
they advanced together.

5 They looked, and froze with fear;
they fled in terror.

6 Trembling seized them there,
agony like that of a woman in labor,

7 as You wrecked the ships of Tarshish
with the east wind.

8 Just as we heard, so we have seen
in the city of the LORD of •Hosts,
in the city of our God;
God will establish it forever.   •*Selah*

NOTES

a **48:11** Lit *daughters*
b **48:14** Some Hb mss, LXX; other Hb mss read *over death*
c **49:2** Lit *both sons of Adam and sons of man*
d **49:7** Or *Certainly he cannot redeem himself*, or *Yet he cannot redeem a brother*
e **49:8** Or *costly, it will cease forever*
f **49:11** LXX, Syr, Tg; MT reads *Their inner thought is that their houses are eternal*

9 God, within Your temple,
we contemplate Your faithful love.
10 Your name, God, like Your praise,
reaches to the ends of the earth;
Your right hand is filled with justice.
11 Mount Zion is glad.
The towns[a] of Judah rejoice
because of Your judgments.
12 Go around Zion, encircle it;
count its towers,
13 note its ramparts; tour its citadels
so that you can tell a future generation:
14 "This God, our God forever and ever—
He will lead us eternally."[b]

PSALM 49

MISPLACED TRUST IN WEALTH

For the choir director. A psalm of the sons of Korah.

1 Hear this, all you peoples;
listen, all who inhabit the world,
2 both low and high,[c]
rich and poor together.
3 My mouth speaks wisdom;
my heart's meditation ⌊brings⌋ understanding.
4 I turn my ear to a proverb;
I explain my riddle with a lyre.
5 Why should I fear in times of trouble?
The iniquity of my foes surrounds me.
6 They trust in their wealth
and boast of their abundant riches.
7 Yet these cannot redeem a person[d]
or pay his ransom to God—
8 since the price of redeeming him is too costly,
one should forever stop trying[e]—
9 so that he may live forever
and not see the •Pit.
10 For one can see that wise men die;
the foolish and the senseless also pass away.
Then they leave their wealth to others.
11 Their graves are their eternal homes,[f]
their homes from generation to generation,
though they have named estates after themselves.

NOTES

a **49:12** Or *honor*

b **49:13** Lit *and after them with their mouth they were pleased*

c **49:16** Or *glory*

d **49:17** Or *glory*

e **49:20** Or *with honor*

f 1 Ch 6:39; 15:19; 16:5,7,37

g **50:1** Or *The Mighty One, God, the* LORD, or *The God of gods, the* LORD

h **50:2** Or *God shines forth*

i **50:5** Ex 24:4-8

j **50:6** Ps 97:6

12 But despite ⌊his⌋ assets,[a] man will not last;
he is like the animals that perish.

13 This is the way of those who are arrogant,
and of their followers, who approve
of their words.[b]   •*Selah*

14 Like sheep they are headed for •Sheol;
Death will shepherd them.
The upright will rule over them in the morning,
and their form will waste away in Sheol, far
from their lofty abode.

15 But God will redeem my life from the power
of •Sheol,
for He will take me.   •*Selah*

16 Do not be afraid when a man gets rich,
when the wealth[c] of his house increases.

17 For when he dies, he will take nothing at all;
his wealth[d] will not follow him down.

18 Though he praises himself during his lifetime—
and people praise you when you do well
for yourself—

19 he will go to the generation of his fathers;
they will never see the light.

20 A man with valuable possessions[e] but without
understanding
is like the animals that perish.

PSALM 50

GOD AS JUDGE

A psalm of Asaph.[f]

1 God, the LORD God,[g] speaks;
He summons the earth from east to west.

2 From Zion, the perfection of beauty,
God appears in radiance.[h]

3 Our God is coming; He will not be silent!
Devouring fire precedes Him,
and a storm rages around Him.

4 On high, He summons heaven and earth
in order to judge His people.

5 "Gather My faithful ones to Me,
those who made a covenant with Me by sacrifice."[i]

6 The heavens proclaim His righteousness,[j]
for God is the judge.   •*Selah*

7   "Listen, My people, and I will speak;
I will testify against you, Israel.
I am God, your God.

8   I do not rebuke you for your sacrifices
or for your •burnt offerings, which are
continually before Me. [a]

9   I will not accept a bull from your household
or male goats from your pens,

10 for every animal of the forest is Mine,
the cattle on a thousand hills.

11 I know every bird of the mountains,
and the creatures of the field are Mine.

12 If I were hungry, I would not tell you,
for the world and everything in it is Mine. [b]

13 Do I eat the flesh of bulls
or drink the blood of goats?

14 Sacrifice a thank offering[c] to God,
and pay your vows to the •Most High.

15 Call on Me in a day of trouble;
I will rescue you, and you will honor Me."

16 But God says to the wicked:
"What right do you have to recite
My statutes
and to take My covenant on your lips?

17 You hate instruction
and turn your back on My words. [d]

18 When you see a thief, you make friends
with him,
and you associate with adulterers.

19 You unleash your mouth for evil
and harness your tongue for deceit.

20 You sit, maligning your brother,
slandering your mother's son.

21 You have done these things,
and I kept silent;
you thought I was just like you.
But I will rebuke you and lay out the case
before you. [e]

22 Understand this, you who forget God,
or I will tear you apart, and there will be
no rescuer.

23 Whoever sacrifices a thank offering honors
Me,
and whoever orders his conduct,
I will show him the salvation of God."

[a] **50:8** Ps 40:6; 51:16; 1 Sm 15:22
[b] **50:12** Ps 24:1
[c] **50:14** Lv 7:12
[d] **50:17** Or *and cast My words behind you*
[e] **50:21** Lit *out before your eyes*

^a 2 Sm 11:1–12:23
^b 51:4 Rm 3:4
^c 51:7 Lv 14:4,49; Nm 19:18
^d 51:9 Lit *Hide Your face*
^e 51:10 Or *right*
^f 51:16 Ps 40:6

PSALM 51

A PRAYER FOR RESTORATION

For the choir director. A Davidic psalm, when Nathan the prophet came to him after he had gone to Bathsheba. [a]

1 Be gracious to me, God, according to
     Your faithful love;
according to Your abundant compassion,
     blot out my rebellion.

2 Wash away my guilt,
and cleanse me from my sin.

3 For I am conscious of my rebellion,
and my sin is always before me.

4 Against You—You alone—I have sinned
and done this evil in Your sight.
So You are right when You pass sentence;
You are blameless when You judge. [b]

5 Indeed, I was guilty ⌊when I⌋ was born;
I was sinful when my mother conceived me.

6 Surely You desire integrity in the inner self,
and You teach me wisdom deep within.

7 Purify me with hyssop, [c] and I will be clean;
wash me, and I will be whiter than snow.

8 Let me hear joy and gladness;
let the bones You have crushed rejoice.

9 Turn Your face away [d] from my sins
and blot out all my guilt.

10 God, create a clean heart for me
and renew a steadfast [e] spirit within me.

11 Do not banish me from Your presence
or take Your Holy Spirit from me.

12 Restore the joy of Your salvation to me,
and give me a willing spirit.

13 Then I will teach the rebellious Your ways,
and sinners will return to You.

14 Save me from the guilt of bloodshed, God,
     the God of my salvation,
and my tongue will sing
     of Your righteousness.

15 Lord, open my lips,
and my mouth will declare Your praise.

16 You do not want a sacrifice, or I would give it;
You are not pleased with a •burnt offering. [f]

17 The sacrifice pleasing to God is[a]
a broken spirit.
God, You will not despise a broken
and humbled heart.

18 In Your good pleasure, cause Zion to prosper;
build[b] the walls of Jerusalem.

19 Then You will delight in righteous sacrifices,
whole •burnt offerings;
then bulls will be offered on Your altar.

[a] **51:17** Lit *The sacrifices of God are*
[b] **51:18** Or *rebuild*
[c] 1 Sm 21:1-9; 22:9-10
[d] **52:1** Or *evil all day long?*
[e] **52:7** Or *riches, and grew strong in his evil desire*; lit *his destruction*
[f] **52:8** Jr 11:16

PSALM 52

GOD JUDGES THE PROUD

*For the choir director. A Davidic •Maskil. When Doeg
the Edomite went and reported to Saul, telling him,
"David went to Ahimelech's house."*[c]

1 "Why brag about evil, you hero!
God's faithful love is constant.[d]

2 Like a sharpened razor,
your tongue devises destruction,
working treachery.

3 You love evil instead of good,
lying instead of speaking truthfully.   •*Selah*

4 You love any words that destroy,
you treacherous tongue!

5 This is why God will bring you down forever.
He will take you, ripping you out of your tent;
He will uproot you from the land of the living.
                                        •*Selah*

6 The righteous will look on with awe
and will ridicule him:

7 "Here's the man who would not make God
his refuge,
but trusted in the abundance of his riches,
taking refuge in his destructive behavior."[e]

8 But I am like a flourishing olive tree in the house
of God;[f]
I trust in God's faithful love forever and ever.

9 I will praise You forever for what
You have done.
In the presence of Your faithful people,
I will place my hope in Your name, for it is
good.

NOTES

a Hb term transliterated because its meaning is unclear; may be the name of a song tune, a musical instrument, or a dance; may be related to Hb for "sickness"

b 53:1 Ps 14:1

c 53:2-3 Rm 3:10-12

d 53:6 Ps 14:7; Is 52:7-9; Jr 30:18-19

e 1 Sm 26:1

PSALM 53

A PORTRAIT OF SINNERS

For the choir director: on Mahalath. [a]
A Davidic •Maskil.

1 The fool says in his heart, "God does not
    exist."
  They are corrupt, and they do vile deeds.
  There is no one who does good. [b]

2 God looks down from heaven
    on the •human race
  to see if there is anyone who is wise
  and who seeks God.

3 Everyone has turned aside;
  they have all become corrupt.
  There is no one who does good,
  not even one. [c]

4 Will those who practice sin never understand?
  They consume My people as they consume
    bread;
  they do not call on God.

5 Then they will be filled with terror—
  terror like no other—
  because God will scatter the bones of those
    who besiege you.
  You will put them to shame,
    for God has rejected them.

6 Oh, that Israel's deliverance would come
    from Zion!
  When God restores His captive people,
  Jacob will rejoice; Israel will be glad. [d]

PSALM 54

PRAYER FOR DELIVERANCE

For the choir director: with stringed instruments.
A Davidic •Maskil. When the Ziphites went and said
to Saul, "Is David not hiding among us?" [e]

1 God, save me by Your name,
  and vindicate me by Your might!

2 God, hear my prayer;
  listen to the words of my mouth.

3 For strangers rise up against me,
and violent men seek my life.
They have no regard for God.[a] [b]   •*Selah*

4 God is my helper;
the Lord is the sustainer of my life.[c]

5 He will repay my adversaries for ⌊their⌋ evil.
Because of Your faithfulness, annihilate them.

6 I will sacrifice a freewill offering to You.
I will praise Your name, LORD, because
it is good.[d]

7 For He has delivered me from every trouble,
and my eye has looked down on my enemies.[e]

PSALM 55

BETRAYAL BY A FRIEND

For the choir director: with stringed instruments.
A Davidic •Maskil.

1 God, listen to my prayer
and do not ignore[f] my plea for help.

2 Pay attention to me and answer me.[g]
I am restless and in turmoil with my complaint,

3 because of the enemy's voice,
because of the pressure[h] of the wicked.
For they bring down disaster on me
and harass me in anger.

4 My heart shudders within me;
terrors of death sweep over me.

5 Fear and trembling come upon me;
horror has overwhelmed me.[i]

6 I said, "If only I had wings like a dove![j]
I would fly away and find rest.

7 How far away I would flee;
I would stay in the wilderness.   •*Selah*

8 I would hurry to my shelter
from the raging wind and the storm."

9 Lord, confuse[k] and confound their speech,[l] [m]
for I see violence and strife in the city;

10 day and night they make the rounds on its walls.
Crime and trouble are within it;[n]

11 destruction is inside it;
oppression and deceit never leave
its marketplace.

NOTES

a 54:3 Lit *They do not set God before them*
b 54:3 Ps 86:14
c 54:4 Or *is with those who sustain my life*
d 54:6 Ps 52:9
e 54:7 Ps 59:10
f 55:1 Lit *hide Yourself from*
g 55:1-2 Ps 4:1; 5:1-2; 54:2
h 55:3 Or *threat*, or *oppression*
i 55:4-5 Ps 18:4-5; 116:3
j 55:6 Lit *"Who will give to me . . . dove?* (as a question)
k 55:9 Or *destroy*
l 55:9 Lit *and divide their tongue*
m 55:9 Gn 10:25; 11:7
n 55:9-10 Hab 1:3

a 55:12-13 Ps 41:9
b 55:20 The evil man
c 55:21 Other Hb mss, Sym, Syr, Tg, Jer read *His speech is smoother than butter*
d 55:23 Ps 5:6
e Possibly a song tune
f 1 Sm 21:10-15

12 Now, it is not an enemy who insults me—
   otherwise I could bear it;
   it is not a foe who rises up against me—
   otherwise I could hide from him.

13 But it is you, a man who is my peer,
   my companion and good friend!ᵃ

14 We used to have close fellowship;
   we walked with the crowd into the house of God.

15 Let death take them by surprise;
   let them go down to •Sheol alive,
   because evil is in their homes and within them.

16 But I call to God,
   and the LORD will save me.

17 I complain and groan morning, noon, and night,
   and He hears my voice.

18 Though many are against me,
   He will redeem me from my battle unharmed.

19 God, the One enthroned from long ago,
   will hear, and will humiliate them   •Selah
   because they do not change
   and do not •fear God.

20 Heᵇ acts violently against those at peace with him;
   he violates his covenant.

21 His buttery words are smooth,ᶜ
   but war is in his heart.
   His words are softer than oil,
   but they are drawn swords.

22 Cast your burden on the LORD,
   and He will support you;
   He will never allow the righteous to be shaken.

23 You, God, will bring them down to the pit
      of destruction;
   men of bloodshed and treachery will not live out
      half their days.ᵈ
   But I will trust in You.

PSALM 56
A CALL FOR GOD'S PROTECTION

*For the choir director: according to "A Silent Dove Far Away."ᵉ A Davidic •Miktam. When the Philistines seized him in Gath.*ᶠ

1 Be gracious to me, God, for man tramples me;
   he fights and oppresses me all day long.

2 My adversaries trample me all day,
   for many arrogantly fight against me. [a]

3 When I am afraid,
   I will trust in You.

4 In God, whose word I praise,
   in God I trust; I will not fear.
   What can man do to me? [b]

5 They twist my words all day long;
   all their thoughts are against me for evil.

6 They stir up strife, [c] they lurk;
   they watch my steps
   while they wait to take my life. [d]

7 Will they escape in spite of such sin?
   God, bring down the nations in wrath.

8 You Yourself have recorded my wanderings. [e]
   Put my tears in Your bottle.
   Are they not in Your records?

9 Then my enemies will retreat on the day when I call.
   This I know: God is for me.

10 In God, whose word I praise,
   in the LORD, whose word I praise,

11 in God I trust; I will not fear.
   What can man do to me?

12 I am obligated by vows [f] to You, God;
   I will make my thank offerings [g] to You.

13 For You delivered me from death,
   even my feet from stumbling,
   to walk before God in the light of life. [h]

PSALM 57
PRAISE FOR GOD'S PROTECTION

For the choir director: "Do Not Destroy." [i]
A Davidic •Miktam. When he fled before Saul
into the cave. [j]

1 Be gracious to me, God, be gracious to me,
   for I take refuge in You.
   I will seek refuge in the shadow of Your wings [k]
   until danger passes.

2 I call to God •Most High,
   to God who fulfills ⌊His purpose⌋ for me. [l]

3 He reaches down from heaven and saves me,
   challenging the one who tramples me.   •*Selah*
   God sends His faithful love and truth.

a **56:2** Or *many fight against me,*
   O exalted One, or *many fight*
   against me from the heights
b **56:4** Ps 27:1; 118:6
c **56:6** Or *They attack*
d **56:6** Ps 10:8-10
e **56:8** Or *misery*
f **56:12** Lit *Upon me the vows*
g **56:12** Lv 7:12
h **56:13** Ps 116:8-9
i Possibly a song tune
j 1 Sm 22:1; 24:1-10
k **57:1** Ps 17:8; 91:1
l **57:2** Or *who avenges me*

NOTES

a 57:6 Ps 9:15; 35:8; Pr 28:10
b 57:8 Lit *glory*
c 57:10 Ps 103:11; Lm 3:22-23
d 57:7-11 Ps 108:1-5
e Possibly a song tune
f 58:1 Or *Can you really speak righteousness in silence?*
g 58:5 Ec 10:11; Jr 8:17
h 58:7 Or *their arrows as if they were circumcised*; Hb uncertain
i 58:7 Or *they wither like trampled grass*

4   I am in the midst of lions;
     I lie down with those who devour •men.
     Their teeth are spears and arrows;
     their tongues are sharp swords.

5   God, be exalted above the heavens;
     let Your glory be above the whole earth.

6   They prepared a net for my steps;
     I was downcast.
     They dug a pit ahead of me,
     but they fell into it![a]   •Selah

7   My heart is confident, God, my heart
       is confident.
     I will sing, I sing praises.

8   Wake up, my soul![b]
     Wake up, harp and lyre!
     I will wake up the dawn.

9   I will praise You, Lord, among the peoples;
     I will sing praises to You among the nations.

10   For Your faithful love is as high as the heavens;
     Your faithfulness reaches to the clouds.[c]

11   God, be exalted above the heavens;
     let Your glory be over the whole earth.[d]

PSALM 58

A CRY AGAINST INJUSTICE

For the choir director: "Do Not Destroy." [e]
A Davidic •Miktam.

1   Do you really speak righteously, you mighty ones?[f]
     Do you judge •people fairly?

2   No, you practice injustice in your hearts;
     with your hands you weigh out violence
       in the land.

3   The wicked go astray from the womb;
     liars err from birth.

4   They have venom like the venom of a snake,
     like the deaf cobra that stops up its ears,

5   that does not listen to the sound of the charmers
     who skillfully weave spells.[g]

6   God, knock the teeth out of their mouths;
     LORD, tear out the young lions' fangs.

7   They will vanish like water that flows by;
     they will aim their useless arrows.[h] [i]

8 Like a slug that moves along in slime,
   like a woman's miscarried ⌊child⌋, they will not
      see the sun.[a]
9 Before your pots can feel the heat of the thorns—
   whether green or burning—He will sweep them
      away.[b]
10 The righteous will rejoice when he sees
      the retribution;[c]
   he will wash his feet in the blood of the wicked.
11 Then people will say, "Yes, there is a reward
      for the righteous!
   There is a God who judges on earth!"[d]

PSALM 59

GOD OUR STRONGHOLD

For the choir director: "Do Not Destroy."[e]
*A Davidic •Miktam. When Saul sent men to watch
the house to kill him.*[f]

1 Deliver me from my enemies, my God;[g]
   protect me from those who rise up against me.[h]
2 Deliver me from those who practice sin,
   and save me from men of bloodshed.
3 LORD, look! They set an ambush for me.
   Powerful men attack me,
   but not because of any sin or rebellion of mine.[i]
4 For no fault of mine, they run and take up
      a position.
   Awake to help me, and take notice.
5 You, LORD God of •Hosts, God of Israel,
   rise up to punish all the nations;
   do not show grace to any wicked traitors. •*Selah*
6 They return at evening, snarling like dogs
   and prowling around the city.
7 Look, they spew from their mouths—
   sharp words from[j] their lips.[k]
   "For who," ⌊they say,⌋ "will hear?"
8 But You laugh[l] at them, LORD;
   You ridicule all the nations.
9 I will keep watch for You, my[m] strength,
   because God is my stronghold.
10 My faithful God[n] will come to meet me;
   God will let me look down on my adversaries.

[a] 58:8 Jb 3:16
[b] 58:9 Or *thorns, He will sweep
    it away, whether raw or cook-
    ing,* or *thorns, He will sweep
    him away alive in fury*
[c] 58:10 Jr 11:20
[d] 58:11 Ps 50:6; 75:7
[e] Possibly a song tune
[f] 1 Sm 19:11-18
[g] 59:1 Ps 143:9
[h] 59:1 Ps 18:17; 91:14; 2 Sm
    22:18
[i] 59:3 1 Sm 20:1; 24:11
[j] 59:7 Lit *swords are on*
[k] 59:7 Ps 52:2; 57:4; 64:3
[l] 59:8 Ps 2:4; 37:13
[m] 59:9 Some Hb mss, LXX, Vg,
    Tg; other Hb mss read *his*
[n] 59:10 Alt Hb traditions read
    God in His faithful love, or *My
    God, His faithful love*

NOTES

a **59:11** Gn 15:1; Dt 33:29; 2 Sm 22:3,31
b **59:13** Ps 104:35
c **59:16** Ps 5:3; 88:13; 92:2
d Possibly a song tune
e 2 Kg 14:7; 1 Ch 18:3-11; 19:6-19
f **60:1** Lit *have burst through*
g **60:1** Or *Turn back to us*
h **60:3** Is 51:17-23; Jr 25:15-17
i **60:4** Or *can rally before the archers*, or *can rally because of the truth*

WORD STUDY

Hebrew word:
misgab [mish GAHV]

HCSB translation:
stronghold

Focus passage:
Psalm 59:9,16-17

Misgab is related to the verb *sagab* (*to be inaccessibly high*). Literally, *misgab* is a high point used for refuge. This could include a rocky cliff (Is 33:16) or fortified walls (Is 25:12). Such means of protection were necessary for survival in the ancient Near East. Metaphorically, *misgab* refers to God as the *stronghold* where His people find shelter from life's troubles. "My" is often attached to *misgab*, indicating that God's people may personally appropriate His protective care (Ps 18:2). *Misgab* is often used with other terms that denote protection, such as crag (Ps 18:2), fortress (Ps 144:2), deliverer (Ps 18:2), shield (Ps 18:2), and savior (2 Sm 22:3). Yahweh is the *stronghold* of His people (Ps 46:7), especially the oppressed (Ps 9:9). He is not only a hiding place to whom His people can run, but also an active ally who fights on their behalf (Ps 144:2).

11 Do not kill them; otherwise, my people will forget.
By Your power, make them homeless wanderers
   and bring them down,
O Lord, our shield.[a]

12 The sin of their mouths is the word of their lips,
so let them be caught in their pride.
They utter curses and lies.

13 Consume ⌊them⌋ in rage;
consume ⌊them⌋ until they are gone.[b]
Then they will know to the ends of the earth
that God rules over Jacob.   •*Selah*

14 And they return at evening, snarling like dogs
and prowling around the city.

15 They scavenge for food;
they growl if they are not satisfied.

16 But I will sing of Your strength
and will joyfully proclaim Your faithful love
   in the morning.[c]
For You have been a stronghold for me,
a refuge in my day of trouble.

17 To You, my strength, I sing praises,
because God is my stronghold—
my faithful God.

PSALM 60

PRAYER IN DIFFICULT TIMES

For the choir director: according to "The Lily of Testimony."[d] *A Davidic •Miktam for teaching. When he fought with Aram-naharaim and Aram-zobah, and Joab returned and struck Edom in the Valley of Salt, ⌊killing⌋ 12,000.*[e]

1 God, You have rejected us; You have
   broken out[f] against us;
You have been angry. Restore us![g]

2 You have shaken the land and split it open.
Heal its fissures, for it shudders.

3 You have made Your people suffer hardship;
You have given us a wine to drink that made us
   stagger.[h]

4 You have given a signal flag to those who •fear
   You,
so that they can flee before the archers.[i]   •*Selah*

62

5 Save with Your right hand,[a] and answer me,
so that those You love may be rescued.

6 God has spoken in His sanctuary:[b]
"I will triumph! I will divide up Shechem.
I will apportion the Valley of Succoth.

7 Gilead is Mine, Manasseh is Mine,
and Ephraim is My helmet;
Judah is My scepter.[c]

8 Moab is My washbasin;
on Edom I throw My sandal.
Over Philistia I shout in triumph."

9 Who will bring me to the fortified city?
Who will lead me to Edom?

10 Is it not You, God, who have rejected us?
God, You do not march out with our armies.

11 Give us aid against the foe,
for human help is worthless.

12 With God we will perform valiantly;[d]
He will trample our foes.[e]

PSALM 61
SECURITY IN GOD

For the choir director: on stringed instruments.
Davidic.

1 God, hear my cry;
pay attention to my prayer.[f]

2 I call to You from the ends of the earth
when my heart is without strength.
Lead me to a rock that is high above me,[g]

3 for You have been a refuge for me,
a strong tower[h] in the face of the enemy.

4 I will live in Your tent forever,
take refuge under the shelter of Your wings.[i]
•*Selah*

5 God, You have heard my vows;
You have given a heritage to those who fear
Your name.

6 Add days to the king's life;
may his years span many generations.

7 May he sit enthroned before God forever;[j]
appoint faithful love and truth to guard him.[k]

8 Then I will continually sing of Your name,
fulfilling my vows day by day.

NOTES

[a] **60:5** Ps 17:7; 20:6; 138:7
[b] **60:6** Or *has promised by His holy nature*
[c] **60:7** Gn 49:10
[d] **60:12** Ps 118:15-16; Nm 24:18
[e] **60:5-12** Ps 108:6-13
[f] **61:1** Ps 17:1; 88:2; 142:6
[g] **61:2** Ps 27:5
[h] **61:3** Pr 18:10
[i] **61:4** Ps 17:8; 91:4; Ru 2:12
[j] **61:7** Ps 9:7; 29:10; 102:12
[k] **61:7** Ps 40:11

NOTES

a 1 Ch 25:1-6
b 62:1-2 Ps 3:8; 4:8; 2 Sm 22:2-3
c 62:2 Ps 37:24; 55:22
d 62:3 Other Hb mss read *you be struck down*
e 62:9 Ps 39:5-6,11
f 62:10 Lit *increases, do not set heart*
g 62:10 Jb 31:24-25; Mk 4:19; 1 Tm 6:10,17-19
h 62:12 Mt 16:27; Rm 2:6; Rv 22:12

WORD STUDY

Hebrew word:
mahseh [mach SEH]

HCSB translation:
refuge, shelter

Focus passage:
Psalm 62:7-8

Mahseh literally refers to any structure providing shelter. The crags of the rocks are a *shelter* for the hyraxes (Ps 104:18). The poor have no *place of shelter* when oppressed by evil men (Jb 24:8). The OT usually uses *mahseh* figuratively to refer to a person or an abstract concept that is trusted as a *shelter*. Men can seek false *shelter* (Is 28:15), or they can trust in Yahweh, the appropriate *shelter* from harm. Believers can proclaim, "Yahweh is my *refuge*," (Ps 46:1) and should teach their children to seek *refuge* in Him (Pr 14:26). Yahweh is a *refuge* for the afflicted (Ps 14:6). *Mahseh* is often used with words such as *stronghold* (Jl 3:16) and *fortress* (Ps 91:2), stressing Yahweh's faithfulness in watching over His people. His glorious presence will one day *shelter* His people from every calamity (Is 4:6).

PSALM 62

TRUST IN GOD ALONE

For the choir director: according to Jeduthun. [a]
A Davidic psalm.

1 I am at rest in God alone;
my salvation comes from Him.
2 He alone is my rock and my salvation, [b]
my stronghold; I will not be greatly shaken. [c]
3 How long will you threaten a man?
Will all of you attack [d]
as if he were a leaning wall
or a tottering stone fence?
4 They only plan to bring him down
from his high position.
They take pleasure in lying;
they bless with their mouths,
but they curse inwardly. •Selah
5 Rest in God alone, my soul,
for my hope comes from Him.
6 He alone is my rock and my salvation,
my stronghold; I will not be shaken.
7 My salvation and glory depend on God;
my strong rock, my refuge, is in God.
8 Trust in Him at all times, you people;
pour out your hearts before Him.
God is our refuge. •Selah
9 •Men are only a vapor; [e]
exalted men, an illusion.
On a balance scale, they go up;
together they ⌊weigh⌋ less than a vapor.
10 Place no trust in oppression,
or false hope in robbery.
If wealth increases,
pay no attention to it. [f] [g]
11 God has spoken once;
I have heard this twice:
strength belongs to God,
12 and faithful love belongs to You, LORD.
For You repay each according to his works. [h]

PSALM 63

PRAISE GOD WHO SATISFIES

A Davidic psalm. When he was in the wilderness of Judah. [a]

1 O God, You are my God; I eagerly seek You. [b]
My soul thirsts for You; [c]
my body faints for You
in a land that is dry, desolate, and without water.

2 So I gaze on You in the sanctuary
to see Your strength and Your glory. [d]

3 My lips will glorify You
because Your faithful love is better than life.

4 So I will praise You as long as I live;
at Your name, I will lift up my hands. [e]

5 You satisfy me as with rich food; [f] [g]
my mouth will praise You with joyful lips.

6 When, on my bed, I think of You, [h]
I meditate on You during the night watches [i]

7 because You are my help; [j]
I will rejoice in the shadow of Your wings. [k]

8 I follow close to You;
Your right hand holds on to me.

9 But those who seek to destroy my life
will go into the depths of the earth. [l]

10 They will be given over to the power
of the sword; [m]
they will become the jackals' prey.

11 But the king will rejoice in God;
all who swear by Him [n] will boast, [o]
for the mouths of liars will be shut.

PSALM 64

PROTECTION FROM EVILDOERS

For the choir director. A Davidic psalm.

1 God, hear my voice when I complain.
Protect my life from the terror of the enemy.

2 Hide me from the scheming of the wicked,
from the mob of evildoers,

3 who sharpen their tongues like swords
and aim bitter words like arrows, [p]

NOTES

a 1 Sm 23–24; 2 Sm 15:23,28; 16:2
b 63:1 Ps 78:34; Is 26:9; Hs 5:15
c 63:1 Ps 42:2; Is 55:1
d 63:2 Ps 17:15; 27:4; Jb 19:26-27
e 63:4 Lm 3:41
f 63:5 Lit *with fat and fatness*
g 63:5 Pr 13:25; Jr 50:19
h 63:6 Ps 42:6; Is 64:5; Jr 20:9
i 63:6 Ps 119:148; Lm 2:19
j 63:7 Ps 27:9; 40:17; 46:1
k 63:7 Ps 17:8; 36:7; 57:1
l 63:9 Ps 86:13; Ezk 26:20; 31:14-18
m 63:10 Jr 18:21; Ezk 35:5
n 63:11 Or *him*, referring to the king; 1 Sm 17:55; 2 Sm 14:19
o 63:11 Ps 34:2; 1 Ch 16:10; Is 41:16
p 64:3 Ps 52:2; 57:4; Pr 25:18

NOTES

[a] 64:5 Lit *word*, or *thing*
[b] 64:5 Or *They hold fast to an evil purpose*, or *They establish for themselves an evil purpose*
[c] 64:5 Ps 35:7; 140:5; 141:9
[d] 64:5 Or *us*, or *it*
[e] 64:8 Jr 48:27
[f] 64:10 Ps 58:10; 68:3; 97:11-12
[g] 65:1 LXX, Syr read *is due to You*
[h] 65:1 Or *Praise is silence to You*, or *Praise awaits You*
[i] 65:1 Jerusalem
[j] 65:2 Ps 86:9; Is 2:2-4; 66:23
[k] 65:3 Or *can forgive*, or *can wipe out*
[l] 65:4 Or *house, Your holy temple*
[m] 65:5 Ps 45:4; 106:22; Is 64:3
[n] 65:5 Ps 79:9; 85:4; 1 Ch 16:35
[o] 65:6 Ps 90:2; Am 4:13

4 shooting from concealed places at the innocent.
They shoot at him suddenly and are not afraid.

5 They encourage each other in an evil plan;[a] [b]
they talk about hiding traps[c] and say,
"Who will see them?"[d]

6 They devise crimes ⌊and say,⌋
"We have perfected a secret plan."
The inner man and the heart are mysterious.

7 But God will shoot them with arrows;
suddenly, they will be wounded.

8 They will be made to stumble;
their own tongues work against them.
All who see them will shake their heads.[e]

9 Then everyone will fear
and will tell about God's work,
for they will understand what He has done.

10 The righteous rejoice in the LORD[f]
and take refuge in Him;
all the upright in heart offer praise.

PSALM 65
GOD'S CARE FOR THE EARTH

For the choir director. A Davidic psalm. A song.

1 Praise is rightfully Yours,[g] [h]
God, in Zion;[i]
vows to You will be fulfilled.

2 All humanity will come to You,
the One who hears prayer.[j]

3 Iniquities overwhelm me;
only You can atone for[k] our rebellions.

4 How happy is the one You choose
and bring near to live in Your courts!
We will be satisfied with the goodness
of Your house,
the holiness of Your temple.[l]

5 You answer us in righteousness,
with awe-inspiring works,[m]
God of our salvation,[n]
the hope of all the ends of the earth
and of the distant seas;

6 You establish the mountains by Your power,[o]
robed with strength;

7   You silence the roar of the seas, the roar
      of their waves,
   and the tumult of the nations.^a

8   Those who live far away are awed
      by Your signs;
   You make east and west shout for joy.

9   You visit the earth and water it abundantly,
      enriching it greatly.^b
   God's stream is filled with water,
   for You prepare the earth^c in this way, providing
   ⌊people⌋ with grain.

10   You soften it with showers and bless its growth,
   soaking its furrows and leveling its ridges.

11   You crown the year with Your goodness;
   Your ways overflow with plenty.^d

12   The wilderness pastures overflow,
   and the hills are robed with joy.^e

13   The pastures are clothed with flocks,
   and the valleys covered with grain.^f
   They shout in triumph; indeed, they sing.^g

PSALM 66

PRAISE FOR GOD'S MIGHTY ACTS

For the choir director. A song. A psalm.

1   Shout joyfully to God, all the earth!
2   Sing the glory of His name;
   make His praise glorious.^h

3   Say to God, "How awe-inspiring are
      Your works!
   Your enemies will cringe before You
   because of Your great strength.

4   All the earth will worship Youⁱ and sing praise
      to You.
   They will sing praise to Your name."   •*Selah*

5   Come and see the works of God;^j
   His acts toward •mankind are awe-inspiring.

6   He turned the sea into dry land,
   and they crossed the river on foot.^k
   There we rejoiced in Him.

7   He rules forever by His might;
   He keeps His eye on the nations.^l
   The rebellious should not exalt themselves. •*Selah*

NOTES

^a **65:7** Ps 93:4; Is 17:13; Jr 51:55
^b **65:9** Ps 104:13; 147:8; Is 45:8
^c **65:9** Lit *prepare it*
^d **65:11** Lit *ways drip with fat*
^e **65:12** Jb 38:26-27; Jl 2:22; 3:18
^f **65:13** Is 30:23
^g **65:13** Is 44:23; 55:12
^h **66:1-2** Ps 48:10; 100:1; 106:47; 1 Ch 16:29,35
ⁱ **66:4** Ps 72:11; Is 66:23; Zph 2:11
^j **66:5** Ps 46:8
^k **66:6** Ex 14:10-31
^l **66:7** Ps 14:2; 33:13-14; Pr 15:3

8 Praise our God, you peoples;
 let the sound of His praise be heard.

9 He keeps us alive[a]
 and does not allow our feet to slip.[b]

10 For You, God, tested us;[c]
 You refined us as silver is refined.[d]

11 You lured us into a trap;[e]
 You placed burdens on our backs.

12 You let men ride over our heads;
 we went through fire and water,[f]
 but You brought us out to abundance.[g] [h]

13 I will enter Your house with •burnt offerings;
 I will pay You my vows

14 that my lips promised
 and my mouth spoke during my distress.

15 I will offer You fattened sheep as •burnt offerings,
 with the fragrant smoke of rams;
 I will sacrifice oxen with goats.   •*Selah*

16 Come and listen, all who •fear God,
 and I will tell what He has done for me.[i]

17 I cried out to Him with my mouth,
 and praise was on my tongue.

18 If I had been aware of malice in my heart,
 the Lord would not have listened.[j]

19 However, God has listened;
 He has paid attention to the sound of my prayer.

20 May God be praised!
 He has not turned away my prayer
 or turned His faithful love from me.

PSALM 67

ALL WILL PRAISE GOD

For the choir director: with stringed instruments.
A psalm. A song.

1 May God be gracious to us and bless us;
 look on us with favor[k]   •*Selah*

2 so that Your way may be known on earth,[l]
 Your salvation among all nations.

3 Let the peoples praise You, God;
 let all the peoples praise You.[m]

4 Let the nations rejoice and shout for joy,
 for You judge the peoples with fairness[n]
 and lead the nations on earth.   •*Selah*

5 Let the peoples praise You, O God,
let all the peoples praise You.

6 The earth has produced its harvest;
God, our God, blesses us.

7 God will bless us,
and all the ends of the earth will •fear Him.[a]

PSALM 68

GOD'S MAJESTIC POWER

For the choir director. A Davidic psalm. A song.

1 God arises. His enemies scatter,
and those who hate Him flee
from His presence.[b]

2 As smoke is blown away,
so You blow ⌊them⌋ away.[c]
As wax melts before the fire,
so the wicked are destroyed before God.

3 But the righteous are glad;
they rejoice before God and celebrate with joy.[d]

4 Sing to God! Sing praises to His name.[e]
Exalt Him who rides on the clouds[f] [g]—
His name is •Yahweh[h]—and rejoice before Him.

5 A father of the fatherless and a champion
of widows[i]
is God in His holy dwelling.

6 God provides homes for those who are deserted.
He leads out the prisoners to prosperity,[j]
but the rebellious live in a scorched land.

7 God, when You went out before Your people,
when You marched through the desert,   •*Selah*

8 the earth trembled, and the skies poured down
⌊rain⌋
before God, the God of Sinai,[k]
before God, the God of Israel.[l]

9 You, God, showered abundant rain;[m]
You revived Your inheritance
when it languished.

10 Your people settled in it;
by Your goodness You provided for the poor,
God.

11 The Lord gave the command;
a great company of women brought
the good news:[n]

NOTES

a 67:7 Ps 33:8; 1 Kg 8:43; 2 Ch 6:33
b 68:1 Ps 7:6; Nm 10:35; Ezk 30:26
c 68:2 Ps 37:20; Hs 13:3
d 68:3 Ps 40:16; 64:10; 1 Sm 2:1; Is 61:10
e 68:4 Ps 7:17; 66:4; Ex 15:1-18
f 68:4 Or *rides through the desert*
g 68:4 Ps 18:10-11; Dt 33:26; Is 19:1
h 68:4 Lit *Yah*
i 68:5 Ps 146:9; Dt 24:17,19; Jr 22:3
j 68:6 Or *prisoners with joyous music*; Hb uncertain
k 68:8 Lit *God, this Sinai*
l 68:7-8 Ex 19:16-18; Jdg 5:4-5
m 68:9 Ps 65:9-13
n 68:11 1 Sm 18:6-7

a 68:13 Or *If*

b 68:13 Or *campfires*, or *saddle-bags*; Hb obscure

c 68:13 Gn 49:14; Jdg 5:16

d 68:14 Or *Black Mountain*

e 68:16 Mount Zion

f 68:15 Ps 48:1-2; 132:13-14; Is 2:2-4

g 68:17 Hab 3:8

h 68:17 Or *in holiness*

i 68:17 Some emend text to *Lord came from Sinai into the holy place*

j 68:18 Lit *among*

k 68:18 Or *even those rebelling against the* LORD *God's living there*, or *even rebels are living with the* LORD *God*; Hb obscure

l 68:18 Dt 21:10; Eph 4:8

m 68:19 Is 46:3-4

n 68:23 LXX, Syr read *dip*

o 68:23 1 Kg 21:19; 22:38; 2 Kg 9:36

p 68:24 Ps 42:4; Is 60:11

q 68:24 Or *in holiness*

r 68:25 Some Hb mss, LXX, Syr read *Officials*

s 68:25 Jdg 11:34; 1 Sm 18:6; Jr 31:4

t 68:27 Hb obscure

12 "The kings of the armies flee—they flee!"
She who stays at home divides the spoil.

13 While[a] you lie among the sheepfolds,[b] [c]
the wings of a dove are covered with silver,
and its feathers with glistening gold.

14 When the Almighty scattered kings in the land,
it snowed on Zalmon.[d]

15 Mount Bashan is God's towering mountain;
Mount Bashan is a mountain of many peaks.

16 Why gaze with envy, you mountain peaks,
at the mountain[e] God desired for His dwelling?[f]
The LORD will live ⌊there⌋ forever!

17 God's chariots[g] are tens of thousands,
thousands and thousands;
the Lord is among them in the sanctuary[h]
as He was at Sinai.[i]

18 You ascended to the heights, taking away captives;
You received gifts from[j] people,
even from the rebellious,
so that the LORD God might live ⌊there⌋.[k] [l]

19 May the Lord be praised!
Day after day He bears our burdens;[m]
God is our salvation.   •*Selah*

20 Our God is a God of salvation,
and escape from death belongs to the Lord GOD.

21 Surely God crushes the heads of His enemies,
the hairy head of one who goes on
in his guilty acts.

22 The Lord said, "I will bring ⌊them⌋ back
from Bashan;
I will bring ⌊them⌋ back from the depths of the sea

23 so that your foot may wade[n] in blood
and your dogs' tongues may have their share
from the enemies."[o]

24 People have seen Your procession,[p] God,
the procession of my God, my King,
in the sanctuary.[q]

25 Singers[r] lead the way, with musicians following;
among them are young women playing
tambourines.[s]

26 Praise God in the assemblies;
⌊praise⌋ the LORD from the fountain of Israel.

27 There is Benjamin, the youngest, leading them,
the rulers of Judah in their assembly,[t]
the rulers of Zebulun, the rulers of Naphtali.

28 Your God has decreed your strength.
Show Your strength, God,
You who have acted on our behalf.

29 Because of Your temple at Jerusalem,
kings will bring tribute to You.[a]

30 Rebuke the beast[b] in the reeds,
the herd of bulls with the calves of the peoples.
Trample underfoot those with bars of silver.[c]
Scatter the peoples who take pleasure in war.

31 Ambassadors will come[d] from Egypt;
Cush[e] will stretch out its hands[f] to God.

32 Sing to God, you kingdoms of the earth;
sing praise to the Lord,   •Selah

33 to Him who rides in the ancient, highest heavens.[g]
Look, He thunders with His powerful voice![h]

34 Ascribe power to God.
His majesty is over Israel,
His power among the clouds.

35 God, You are awe-inspiring in Your sanctuaries.
The God of Israel gives power and strength
to His people.[i]
May God be praised!

PSALM 69
A PLEA FOR RESCUE

*For the choir director: according to "The Lilies."[j]
Davidic.*

1 Save me, God,[k]
for the water has risen to my neck.

2 I have sunk in deep mud with no footing;
I have come into deep waters,
and a flood sweeps over me.[l]

3 I am weary from my crying; my throat
is parched.
My eyes fail, looking for my God.[m]

4 Those who hate me without cause[n]
are more numerous than the hairs of my head;
my deceitful enemies, who would destroy me,
are powerful.
Though I did not steal, I must repay.[o]

5 God, You know my foolishness,
and my guilty acts are not hidden from You.

NOTES

[a] **68:29** Is 18:7; 66:20; Hg 2:7
[b] **68:30** Probably Egypt
[c] **68:30** Or *peoples, trampling on those who take pleasure in silver*, or *peoples, trampling on the bars of silver*, or *peoples, who trample each other for bars of silver*
[d] **68:31** Or *They bring red cloth*, or *They bring bronze*
[e] **68:31** Modern Sudan
[f] **68:31** Probably with tribute or in submission
[g] **68:33** Dt 33:26
[h] **68:33** Ps 29:3-5; 46:6; Is 30:30
[i] **68:35** Ps 29:11; Is 40:29
[j] Apparently a hymn tune; compare Pss 45; 60; 80
[k] **69:1** Ps 3:7; 1 Ch 16:35
[l] **69:2** Ps 40:2; 69:14; 124:4
[m] **69:3** Ps 6:6; Jr 45:3; Lm 4:17
[n] **69:4** Ps 35:19; Jn 15:25
[o] **69:4** Lv 6:2-5

WORD STUDY

Hebrew word:
adonay [a doh NIGH]

HCSB translation:
Lord

Focus passage:
Psalm 68:12,18,20,21,23,33

Adonay, related to *adon* (*lord, master*), is a title showing honor and respect for God. *Adonay*, emphasizing God's authority or kingship, indicates the speaker's recognition of God's authority over him. While forms related to *adon* are used of other people – for example, *adoni* (*my lord*; Nm 32:25)—*adonay* is used exclusively in reference to God. The ending *–ay* may add emphasis to *adon*, showing that God is "Lord over all." For this reason, the term is frequently used in such contexts as appeals for deliverance from danger (Ps 40:18), in which God's sovereignty is acknowledged.

NOTES
a 69:6 Ps 25:3
b 69:7 Ps 44:15
c 69:8 Ps 38:11; Jb 19:13-14; Jr 12:6
d 69:9 Jn 2:17
e 69:9 Rm 15:3
f 69:10 Ps 35:13; 109:24-25
g 69:11 Jb 30:9
h 69:17 Ps 27:9; 44:24; Is 54:8
i 69:20 Lm 1:2-9,17,21

6 Do not let those who hope in You be disgraced[a]
   because of me,
Lord GOD of •Hosts;
do not let those who seek You be humiliated
   because of me,
God of Israel.

7 For I have endured insults because of You,
and shame has covered my face.[b]

8 I have become a stranger to my brothers
and a foreigner to my mother's sons[c]

9 because zeal for Your house has consumed me,[d]
and the insults of those who insult You
   have fallen on me.[e]

10 I mourned and fasted,[f]
but it brought me insults.

11 I wore •sackcloth as my clothing,
and I was a joke to them.[g]

12 Those who sit at the city gate talk about me,
and drunkards make up songs about me.

13 But as for me, LORD, my prayer to You is
   for a time of favor.
In Your abundant, faithful love, God,
answer me with Your sure salvation.

14 Rescue me from the miry mud; don't let me sink.
Let me be rescued from those who hate me,
and from the deep waters.

15 Don't let the floodwaters sweep over me
or the deep swallow me up;
don't let the pit close its mouth over me.

16 Answer me, LORD, for Your faithful love is
   good;
in keeping with Your great compassion, turn
   to me.

17 Don't hide Your face from Your servant,
for I am in distress.[h]
Answer me quickly!

18 Draw near to me and redeem me;
ransom me because of my enemies.

19 You know the insults I endure—my shame
   and disgrace.
You are aware of all my adversaries.

20 Insults have broken my heart, and I am
   in despair.
I waited for sympathy, but there was none;
for comforters, but found no one.[i]

21 Instead, they gave me gall[a] for my food,
and for my thirst they gave me vinegar
to drink.[b]

22 Let their table set before them be a snare,
and let it be a trap for ⌊their⌋ allies.[c]

23 Let their eyes grow too dim to see,
and let their loins continually shake.[d]

24 Pour out Your rage on them,
and let Your burning anger overtake them.[e]

25 Make their fortification desolate;
may no one live in their tents.[f]

26 For they persecute the one You struck
and talk about the pain of those You wounded.

27 Add guilt to their guilt;
do not let them share in Your righteousness.

28 Let them be erased from the book of life
and not be recorded with the righteous.[g]

29 But as for me—poor and in pain—
let Your salvation protect me, God.[h]

30 I will praise God's name with song
and exalt Him with thanksgiving.[i]

31 That will please the LORD more than an ox,
more than a bull with horns and hooves.

32 The humble will see it and rejoice.
You who seek God, take heart!

33 For the LORD listens to the needy
and does not despise His own who are
prisoners.[j]

34 Let heaven and earth praise Him,
the seas and all that moves in them,

35 for God will save Zion
and build up[k] the cities of Judah.[l]
They will live there and possess it.

36 The descendants of His servants will inherit it,
and those who love His name will live in it.[m]

PSALM 70

A CALL FOR DELIVERANCE

For the choir director. Davidic.
To bring remembrance.

1 God, deliver me.
Hurry to help me, LORD![n]

[a] **69:21** A bitter substance
[b] **69:21** Mt 27:34,48; Jn 19:29
[c] **69:22** Rm 11:9-10; 1 Th 5:3
[d] **69:23** Ec 12:3; Ezk 29:7; Rm 11:10
[e] **69:24** Ps 79:6; Ezk 21:31; Zph 3:8
[f] **69:25** Ac 1:20
[g] **69:28** Ex 32:32; Dn 12:1; Mal 3:16; Rv 3:5
[h] **69:29** Ps 91:14; 107:41; Pr 29:25
[i] **69:30** Ps 100:4; 107:22; Jr 33:11
[j] **69:33** Ps 68:6; 107:10-16; 146:7
[k] **69:35** Or *and rebuild*
[l] **69:35** Is 44:26; 61:4; Ezk 36:10
[m] **69:36** Ps 102:29; Is 65:9,23
[n] **70:1** Ps 22:20; 38:23

NOTES

a **70:2-3** Ps 35:25; 40:14-15
b **70:4** Ps 35:27
c **70:5** Ps 40:17; Dn 9:19
d **71:1** Ps 18:2,30; Ru 2:12; 2 Sm 22:3,31
e **71:1** Ps 25:2,20; 31:2
f **71:3** Some Hb mss, LXX, Sym, Tg; other Hb mss read *habitation*
g **71:1-3** Ps 31:1-3
h **71:3** Ps 18:2; 31:3; 2 Sm 22:2
i **71:5-6** Ps 22:9-10
j **71:7** Ps 62:7; 73:28; 91:2,9
k **71:8** 1 Ch 29:13; Is 60:19
l **71:9** Ps 27:9; 71:18; Is 46:3-4
m **71:10-11** Ps 56:6; Jr 20:10

2 Let those who seek my life
    be disgraced and confounded;
    let those who wish me harm
    be driven back and humiliated.

3 Let those who say, "Aha, aha!"
    retreat because of their shame. [a]

4 Let all who seek You rejoice and be glad in You;
    let those who love Your salvation
    continually say, "God is great!" [b]

5 But I am afflicted and needy;
    hurry to me, God.
    You are my help and my deliverer;
    LORD, do not delay. [c]

PSALM 71

GOD'S HELP IN OLD AGE

1 LORD, I seek refuge in You; [d]
    never let me be disgraced. [e]

2 In Your justice, rescue and deliver me;
    listen closely to me and save me.

3 Be a rock of refuge [f] for me,
    where I can always go.
    Give the command to save me,
    for You are my rock and fortress. [g] [h]

4 Deliver me, My God, from the hand
      of the wicked,
    from the grasp of the unjust and oppressive.

5 For You are my hope, Lord GOD,
    my confidence from my youth.

6 I have leaned on You from birth;
    You took me from my mother's womb. [i]
    My praise is always about You.

7 I have become an ominous sign to many,
    but You are my strong refuge. [j]

8 My mouth is full of praise
    and honor to You all day long. [k]

9 Don't discard me in my old age:
    as my strength fails, do not abandon me. [l]

10 For my enemies talk about me,
    and those who spy on me plot together,

11 saying, "God has abandoned him;
    chase him and catch him,
    for there is no one to rescue ⌊him⌋." [m]

12 God, do not be far from me;
my God, hurry to help me.[a]

13 May my adversaries be disgraced
and confounded;
may those who seek my harm
be covered with disgrace
and humiliation.[b]

14 But I will hope continually[c]
and will praise You more and more.

15 My mouth will tell
about Your righteousness
and Your salvation all day long,
though I cannot sum them up.

16 I come because of the mighty acts[d]
of the Lord GOD;
I will proclaim Your righteousness,
Yours alone.

17 God, You have taught me from my youth,
and I still proclaim Your wonderful works.

18 Even when I am old and gray,
God, do not abandon me.[e]
Then I will[f] proclaim Your power to ⌊another⌋
generation,
Your strength to all who are to come.[g]

19 Your righteousness reaches heaven, God,
You who have done great things.
God, who is like You?[h]

20 You caused me[i] to experience many troubles
and misfortunes,
but You will revive me[j] again.
You will bring me[k] up again, even
from the depths of the earth.

21 You will increase my honor
and comfort me once again.

22 Therefore, with a lute I will praise You
for Your faithfulness, my God;
I will sing to You with a harp,
Holy One of Israel.

23 My lips will shout for joy when I sing praise
to You,
because You have redeemed me.

24 Therefore, my tongue will proclaim
Your righteousness all day long,
for those who seek my harm
will be disgraced and confounded.

a 71:12 Ps 22:11,19; 38:21-22; 40:13
b 71:13 Ps 71:24; Est 9:2
c 71:14 Ps 33:18; 130:7; 147:11
d 71:16 Some Hb mss, LXX, Jer read *come with the might*
e 71:18 Is 46:4
f 71:18 Lit *me until I*
g 71:18 Ps 22:30-31
h 71:19 Ps 86:8; Ex 15:11; Mc 7:18
i 71:20 Alt Hb tradition, Aq read *us*
j 71:20 Alt Hb tradition, Tg, Jer read *us*
k 71:20 Other Hb mss, Tg, Jer read *us*

NOTES

[a] 72:1 1 Kg 3:6–9:28

[b] 72:3 Or *peace*

[c] 72:3 Is 11:9; 52:7; 55:12

[d] 72:4 Ps 72:13; 109:31

[e] 72:5 LXX; MT reads *May they fear you*

[f] 72:6 Dt 32:2; 2 Sm 23:3-4; Pr 16:15

[g] 72:7 Some Hb mss, LXX, Syr, Jer read *May righteousness*

[h] 72:7 Or *peace*

[i] 72:7 Ps 37:11; Is 60:21

[j] 72:8 Gn 15:18; Ex 23:31; Zch 9:10

[k] 72:9 Is 49:23; Zch 14:16-17

[l] 72:10 1 Kg 10:22; Is 60:9; Ezk 27:15

[m] 72:10 1 Kg 10:1-10; Is 60:6

[n] 72:12 Jb 29:12; Lm 1:7

[o] 72:14 Or *valuable*

[p] 72:14 Ps 69:18; 116:15

PSALM 72

A PRAYER FOR THE KING

Solomonic.

1 God, give Your justice to the king
and Your righteousness to the king's son.[a]

2 He will judge Your people with righteousness
and Your afflicted ones with justice.

3 May the mountains bring prosperity[b]
to the people,
and the hills, righteousness.[c]

4 May he vindicate the afflicted among the people,
help the poor,[d]
and crush the oppressor.

5 May he continue[e] while the sun endures,
and as long as the moon,
throughout all generations.

6 May he be like rain that falls on the cut grass,
like spring showers that water the earth.[f]

7 May the righteous[g] flourish in his days,
and prosperity[h] abound till the moon is
no more.[i]

8 And may he rule from sea to sea
and from the Euphrates to the ends of the earth.[j]

9 May desert tribes kneel before him
and his enemies lick the dust.[k]

10 May the kings of Tarshish and the coastlands
bring tribute,[l]
the kings of Sheba and Seba offer gifts.[m]

11 And let all kings bow down to him,
all nations serve him.

12 For he will rescue the poor who cry out
and the afflicted who have no helper.[n]

13 He will have pity on the poor and helpless
and save the lives of the poor.

14 He will redeem them from oppression
and violence,
for their lives are precious[o] in his sight.[p]

15 May he live long!
May gold from Sheba be given to him.
May prayer be offered for him continually,
and may he be blessed all day long.

16 May there be plenty of grain in the land;
may it wave on the tops of the mountains.

May its crops be like Lebanon.
May people flourish in the cities like the grass
    of the field.

17 May his name endure forever;
as long as the sun shines, may his fame increase.
May all nations be blessed by him and call him
    blessed.^a

18 May the LORD God, the God of Israel,
    be praised,
who alone does wonders.^b

19 May His glorious name be praised forever;
the whole earth is filled with His glory.^c
Amen and amen.

20 The prayers of David son of Jesse are concluded.

a **72:17** Gn 12:2–3; 22:18
b **72:18** Ps 136:4; Ex 15:1; Jb 9:10
c **72:19** Nm 14:21; Is 6:3
d **73:3** Ps 37:1; Pr 23:17; 24:1
e **73:4** Lit *For there are no pangs to their death*
f **73:4** Lit *fat*
g **73:10** Lit *turn here*
h **73:10** Lit *and waters of fullness are drained by them*

BOOK III
(PSALMS 73–89)
PSALM 73
GOD'S WAYS VINDICATED

A psalm of Asaph.

1 God is indeed good to Israel,
to the pure in heart.

2 But as for me, my feet almost slipped;
my steps nearly went astray.

3 For I envied the arrogant;
I saw the prosperity of the wicked.^d

4 They have an easy time until they die,^e
and their bodies are well-fed.^f

5 They are not in trouble like others;
they are not afflicted like most people.

6 Therefore, pride is their necklace,
and violence covers them like a garment.

7 Their eyes bulge out from fatness;
the imaginations of their hearts run wild.

8 They mock, and they speak maliciously;
they arrogantly threaten oppression.

9 They set their mouths against heaven,
and their tongues strut across the earth.

10 Therefore His people turn to them^g
and drink in their overflowing waters.^h

a 73:11 Ps 10:4,11; Is 29:15
b 73:13 Ps 24:4; 26:6; Mt 27:24
c 73:15 Lit *betrayed the genera-tion of Your sons*
d 73:16 Lit *it was trouble in my eyes*
e 73:17 Dt 32:20; Pr 14:12; Jr 29:11
f 73:20 Ps 35:23; 59:5
g 73:21 Lit *my kidneys were*
h 73:24 Or *will receive me with honor*
i 73:26 Lit *rock*
j 73:25-26 1 Sm 2:2; 2 Sm 22:31-32; Is 26:4

11 They say, "How can God know?
Does the •Most High know everything?"ᵃ

12 Look at them—the wicked!
They are always at ease, and they increase
their wealth.

13 Did I purify my heart
and wash my hands in innocenceᵇ for nothing?

14 For I am afflicted all day long,
and punished every morning.

15 If I had decided to say these things ⌊aloud⌋,
I would have betrayed Your people.ᶜ

16 When I tried to understand all this,
it seemed hopelessᵈ

17 until I entered God's sanctuary.
Then I understood their destiny.ᵉ

18 Indeed You put them in slippery places;
You make them fall into ruin.

19 How suddenly they become a desolation!
They come to an end, swept away by terrors.

20 Like one waking from a dream,
Lord, when arising, You will despise
their image.ᶠ

21 When I became embittered
and my innermost being wasᵍ wounded,

22 I was a fool and didn't understand;
I was an unthinking animal toward You.

23 Yet I am always with You;
You hold my right hand.

24 You guide me with Your counsel,
and afterward You will take me up in glory.ʰ

25 Whom do I have in heaven but You?
And I desire nothing on earth but You.

26 My flesh and my heart may fail,
but God is the strengthⁱ of my heart, my portion
forever.ʲ

27 Those far from You will certainly perish;
You destroy all who are unfaithful to You.

28 But as for me, God's presence is my good.
I have made the Lord GOD my refuge,
so I can tell about all You do.

PSALM 74

PRAYER FOR ISRAEL

A •Maskil of Asaph. [a]

NOTES

[a] 1 Ch 6:39; 15:19; 16:5,7,37
[b] 74:1 Ps 60:1,10; 108:11
[c] 74:1 Ps 79:13; 95:7; 100:3
[d] 74:2 Is 63:17; Jr 10:16; 51:19
[e] 74:2 Is 8:18
[f] 74:3 Lit *Lift up Your steps*
[g] 74:4 Lit *in Your meeting place*
[h] 74:7 Lit *they to the ground*
[i] 74:8 Lit *every meeting place of God in the land*
[j] 74:9 1 Sm 3:1; Lm 2:9; Ezk 7:26
[k] 74:10 Ps 74:18,22; Ex 32:12-13; Dt 32:27
[l] 74:11 Lit *From Your bosom*
[m] 74:12 Ps 47:6-8; 95:3; Jr 10:10
[n] 74:13 Is 27:1; Ezk 32:2
[o] 74:14 Is 27:1

1 Why have You rejected ⌊us⌋ forever, God? [b]
Why does Your anger burn against the sheep
    of Your pasture? [c]

2 Remember Your congregation,
    which You purchased long ago
and redeemed as the tribe
    for Your own possession. [d]
⌊Remember⌋ Mount Zion where You dwell. [e]

3 Make Your way [f] to the everlasting ruins,
to all that the enemy has destroyed
    in the sanctuary.

4 Your adversaries roared in the meeting place
    where You met with us. [g]
They set up their emblems as signs.

5 It was like men in a thicket of trees,
wielding axes,

6 then smashing all the carvings
with hatchets and picks.

7 They set Your sanctuary on fire;
they utterly [h] desecrated the dwelling place
    of Your name.

8 They said in their hearts, "Let us oppress them
    relentlessly."
They burned down every place throughout
    the land where God met with us. [i]

9 We don't see any signs for us.
There is no longer a prophet. [j]
And none of us knows how long this will last.

10 God, how long will the foe mock?
Will the enemy insult Your name forever? [k]

11 Why do You hold back Your hand?
Stretch out [l] Your right hand
    and destroy ⌊them⌋!

12 God my king [m] is from ancient times,
performing saving acts on the earth.

13 You divided the sea with Your strength;
You smashed the heads of the sea monsters
    in the waters; [n]

14 You crushed the heads of Leviathan; [o]
You fed him to the creatures of the desert.

NOTES

a 74:15 Ps 78:15; 104:10-11; Hab 3:9
b 74:15 Jos 4:23; Is 42:15; 44:27
c 74:16 Gn 1:14,16
d 74:17 Jb 38:10-11; Pr 8:29; Jr 5:22
e 74:17 Ps 104:19; Gn 1:14; 8:22
f 74:18 Ps 14:1; Dt 32:6,21
g 74:19 One Hb ms, LXX, Syr read *Do not hand over to beasts a soul that praises You*
h 74:20 Lv 26:9; Dt 4:31; 7:9,12
i 74:22 Ps 9:19; 82:8; Nm 10:35
j Apparently a tune for the psalm
k 75:1 Ps 119:151; 145:18; Dt 4:7
l 75:2 Ps 9:8; 96:10
m 75:4 Pr 27:1; Jr 9:23
n 75:4 Ps 89:17,24; 92:10; 1 Sm 2:1,10

15 You opened up springs and streams;[a]
You dried up ever-flowing rivers.[b]

16 The day is Yours, also the night;
You established the moon and the sun.[c]

17 You set all the boundaries of the earth;[d]
You made summer and winter.[e]

18 Remember this: the enemy has mocked
the LORD,
and a foolish people has insulted Your name.[f]

19 Do not give the life of Your dove to beasts;[g]
do not forget the lives of Your poor people
forever.

20 Consider the covenant,[h]
for the dark places of the land are full
of violence.

21 Do not let the oppressed turn away in shame;
let the poor and needy praise Your name.

22 Arise, God, defend Your cause![i]
Remember the insults that fools bring against
You all day long.

23 Do not forget the clamor of Your adversaries,
the tumult of Your opponents that goes up
constantly.

PSALM 75

GOD JUDGES THE WICKED

For the choir director: "Do Not Destroy."[j] *A psalm of Asaph. A song.*

1 We give thanks to You, God;
we give thanks to You, for Your name is near.[k]
People tell about Your wonderful works.

2 "When I choose a time,
I will judge fairly.[l]

3 When the earth and all its inhabitants shake,
I am the One who steadies its pillars.   •*Selah*

4 I say to the boastful, 'Do not boast,'[m]
and to the wicked, 'Do not lift up
your •horn.[n]

5 Do not lift up your •horn against heaven
or speak arrogantly.' "

6 Exaltation does not come
from the east, the west, or the desert,

7   for God is the judge: [a]
     He brings down one and exalts another. [b]

8   For there is a cup in the LORD's hand,
     full of wine blended with spices, and He pours
       from it.
     All the wicked of the earth will drink,
     draining it to the dregs. [c]

9   As for me, I will tell about Him forever;
     I will sing praise to the God of Jacob. [d]

10   "I will cut off all the •horns of the wicked,
     but the horns of the righteous will be lifted up."

PSALM 76

GOD, THE POWERFUL JUDGE

For the choir director: with stringed instruments.
A psalm of Asaph. A song.

1   God is known in Judah;
     His name is great [e] in Israel.

2   His tent is in Salem, [f] [g]
     His dwelling place in Zion.

3   There He shatters the bow's flaming arrows,
     the shield, the sword, and the weapons of war. [h]
                     •*Selah*

4   You are resplendent and majestic
     ⌊coming down⌋ from the mountains of prey.

5   The brave-hearted have been plundered;
     they have slipped into their ⌊final⌋ sleep.
     None of the warriors was able to lift a hand.

6   At Your rebuke, God of Jacob,
     both chariot and horse lay still.

7   And You—You are to be •feared. [i]
     When You are angry, who can stand before You? [j]

8   From heaven You pronounced judgment.
     The earth feared and grew quiet

9   when God rose up to judge
     and to save all the lowly of the earth. [k]   •*Selah*

10   Even human wrath will praise You;
     You will clothe Yourself with
       their remaining wrath. [l]

11   Make and keep your vows to the LORD your God;
     let all who are around Him bring tribute [m]
       to the awe-inspiring One. [n]

[a] **75:7** Ps 50:6; 58:11; Is 33:22
[b] **75:7** 1 Sm 2:7-8; Lk 1:52-53
[c] **75:8** Is 51:17,22; Jr 25:15-17
[d] **75:9** Ps 7:17; 9:2; 18:49
[e] **76:1** Jr 10:6; Mal 1:11
[f] **76:2** Jerusalem
[g] **76:2** Gn 14:18
[h] **76:3** Ps 46:9; Is 2:4; Jr 49:35
[i] **76:7** Or *are awe-inspiring*
[j] **76:7** Ps 1:5; 130:3; Nah 1:6
[k] **76:9** Is 3:13-15
[l] **76:10** Hb obscure
[m] **76:11** Ps 68:29; Is 18:7
[n] **76:11** Or *tribute with awe*

NOTES

a 1 Ch 25:1-6
b 1 Ch 6:39; 15:19; 16:5,7,37
c 77:2 Gn 37:35; Jr 31:15
d 77:3 Ps 42:5,11; 55:17; Ezk 7:16
e 77:3 Ps 143:4
f 77:7 Lm 2:7; 3:31
g 77:8 Ps 33:11; 85:5; 89:1,4
h 77:7-9 Ex 34:6-7
i 77:10 Lit "My piercing
j 77:11 Ps 88:12; 89:5
k 77:13-14 Ps 72:18; Ex 15:11; 34:10
l 77:15 Ex 6:6

12 He humbles the spirit of leaders;
He is •feared by the kings of the earth.

PSALM 77
CONFIDENCE IN A TIME OF CRISIS

For the choir director: according to Jeduthun.[a]
Of Asaph.[b] *A psalm.*

1 I cry aloud to God,
aloud to God, and He will hear me.
2 In my day of trouble I sought the Lord.
My hands were lifted up all night long;
I refused to be comforted.[c]
3 I think of God; I groan;[d]
I meditate; my spirit becomes weak.[e]   •*Selah*
4 You have kept me from closing my eyes;
I am troubled and cannot speak.
5 I consider days of old,
years long past.
6 At night I remember my music;
I meditate in my heart, and my spirit ponders.
7 "Will the Lord reject forever[f]
and never again show favor?
8 Has His faithful love ceased forever?
Is ⌊His⌋ promise at an end for all time?[g]
9 Has God forgotten to be gracious?
Has He in anger withheld His compassion?"[h]
        •*Selah*
10 So I say, "It is my sorrow[i]
that the right hand of the •Most High
has changed."
11 I will remember the LORD's works;
yes, I will remember Your ancient wonders.[j]
12 I will reflect on all You have done
and meditate on Your actions.
13 God, Your way is holy.
What god is great like God?
14 You are the God who works wonders;
You revealed Your strength
among the peoples.[k]
15 With power You redeemed
Your people,[l]
the descendants of Jacob and Joseph.   •*Selah*

16 The waters saw You, God.
The waters saw You; they trembled.
Even the depths shook.

17 The clouds poured down water.
The storm clouds thundered;
Your arrows flashed back and forth.^a

18 The sound of Your thunder was
in the whirlwind;
lightning lit up the world.^b
The earth shook and quaked.^c

19 Your way went through the sea,
and Your path through the great waters,^d
but Your footprints were unseen.

20 You led Your people like a flock^e
by the hand of Moses and Aaron.^{f g}

PSALM 78

LESSONS FROM ISRAEL'S PAST

A •Maskil of Asaph.^h

1 My people, hear my instruction;
listen to what I say.ⁱ

2 I will declare wise sayings;
I will speak mysteries from the past^j—

3 things we have heard and known
and that our fathers have passed down to us.

4 We must not hide them from their children,
but must tell a future generation the praises
of the LORD,
His might, and the wonderful works
He has performed.^k

5 He established a •testimony in Jacob
and set up a law in Israel,
which He commanded our fathers
to teach to their children

6 so that a future generation—children yet
to be born—might know.
They were to rise and tell their children

7 so that they might put their confidence in God
and not forget God's works,
but keep His commandments.^l

8 Then they would not be like their fathers,
a stubborn and rebellious generation,

NOTES

^a **77:17** Hab 3:11; Zch 9:14
^b **77:16-18** Ps 29:3-9; 97:4
^c **77:18** Ps 18:7; 2 Sm 22:8; Is 13:13
^d **77:19** Is 43:16
^e **77:20** Ps 23:1-4; 78:52-53; Ezk 34
^f **77:20** Nm 33:1; 1 Sm 12:6; Mc 6:4
^g **77:16-20** Ps 74:12-17; 114:3-5; Ex 15:5-10
^h 1 Ch 6:39; 15:19; 16:5,7,37
ⁱ **78:1** Pr 5:7; 7:24; Is 55:3
^j **78:2** Mt 13:35
^k **78:3-4** Ps 44:1; Ex 13:14; Jos 4:21-22
^l **78:7** Ps 103:2; 106:13; Pr 3:1

NOTES

a **78:8** Ps 78:37; 2 Ch 12:14

b **78:10** 1 Kg 11:11; 2 Kg 17:15; Jr 32:23

c **78:12** Ps 78:43; Ex 6-15

d **78:13** Ex 14:21; 15:8

e **78:14** Ex 13:21; Nm 14:14

f **78:15** Ex 17:6; Nm 20:8-13; Is 48:21

g **78:17** Is 63:10

h **78:18** Lit *in their heart*

i **78:18** Ex 17:2,7; Nm 14:22; 1 Co 10:5-10

j **78:20** Ex 16:3-36; Nm 11:4-34

k **78:22** Dt 9:23

l **78:25** Lit *Man*

m **78:25** Lit *mighty ones*

n **78:24-25** Ex 16:3-36; Jn 6:31

WORD STUDY

Hebrew word :
sur [TSOOR]

HCSB translation:
rock

Focus passage:
Psalms 78:15,20,35

Sur refers to a rock or rock formation. During Israel's wilderness wanderings, God brought water from a rock (Ex 17:6). This incident became a landmark event reminding Israel of God's provision for His people. *Rocks* provided refuge from calamity (Ps 27:5). They were used for offering sacrifices (Jdg 6:21) and for engraving documents and records (Jb 19:24). Figuratively, *sur* may refer to someone considered a source of protection. *Rock* is most often a title for Yahweh, emphasizing His strength and protective power (Dt 32:4). The term is used of God as the One who gave birth to His covenant people, Israel (Dt 32:18), and of Abraham as Israel's forefather (Is 51:1-2). Isaiah utilizes a *rock's* potential for harm to describe the Messiah as "a *rock* that makes men fall" (Is 8:14), emphasizing the fact that men cannot ignore an encounter with Him.

84

a generation whose heart was not loyal
and whose spirit was not faithful to God.[a]

9 The Ephraimite archers turned back
on the day of battle.

10 They did not keep God's covenant
and refused to live by His law.[b]

11 They forgot what He had done,
the wonderful works He had shown them.

12 He worked wonders in the sight of their fathers,
in the land of Egypt, the region of Zoan.[c]

13 He split the sea and brought them across;
the water stood up like a wall.[d]

14 He led them with a cloud by day
and with a fiery light throughout the night.[e]

15 He split rocks in the wilderness
and gave them drink as abundant as the deep.[f]

16 He brought streams out of the stone
and made water flow down like rivers.

17 But they continued to sin against Him,
rebelling in the desert against the •Most High.[g]

18 They deliberately[h] tested God,
demanding the food they craved.[i]

19 They spoke against God,
saying, "Is God able to provide food
in the wilderness?

20 Look! He struck the rock and water
gushed out;
torrents overflowed.
But can He also provide bread
or furnish meat for His people?"[j]

21 Therefore, the LORD heard and became furious;
then fire broke out against Jacob,
and anger flared up against Israel

22 because they did not believe God[k]
or rely on His salvation.

23 He gave a command to the clouds above
and opened the doors of heaven.

24 He rained manna for them to eat;
He gave them grain from heaven.

25 People[l] ate the bread of angels.[m]
He sent them an abundant supply of food.[n]

26 He made the east wind blow in the skies
and drove the south wind by His might.

27 He rained meat on them like dust,
and winged birds like the sand of the seas.

| | | |

28 He made ⌊them⌋ fall in His camp,
all around His tent.^{a b}

29 They ate and were completely satisfied,
for He gave them what they craved.

30 Before they had satisfied their desire,
while the food was still in their mouths,

31 God's anger flared up against them,
and He killed some of their best men.
He struck down Israel's choice young men.^c

32 Despite all this, they kept sinning
and did not believe His wonderful works.

33 He made their days end in futility,
their years in sudden disaster.

34 When He killed ⌊some of⌋ them, ⌊the rest⌋ began
    to seek Him;
they repented and searched for God.

35 They remembered that God was their rock,
the •Most High God,^d their Redeemer.^e

36 But they deceived Him with their mouths,
they lied to Him with their tongues,

37 their hearts were insincere toward Him,
and they were unfaithful to His covenant.^f

38 Yet He was compassionate;
He atoned for^g ⌊their⌋ guilt^h
and did not destroy ⌊them⌋.ⁱ
He often turned His anger aside
and did not unleash^j all His wrath.^k

39 He remembered that they were ⌊only⌋ flesh,^l
a wind that passes and does not return.

40 How often they rebelled against Him
    in the wilderness^m
and grieved Him in the desert.

41 They constantly tested God
and provoked the Holy One of Israel.

42 They did not remember His power ⌊shown⌋
on the day He redeemed them from the foe,

43 when He performed His miraculous signs in Egypt
and His marvels in the region of Zoan.ⁿ

44 He turned their rivers into blood,
and they could not drink from their streams.^o

45 He sent among them swarms of flies,^p which fed
    on them,
and frogs, which devastated them.^q

46 He gave their crops to the caterpillar
and the fruit of their labor to the locust.^r

^a **78:28** LXX, Syr read *in their camp . . . their tents*
^b **78:28** Or *in its camp, all around its tents*
^c **78:31** Nm 11:4-33
^d **78:35** Gn 14:18-20
^e **78:35** Ps 19:14; Dt 32:4,15; Is 44:6,8
^f **78:37** Ac 8:21
^g **78:38** Or *He wiped out,* or *He forgave*
^h **78:38** Pr 16:6; Is 27:9; Dn 9:24
ⁱ **78:38** Dt 4:31; 2 Ch 7:14
^j **78:38** Or *stir up*
^k **78:38** Is 12:1
^l **78:39** Gn 6:3
^m **78:40** Nm 27:14; Dt 9:7,23-24; 31:27
ⁿ **78:42-43** Dt 7:8; 15:15; Neh 1:10; Mc 6:4
^o **78:44** Ex 7:14-25
^p **78:45** Ps 105:31; Ex 8:17
^q **78:45** Ps 105:30; Ex 8:3-6
^r **78:46** Ps 105:34; Ex 10:14-15

NOTES

a 78:47-48 Ps 105:32; Ex 9:22-26
b 78:49 Or *angels*
c 78:51 Ham's descendants who settled in Egypt; Ps 105:23,27
d 78:51 Ps 105:36; Ex 12:29; 13:15
e 78:53 Ex 14; 15:19; Jos 24:7
f 78:54 Ps 74:2; Ex 15:17
g 78:55 Jos 1–12
h 78:55 Jos 13–22
i 78:58 Places for the worship of pagan gods
j 78:60 Hb *adam*
k 78:61 See Ps 132:8 where the ark of the covenant is the *ark of His strength.*
l 78:61 1 Sm 4
m 78:63 Lit *His virgins were not praised*
n 78:64 Lit *His*
o 78:64 War probably prevented customary funerals.
p 78:65 Ps 35:23; 59:5; 121:4
q 78:65 Is 42:13; 51:9

47 He killed their vines with hail
and their sycamore-fig trees with a flood.

48 He handed over their livestock to hail
and their cattle to lightning bolts.[a]

49 He sent His burning anger against them:
fury, indignation, and calamity—
a band of deadly messengers.[b]

50 He cleared a path for His anger.
He did not spare them from death,
but delivered their lives to the plague.

51 He struck all the firstborn in Egypt,
the first progeny of the tents of Ham.[c] [d]

52 He led His people out like sheep
and guided them like a flock in the wilderness.

53 He led them safely, and they were not afraid;
but the sea covered their enemies.[e]

54 He brought them to His holy land,
to the mountain His right hand acquired.[f]

55 He drove out nations before them.[g]
He apportioned their inheritance by lot
and settled the tribes of Israel in their tents.[h]

56 But they rebelliously tested the •Most High God,
for they did not keep His decrees.

57 They treacherously turned away
like their fathers;
they became warped like a faulty bow.

58 They enraged Him with their high places[i]
and provoked His jealousy
with their carved images.

59 God heard and became furious;
He completely rejected Israel.

60 He abandoned the tabernacle at Shiloh,
the tent where He resided among men.[j]

61 He gave up His strength[k] to captivity
and His splendor to the hand of a foe.[l]

62 He surrendered His people to the sword
because He was enraged with His heritage.

63 Fire consumed His chosen young men,
and His young women had no wedding songs.[m]

64 His priests fell by the sword,
but the[n] widows could not lament.[o]

65 Then the Lord awoke as if from sleep,[p]
like a warrior[q] from the effects of wine.

66 He beat back His foes;
He gave them lasting shame.

67 He rejected the tent of Joseph
and did not choose the tribe of Ephraim.

68 He chose instead the tribe of Judah,
Mount Zion, which He loved.

69 He built His sanctuary like the heights,[a]
like the earth that He established forever.

70 He chose David His servant
and took him from the sheepfolds;

71 He brought him from tending ewes
to be shepherd over His people Jacob—
over Israel, His inheritance.

72 He shepherded them[b] with a pure heart
and guided them with his skillful hands.

a **78:69** Either the heights of heaven or the mountain heights
b **78:72** 2 Sm 6:21; 7:8; 1 Kg 8:16
c 1 Ch 6:39; 15:19; 16:5,7,37
d **79:1** Jr 12:14; 16:18; Lm 1:10
e **79:1** Jr 26:18; Mc 3:12
f **79:2** Dt 28:26; Jr 7:33; 16:4
g **79:3** Jr 14:16; 22:19
h **79:4** Ps 44:14
i **79:5** Ps 80:4; 89:46; Zch 1:12
j **79:6-7** Is 10:24-26; Jr 10:25
k **79:8** Or *hold the sins of past generations*

PSALM 79

FAITH AMID CONFUSION

A psalm of Asaph.[c]

1 God, the nations have invaded
Your inheritance,
desecrated Your holy temple,[d]
and turned Jerusalem into ruins.[e]

2 They gave the corpses of Your servants
to the birds of the sky for food,[f]
the flesh of Your godly ones to the beasts
of the earth.

3 They poured out their blood like water all
around Jerusalem,
and there was no one to bury ⌊them⌋.[g]

4 We have become an object of reproach
to our neighbors,
a source of mockery and ridicule to those
around us.[h]

5 How long, LORD? Will You be angry forever?
Will Your jealousy keep burning like fire?[i]

6 Pour out Your wrath on the nations that don't
acknowledge You,
on the kingdoms that don't call on Your name,

7 for they have devoured Jacob
and devastated his homeland.[j]

8 Do not hold past sins[k] against us;
let Your compassion come to us quickly,
for we have become weak.

NOTES

a **79:9** Ps 85:4; 1 Ch 16:35
b **79:9** Or *and wipe out,* or *and forgive*
c **79:9** Ps 23:3; 25:11; 106:8
d **79:10** Ps 115:2; Jl 2:17; Mc 7:10
e **79:10** Dt 32:43; Jr 20:12; 46:10
f **79:11** Ps 12:6; 102:20; Mal 2:13
g **79:12** Lv 26:18,21,24; Is 65:6-7; Jr 32:18
h **79:13** Ps 74:1; 95:7; 100:3
i Possibly a hymn tune; compare Pss 45; 60; 69
j 1 Ch 6:39; 15:19; 16:5,7,37
k **80:1** Ps 100:3; Gn 48:15; Ezk 34:11-16,31
l **80:1** 1 Sm 4:4; 2 Sm 6:2; 2 Kg 19:14-15
m **80:2** See Nm 2:17-24 for the order of these names in the marching order of the camp of Israel.
n **80:3** Ps 4:6; 67:1; Nm 6:24-26
o **80:5** Lit *a one-third measure*
p **80:5** Ps 102:9; Is 30:20; Hs 9:4

9 God of our salvation, help us[a]—
for the glory of Your name.
Deliver us and atone for[b] our sins,
for Your name's sake.[c]

10 Why should the nations ask, "Where is
their God?"[d]
Before our eyes, let vengeance for the shed blood
of Your servants
be known among the nations.[e]

11 Let the groans of the prisoners reach You;[f]
according to Your great power,
preserve those condemned to die.

12 Pay back sevenfold to our neighbors[g]
the reproach they have hurled at You, Lord.

13 Then we, Your people, the sheep
of Your pasture,[h]
will thank You forever;
we will declare Your praise to generation
after generation.

PSALM 80

A PRAYER FOR RESTORATION

For the choir director: according to "The Lilies."[i]
A testimony of Asaph.[j] *A psalm.*

1 Listen, Shepherd of Israel,
who guides Joseph like a flock;[k]
You who sit enthroned on the cherubim,[l] rise up

2 at the head of Ephraim, Benjamin,
and Manasseh.[m]
Rally Your power and come to save us.

3 Restore us, God;
look ⌊on us⌋ with favor,[n] and we will be saved.

4 LORD God of •Hosts,
how long will You be angry with
Your people's prayers?

5 You fed them the bread of tears
and gave them a full measure[o] of tears
to drink.[p]

6 You set us at strife with our neighbors;
our enemies make fun of us.

7 Restore us, God of •Hosts;
look ⌊on us⌋ with favor, and we will be saved.

8   You uprooted a vine from Egypt;
You drove out the nations[a] and planted it.[b]

9   You cleared ⌊a place⌋ for it;
it took root and filled the land.

10 The mountains were covered by its shade,
and the mighty cedars[c] with its branches.

11 It sent out sprouts toward the Sea[d]
and shoots toward the River.[e] [f]

12 Why have You broken down its walls
so that all who pass by pick its fruit?[g]

13 The boar from the forest gnaws at it,
and creatures of the field feed on it.

14 Return, God of •Hosts.
Look down from heaven and see;[h]
take care of this vine,

15 the root[i] Your right hand has planted,
the shoot[j] that You made strong for Yourself.

16 It was cut down and burned up;[k]
they[l] perish at the rebuke of Your countenance.

17 Let Your hand be with the man at Your right hand,
with the son of man You have made strong
for Yourself.

18 Then we will not turn away from You;
revive us, and we will call on Your name.

19 Restore us, LORD God of •Hosts;[m]
look ⌊on us⌋ with favor, and we will be saved.

[a] 80:8 Ex 23:28-30; 33:2; 34:11
[b] 80:8 Ex 15:17; 2 Sm 7:10; 1 Ch 17:9
[c] 80:10 Lit *the cedars of God*
[d] 80:11 The Mediterranean
[e] 80:11 The Euphrates
[f] 80:11 Ex 23:31; Dt 11:24; Jos 1:4
[g] 80:12 Ps 89:40-41
[h] 80:14 Ps 33:13; Is 63:15
[i] 80:15 Hb obscure
[j] 80:15 Or *son*
[k] 80:16 Lit *burned with fire*
[l] 80:16 Or *may they*
[m] 80:18-19 Ps 85:6; Hs 6:2
[n] 1 Ch 6:39; 15:19; 16:5,7,37
[o] 81:1 Ex 15:2; Is 12:2; 49:5
[p] 81:1-2 Ps 95:1-2; 98:4-6
[q] 81:3 Nm 29:6; Ezk 46:3
[r] 81:3 Either Passover or Tabernacles
[s] 81:5 LXX, Syr, Jer read *out of*
[t] 81:5 Ex 11:4; Lv 23:41-43

PSALM 81

A CALL TO OBEDIENCE

For the choir director: on the •Gittith. Of Asaph.[n]

1   Sing for joy to God our strength;[o]
shout in triumph to the God of Jacob.

2   Lift up a song—play the tambourine,
the melodious lyre, and the harp.[p]

3   Blow the horn during the new moon[q]
and during the full moon, on the day
of our feast.[r]

4   For this is a statute for Israel,
a judgment of the God of Jacob.

5   He set it up as an ordinance for Joseph
when He went throughout[s] the land of Egypt.[t]
I heard an unfamiliar language:

6 "I relieved his shoulder from the burden;
his hands were freed from ⌊carrying⌋ the basket.[a]
7 You called out in distress, and I rescued you;
I answered you from the thundercloud.[b]
I tested you at the waters of Meribah.[c] •*Selah*
8 Listen, My people, and I will admonish you.
O Israel, if you would only listen to Me!
9 There must not be a strange god among you;
you must not bow down to a foreign god.[d]
10 I am •Yahweh[e] your God,
who brought you up from the land of Egypt.
Open your mouth wide, and I will fill it.
11 But My people did not listen to Me;
Israel did not obey Me.
12 So I gave them over to their stubborn hearts
to follow their own plans.[f]
13 If only My people would listen to Me
and Israel would follow My ways,[g]
14 I would quickly subdue their enemies
and turn My hand against their foes."
15 Those who hate the LORD would pretend
submission to Him;[h]
their doom would last forever.
16 But He would feed Israel[i] with the best wheat.
"I would satisfy you with honey
from the rock."[j]

PSALM 82

A PLEA FOR RIGHTEOUS JUDGMENT

A psalm of Asaph.[k]

1 God has taken His place in the divine assembly;
He judges among the gods:[l] [m]
2 "How long will you judge unjustly
and show partiality to the wicked?[n] •*Selah*
3 Provide justice for the needy and the fatherless;
uphold the rights of the oppressed
and the destitute.[o]
4 Rescue the poor and needy;
save them from the hand of the wicked."[p]
5 They do not know or understand;[q]
they wander in darkness.
All the foundations of the earth are shaken.

NOTES

[a] **81:6** Ex 1:14
[b] **81:7** Ex 14:24; 20:18-20
[c] **81:7** Ex 17:1-7; Nm 20:2-13
[d] **81:9** Ex 20:3-5; 22:20; 34:14
[e] **81:10** The personal name of God in Hb
[f] **81:11-12** Jr 7:24; 11:8; 13:10
[g] **81:13** Is 42:24
[h] **81:15** Ps 18:44; 66:3
[i] **81:16** Lit *him*
[j] **81:16** Ps 147:14; Nm 18:12; Dt 32:13-14
[k] 1 Ch 6:39; 15:19; 16:5,7,37
[l] **82:1** Either heavenly beings or earthly rulers
[m] **82:1** Ps 7:8; Jb 21:22; Is 2:4
[n] **82:2** Lv 19:15; Pr 18:5; Mal 2:9
[o] **82:3** Dt 27:19; Pr 17:5; Is 11:4
[p] **82:4** Ps 18:43,48; 37:40; 71:4
[q] **82:5** Is 44:18

WORD STUDY

Hebrew word:
'El [EHL]/*'Elohim* [eh loh HEEM]

HCSB translation:
God, gods

Focus passage:
Psalm 82:1,6,8

'El is the general name for *God* in the OT. It is used primarily in emphasizing God's universal cosmic actions rather than His personal contacts with His creation. The plural form *'elohim* has three uses. It can be a numerical plural referring either to rulers or judges who act on God's behalf (Ex 22:8), to *gods* of other nations (Ex 18:11), or to angels (Ps 97:7). It can also serve to intensify a singular object or person by attaching "*of God*" to the term (Ex 4:16). In its third usage—as a plural of majesty—*'Elohim* refers to singular *God,* but uses the plural form to emphasize His majesty and greatness (Gn 1:1). This third usage is usually associated with actions, such as creation, that are unique to God.

6 I said, "You are gods;[a]
you are all sons of the •Most High.[b]

7 However, you will die like men
and fall like any other ruler."

8 Rise up, God, judge the earth,
for all the nations belong to You.

PSALM 83

PRAYER AGAINST ENEMIES

A song. A psalm of Asaph.[c]

1 God, do not keep silent.
Do not be deaf, God; do not be idle.[d]

2 See how Your enemies make an uproar;[e]
those who hate You have acted arrogantly.[f]

3 They devise clever schemes against Your people;
they conspire against Your treasured ones.[g]

4 They say, "Come, let us wipe them out
as a nation
so that Israel's name will no longer
be remembered."

5 For they have conspired with one mind;
they form an alliance[h] against You—

6 the tents of Edom and the Ishmaelites,[i]
Moab and the Hagrites,

7 Gebal, Ammon, and Amalek,
Philistia with the inhabitants of Tyre.

8 Even Assyria has joined them;
they lend support[j] to the sons of Lot.[k]   •*Selah*

9 Deal with them as ⌊You did⌋ with Midian,
as ⌊You did⌋ with Sisera and Jabin
at the Kishon River.[l]

10 They were destroyed at En-dor;
they became manure for the ground.[m]

11 Make their nobles like Oreb and Zeeb,[n]
and all their tribal leaders like Zebah
and Zalmunna,[o]

12 who said, "Let us seize God's pastures
for ourselves."

13 Make them like tumbleweed, my God,
like straw before the wind.[p]

14 As fire burns a forest,
as a flame blazes through mountains,

NOTES

[a] **82:6** Is 41:23
[b] **82:6** Jn 10:34-35
[c] **1 Ch 6:39; 15:19; 16:5,7,37**
[d] **83:1** Ps 28:1; 39:12; Is 62:1
[e] **83:2** Ps 46:6; Is 17:12
[f] **83:2** Lit *have lifted their head*
[g] **83:1-3** Jb 5:12-13
[h] **83:5** Lit *they cut a covenant*
[i] **83:6** Gn 17:20; 37:25-28; 39:1
[j] **83:8** Lit *they are an arm*
[k] **83:8** Moab and Edom
[l] **83:9** Jdg 4:1-16
[m] **83:10** Jr 9:22; 16:4; 25:33
[n] **83:11** Jdg 7:24-25
[o] **83:11** Jdg 8:5-21
[p] **83:13** Ps 1:4; Jb 21:18; Is 17:13

NOTES

a 1 Ch 9:19
b 84:2 Or *flesh shout for joy to*
c 84:2 Ps 42:2
d 84:6 Or *Valley of Tears*
e 84:6 Or *pools*
f 84:8 Ps 46:7,11; 76:6
g 84:9 The king
h 84:9 Ps 18:2; 89:18
i 84:9 1 Sm 2:10; 2 Sm 22:51; 2 Ch 6:42
j 84:10 Jb 8:22; 21:28

15 so pursue them with Your tempest
and terrify them with Your storm.

16 Cover their faces with shame
so that they will seek Your name, LORD.

17 Let them be put to shame and terrified forever;
let them perish in disgrace.

18 May they know that You alone—
whose name is •Yahweh—
are the •Most High over all the earth.

PSALM 84

LONGING FOR GOD'S HOUSE

For the choir director: on the •Gittith. A psalm of the sons of Korah. a

1 How lovely is Your dwelling place,
LORD of •Hosts.

2 My soul longs, even languishes,
for the courts of the LORD;
my heart and flesh cry out for b the living God. c

3 Even a sparrow finds a home,
and a swallow, a nest for herself
where she places her young—
near Your altars, LORD of •Hosts,
my King and my God.

4 How happy are those who reside in Your house,
who praise You continually.   •Selah

5 Happy are the people whose strength is in You,
whose hearts are set on pilgrimage.

6 As they pass through the Valley of Baca, d
they make it a source of springwater;
even the autumn rain will cover it with blessings. e

7 They go from strength to strength;
each appears before God in Zion.

8 LORD God of •Hosts, hear my prayer;
listen, God of Jacob. f   •Selah

9 Consider our shield, g God; h
look on the face of Your anointed one. i

10 Better a day in Your courts than a thousand
⌊anywhere else⌋.
I would rather be at the door of the house
of my God
than to live in the tents of the wicked. j

11 For the LORD God is a sun and shield.[a]
The LORD gives grace[b] and glory;
He does not withhold the good from those
who live with integrity.

12 LORD of •Hosts,
happy is the person who trusts in You!

PSALM 85

RESTORATION OF FAVOR

For the choir director. A psalm of the sons of Korah.[c]

1 LORD, You showed favor to Your land;[d]
You restored Jacob's prosperity.[e] [f]

2 You took away Your people's guilt;
You covered all their sin.[g]   •*Selah*

3 You withdrew all Your fury;
You turned from Your burning anger.[h]

4 Return to us, God of our salvation,[i]
and abandon Your displeasure with us.

5 Will You be angry with us forever?
Will You prolong Your anger for all
generations?[j]

6 Will You not revive us again[k]
so that Your people may rejoice in You?[l]

7 Show us Your faithful love, LORD,
and give us Your salvation.

8 I will listen to what God will say;
surely the LORD will declare peace[m]
to His people, His godly ones,
and not let them go back to foolish ways.

9 His salvation is very near those who fear Him,
so that glory may dwell in our land.

10 Faithful love and truth[n] will join together;
righteousness and peace will embrace.

11 Truth will spring up from the earth,[o]
and righteousness will look down from heaven.

12 Also, the LORD will provide what is good,
and our land will yield its crops.[p]

13 Righteousness will go before Him
to prepare the way for His steps.[q]

NOTES

a **84:11** Ps 3:3; Gn 15:1; 2 Sm 22:3
b **84:11** Gn 6:8; 39:21; Ex 33:12-13
c 1 Ch 9:19
d **85:1** Lv 25:23; Dt 33:13
e **85:1** Or *restored Jacob from captivity*
f **85:1** Ps 14:7; Dt 30:3; Jr 29:14
g **85:2** Ps 32:1,5; Ex 34:7; Nm 14:18
h **85:3** Ps 69:24; Jr 30:24; Lm 4:11
i **85:4** Ps 27:9; 79:9; Mc 7:7
j **85:5** Jr 17:4
k **85:6** Ps 71:20; 143:11; Hs 6:2
l **85:6** Ps 40:16; 70:4; 118:24
m **85:8** Zch 9:10
n **85:10** Ps 25:10; 40:10-11; 86:15
o **85:11** Is 45:8
p **85:12** Ps 65:12-13; Jr 31:12; Ezk 34:27
q **85:13** Is 40:3,10; 46:12-13; 62:1

NOTES

a **86:1** Ps 4:1; 17:6; 71:2; 102:2
b **86:2** Ps 37:28; 97:10; 1 Sm 2:9
c **86:3** Ps 27:7; 57:1; 119:58
d **86:4** Ps 90:15; 92:4
e **86:4** Ps 43:8
f **86:5** Ex 34:6; Nm 14:18; Neh 9:17
g **86:7** Ps 20:1; 50:15; Gn 35:3
h **86:8** Ex 15:11; Dt 3:24; Is 45:21
i **86:9** Ps 22:27; 66:4; Zch 14:16
j **86:10** Ps 83:19; 2 Kg 19:15; Jr 10:6
k **86:11** Ps 26:3; 27:11; Is 2:3
l **86:11** Ps 111:9; Dt 28:58; 1 Kg 8:43
m **86:13** Ps 57:10; 145:8
n **86:13** Ps 30:3; 49:14-15; Jnh 2:3-6
o **86:14** Ps 119:69,85
p **86:15** Ex 34:6; Nm 14:18; Neh 9:17

PSALM 86

LAMENT AND PETITION

A Davidic prayer.

1 Listen, LORD, and answer me,[a]
for I am poor and needy.

2 Protect my life, for I am faithful.[b]
You are my God; save Your servant who trusts
in You.

3 Be gracious to me, Lord,
for I call to You all day long.[c]

4 Bring joy to Your servant's life,[d]
since I set my hope on You, Lord.[e]

5 For You, Lord, are kind and ready to forgive,
abundant in faithful love[f] to all who call on You.

6 LORD, hear my prayer;
listen to my plea for mercy.

7 I call on You in the day of my distress,
for You will answer me.[g]

8 Lord, there is no one like You among the gods,
and there are no works like Yours.[h]

9 All the nations You have made
will come and bow down before You, Lord,
and will honor Your name.[i]

10 For You are great and perform wonders;
You alone are God.[j]

11 Teach me Your way, LORD,
and I will live by Your truth.[k]
Give me an undivided mind to fear Your name.[l]

12 I will praise You with all my heart, Lord my God,
and will honor Your name forever.

13 For Your faithful love for me is great,[m]
and You deliver my life from the depths
of •Sheol.[n]

14 God, arrogant people have attacked me;
a gang of ruthless men seeks my life.[o]
They have no regard for You.

15 But You, Lord, are a compassionate
and gracious God,
slow to anger and abundant in faithful love
and truth.[p]

16 Turn to me and be gracious to me.
Give Your strength to Your servant;
save the son of Your female servant.

17 Show me a sign of Your goodness;
my enemies will see and be put to shame
because You, LORD, have helped and comforted
me.

PSALM 87
ZION, THE CITY OF GOD

A psalm of the sons of Korah.[a] *A song.*

1 His foundation[b] is on the holy mountains.
2 The LORD loves the gates of Zion
more than all the dwellings of Jacob.[c]
3 Glorious things are said about you,
city of God.[d]   •*Selah*
4 "I will mention those who know Me:[e]
Rahab,[f] Babylon, Philistia, Tyre, and Cush[g]—
each one was born there."
5 And it will be said of Zion,
"This one and that one were born in her."
The •Most High Himself will establish her.[h]
6 When He registers the peoples, the LORD
will record,
"This one was born there."[i]   •*Selah*
7 Singers and dancers alike ⌊will say⌋,
"All my springs[j] are in you."

PSALM 88
A CRY OF DESPERATION

A song. A psalm of the sons of Korah.
For the choir director: according to Mahalath
Leannoth.[k] *A •Maskil of Heman the Ezrahite.*[l]

1 O LORD, God of my salvation,
I cry out before You day and night.
2 May my prayer reach Your presence;
listen to my cry.
3 For I have had enough troubles,
and my life is near •Sheol.
4 I am counted among those going down
to the •Pit.[m]
I am like a man without strength,

NOTES
[a] 1 Ch 9:19
[b] 87:1 Is 14:32
[c] 87:2 Places in Israel
[d] 87:3 Ps 48:1,8; Is 60:14
[e] 87:4 Is 56:6-7; Zch 2:10-12
[f] 87:4 Egypt
[g] 87:4 Modern Sudan
[h] 87:5 Ps 46:4; 48:8; Is 2:2
[i] 87:4-6 Is 49:19-26; 60:4-5; 66:7-8
[j] 87:7 Is 12:3; 41:18; Jl 3:18
[k] Ps 53:1
[l] 1 Ch 2:6; 6:33; 15:17-19
[m] 88:3-4 Ps 28:1; 143:7; Is 38:18

NOTES

a 88:5 Or *set free*
b 88:5 Ezk 32:20-32
c 88:5 Or *hand*
d 88:6 Ps 86:13; Lm 3:55; Ezk 26:20
e 88:8 Jb 19:13-22
f 88:10 Is 14:9; 26:14,19
g 88:11 Pr 15:11; 27:20; Jb 26:6
h 88:12 Ec 9:5
i 88:14 Ps 74:1; 89:38
j 88:14 Ps 10:1; 13:1; 27:9
k 88:16 Jb 6:4
l 1 Ch 15:17,19; 1 Kg 4:31
m 89:1 Ps 17:7; 101:1; 107:43

5   abandoned[a] among the dead.
I am like the slain lying in the grave,[b]
whom You no longer remember,
and who are cut off from Your care.[c]

6   You have put me in the lowest part of the •Pit,[d]
in the darkest places, in the depths.

7   Your wrath weighs heavily on me;
You have overwhelmed me with all Your waves.
                        •*Selah*

8   You have distanced my friends from me;
You have made me repulsive to them.[e]
I am shut in and cannot go out.

9   My eyes are worn out from crying.
LORD, I cry out to You all day long;
I spread out my hands to You.

10   Do You work wonders for the dead?
Do departed spirits rise up to praise You?[f] •*Selah*

11   Will Your faithful love be declared in the grave,
Your faithfulness in •Abaddon?[g]

12   Will Your wonders be known in the darkness,
or Your righteousness in the land of oblivion?[h]

13   But I call to You for help, LORD;
in the morning my prayer meets You.

14   LORD, why do You reject me?[i]
Why do You hide Your face from me?[j]

15   From my youth, I have been afflicted and near death.
I suffer Your horrors; I am desperate.

16   Your wrath sweeps over me;
Your terrors destroy me.[k]

17   They surround me like water all day long;
they close in on me from every side.

18   You have distanced loved one and neighbor from me;
darkness is my ⌊only⌋ friend.

PSALM 89

PERPLEXITY ABOUT GOD'S PROMISES

A •Maskil of Ethan the Ezrahite.[l]

1   I will sing about the LORD's faithful love forever;[m]
with my mouth I will proclaim Your faithfulness to all generations.

2   For I will declare, "Faithful love is built up
     forever;
You establish Your faithfulness in the heavens."

3   ⌊The LORD said,⌋ "I have made a covenant
     with My chosen one;
I have sworn an oath to David My servant:

4   'I will establish your offspring forever
and build up your throne for all generations.' " ᵃ
                       •*Selah*

5   LORD, the heavens praise Your wonders—
Your faithfulness also—in the assembly
     of the holy ones.

6   For who in the skies can compare
     with the LORD?
Who among the heavenly beings ᵇ is
     like the LORD?

7   God is greatly feared in the council
     of the holy ones,
more awe-inspiring than ᶜ all who surround Him. ᵈ

8   O LORD God of •Hosts,
who is strong like You, LORD? ᵉ
Your faithfulness surrounds You.

9   You rule the raging sea;
when its waves surge, You still them. ᶠ

10   You crushed Rahab ᵍ ʰ like one who is slain;
You scattered Your enemies
     with Your powerful arm.

11   The heavens are Yours; the earth also is Yours. ⁱ
The world and everything in it—
     You founded them.

12   North and south—You created them.
Tabor and Hermon shout for joy at Your name.

13   You have a mighty arm;
Your hand is powerful; Your right hand is lifted
     high. ʲ

14   Righteousness and justice are the foundation
     of Your throne; ᵏ
faithful love and truth ˡ go before You.

15   Happy are the people who know
     the joyful shout;
LORD, they walk in the light of Your presence.

16   They rejoice in Your name all day long,
and they are exalted by Your righteousness.

17   For You are their magnificent strength;
by Your favor our •horn is exalted.

NOTES

ᵃ **89:3-4** Ps 132:11-12; 2 Sm 7; 1 Ch 17
ᵇ **89:6** Or *the angels,* or *the sons of the mighty*
ᶜ **89:7** Or *ones, revered by*
ᵈ **89:5-7** Ps 29:1; 82:1; Jb 1–2; Is 6:1-3
ᵉ **89:8** Ex 15:11; 2 Sm 7:22
ᶠ **89:9** Ps 104:9; Jb 38:11; Mt 8:23-27
ᵍ **89:10** Legendary sea monster; sometimes refers to Egypt
ʰ **89:10** Is 30:7; 51:9-10
ⁱ **89:11** Ps 50:12; Gn 14:19; Ex 19:5
ʲ **89:13** Ex 6:6; Dt 5:15; 26:8
ᵏ **89:14** Ps 97:2
ˡ **89:14** Ps 25:10; 40:10-11; 57:3

^a **89:18** The king
^b **89:18** Ps 84:9
^c **89:19** Or *exalted a young man*
^d **89:20** Ps 18:50; 1 Sm 16:13
^e **89:22** Or *not exact tribute from*
^f **89:24** Ps 21:7
^g **89:25** Dt 11:24; Jos 1:4
^h **89:26** 2 Sm 7:14
ⁱ **89:26** Ps 18:2; 95:1
^j **89:27** Col 1:15
^k **89:29** Lit *as days of heaven*
^l **89:29** Ps 89:36-37
^m **89:30-32** 2 Sm 7:14-15; 1 Kg 9:6-7
ⁿ **89:33-34** Lv 26:44; Jdg 2:1; 1 Sm 15:29
^o **89:35** Ex 32:13; Is 45:23; Jr 44:26; Am 8:7
^p **89:37** Jb 16:19

18 Surely our shield[a] [b] belongs to the LORD,
our king to the Holy One of Israel.

19 You once spoke in a vision to Your loyal ones
and said:
"I have granted help to a warrior;
I have exalted one chosen[c] from the people.

20 I have found David My servant;
I have anointed him with My sacred oil.[d]

21 My hand will always be with him,
and My arm will strengthen him.

22 The enemy will not afflict[e] him;
no wicked man will oppress him.

23 I will crush his foes before him
and strike those who hate him.

24 My faithfulness and love will be with him,
and through My name his •horn will be exalted.[f]

25 I will extend his power to the sea
and his right hand to the rivers.[g]

26 He will call to Me, 'You are my Father,[h]
my God, the rock of my salvation.'[i]

27 I will also make him My firstborn,[j]
greatest of the kings of the earth.

28 I will always preserve My faithful love for him,
and My covenant with him will endure.

29 I will establish his line forever,
his throne as long as heaven lasts.[k] [l]

30 If his sons forsake My instruction
and do not live by My ordinances,

31 if they dishonor My statutes
and do not keep My commandments,

32 then I will call their rebellion to account
with the rod,
their sin with blows.[m]

33 But I will not withdraw My faithful love
from him
or betray My faithfulness.

34 I will not violate My covenant
or change what My lips have said.[n]

35 Once and for all I have sworn an oath
by My holiness;[o]
I will not lie to David.

36 His offspring will continue forever,
his throne like the sun before Me,

37 like the moon, established forever,
a faithful witness in the sky."[p]
•*Selah*

38 But You have spurned and rejected him;
You have become enraged with Your anointed.

39 You have repudiated the covenant
with Your servant;
You have completely dishonored his crown.[a] [b]

40 You have broken down all his walls;
You have reduced his fortified cities to ruins.

41 All who pass by plunder him;[c]
he has become a joke to his neighbors.

42 You have lifted high the right hand of his foes;
You have made all his enemies rejoice.

43 You have also turned back his sharp sword
and have not let him stand in battle.

44 You have made his splendor[d] cease
and have overturned his throne.

45 You have shortened the days of his youth;
You have covered him with shame.[e]   •Selah

46 How long, LORD? Will You hide Yourself
forever?
Will Your anger keep burning like fire?[f]

47 Remember how short my life is.[g]
Have You created •everyone for nothing?

48 What man can live and never see death?
Who can save himself from the power of •Sheol?
•Selah

49 Lord, where are the former acts
of Your faithful love
that You swore to David in Your faithfulness?

50 Remember, Lord, the ridicule
against Your servants—
in my heart I carry ⌊abuse⌋ from all
the peoples—

51 how Your enemies have ridiculed, LORD,
how they have ridiculed every step
of Your anointed.

52 May the LORD be praised forever.
Amen and amen.[h]

[a] 89:39 Lit *have dishonored his crown to the ground*
[b] 89:39 Jr 13:18-19; Lm 5:16; Ezk 21:26-27
[c] 89:41 Jdg 2:14; Jr 30:16
[d] 89:44 Hb obscure
[e] 89:45 Is 54:4; Ezk 7:18; Ob 10
[f] 89:46 Ps 6:3; 13:1; 35:17; 79:5
[g] 89:47 Ps 39:6-7; 90:5-6,9-10
[h] 89:52 Ps 41:13; 72:19-20; 106:48

NOTES

a 90:1 A few Hb mss, LXX; MT reads *dwelling place*
b 90:2 LXX, Aq, Sym, Jer, Tg read *before the earth and the world were brought forth*
c 90:3 Ps 90:3; Gn 3:19; Jb 10:9
d 90:4 2 Pt 3:8
e 90:5 Or *You overwhelm them;* Hb uncertain
f 90:5 Ps 76:5-6; Jb 14:12; Jr 51:39,57
g 90:5-6 Ps 37:2; 103:15-16; Jb 14:1-2
h 90:10 Lit *The days of our years in them*
i 90:10 LXX, Tg, Syr, Vg read *Even their breadth is;* Hb uncertain
j 90:12 Or *develop a heart of wisdom*
k 90:12 Dt 32:29; Pr 2:6-15; Eph 5:15-16

BOOK IV

(PSALMS 90–106)

PSALM 90
ETERNAL GOD AND MORTAL MAN

A prayer of Moses the man of God.

1 Lord, You have been our refuge[a]
in every generation.

2 Before the mountains were born,
before You gave birth to the earth and the world,[b]
from eternity to eternity, You are God.

3 You return mankind to the dust,[c]
saying, "Return, descendants of Adam."

4 For in Your sight a thousand years
are like yesterday that passes by,
like a few hours of the night.[d]

5 You end their life;[e] they sleep.[f]
They are like grass that grows in the morning—

6 in the morning it sprouts and grows;
by evening it withers and dries up.[g]

7 For we are consumed by Your anger;
we are terrified by Your wrath.

8 You have set our unjust ways before You,
our secret sins in the light of Your presence.

9 For all our days ebb away under Your wrath;
we end our years like a sigh.

10 Our lives last[h] seventy years
or, if we are strong, eighty years.
Even the best of them are[i] toil and sorrow;
indeed, they pass quickly and we fly away.

11 Who understands the power of Your anger?
Your wrath matches the fear that is due You.

12 Teach us to number our days carefully
so that we may develop wisdom in our hearts.[j] [k]

13 LORD—how long?
Turn and have compassion on Your servants.

14 Satisfy us in the morning with Your faithful love
so that we may shout with joy and be glad all
our days.

15 Make us rejoice for as many days as
You have humbled us,
for as many years as we have seen adversity.

16 Let Your work be seen by Your servants,
    and Your splendor by their children.[a]

17 Let the favor of the Lord our God be upon us;
    establish for us the work of our hands—
    establish the work of our hands![b]

PSALM 91

THE PROTECTION OF THE MOST HIGH

1 The one who lives under the protection
        of the •Most High
    dwells in the shadow of the Almighty.[c]

2 I will say[d] to the LORD, "My refuge
        and my fortress,
    my God, in whom I trust."[e]

3 He Himself will deliver you
        from the hunter's net,[f]
    from the destructive plague.[g]

4 He will cover you with His feathers;
    you will take refuge under His wings.[h]
    His faithfulness will be a protective shield.

5 You will not fear the terror of the night,
    the arrow that flies by day,

6 the plague[i] that stalks in darkness,
    or the pestilence that ravages at noon.

7 Though a thousand fall at your side
    and ten thousand at your right hand,
    the pestilence will not reach you.

8 You will only see it with your eyes
    and witness the punishment of the wicked.

9 Because you have made the LORD—
        my refuge,[j]
    the •Most High—your dwelling place,[k]

10 no harm will come to you;
    no plague will come near your tent.

11 For He will give His angels orders
        concerning you,
    to protect you in all your ways.

12 They will support you with their hands[l]
    so that you will not strike your foot
        against a stone.[m]

13 You will tread on the lion and the cobra;
    you will trample the young lion
        and the serpent.[n]

NOTES

[a] **90:16** Ps 92:4; 143:5; Is 52:10
[b] **90:17** 1 Co 15:58
[c] **91:1** Ps 121:5; Is 49:2; Hs 14:7
[d] **91:1-2** LXX, Syr, Jer read *Almighty, saying,* or *Almighty, he will say*
[e] **91:2** Ps 18:2; 61:4; 62:7-8
[f] **91:3** Ps 124:7; 141:9; Ec 9:12
[g] **91:3** Ex 5:3; Lv 26:25; Nm 14:12
[h] **91:4** Ps 57:1; Dt 32:11; Ru 2:12
[i] **91:6** Ex 5:3; Lv 26:25; Nm 14:12
[j] **91:9** Ps 18:2; 61:4; 62:7-8
[k] **91:9** Ps 121:5; Is 49:2; Hs 14:7
[l] **91:12** Ex 19:4; Is 63:9
[m] **91:11-12** Mt 4:6; Lk 4:10-11
[n] **91:13** Lk 10:19

NOTES

a **91:14** Ps 9:10; 37:40; 107:41
b **91:15** Ps 6:4; 18:19; 2 Sm 22:20
c **91:16** Ps 21:4; Ex 20:12; Dt 4:40
d **91:16** Gn 49:18; Ex 14:13; 15:2
e **92:2** Ps 103:17; 136; Lm 3:22-23
f **92:4** Ps 19:1; 143:5; Is 29:23
g **92:5** Is 55:8-9; Jr 29:11; Mc 4:12
h **92:10** Ps 89:17,24; 112:9; 1 Sm 2:1

14 Because he is lovingly devoted to Me,
     I will deliver him;
   I will exalt him because he knows My name. [a]
15 When he calls out to Me, I will answer him;
   I will be with him in trouble.
   I will rescue him and give him honor. [b]
16 I will satisfy him with a long life [c]
   and show him My salvation. [d]

PSALM 92

GOD'S LOVE AND FAITHFULNESS

A psalm. A song for the Sabbath day.

1 It is good to praise the LORD,
   to sing praise to Your name, •Most High,
2 to declare Your faithful love in the morning
   and Your faithfulness at night, [e]
3 with a ten-stringed harp
   and the music of a lyre.
4 For You have made me rejoice, LORD, by what
     You have done;
   I will shout for joy because of the works
     of Your hands. [f]
5 How magnificent are Your works, LORD,
   how profound Your thoughts! [g]
6 A stupid person does not know,
   a fool does not understand this:
7 though the wicked sprout like grass
   and all evildoers flourish,
   they will be eternally destroyed.
8 But You, LORD, are exalted forever.
9 For indeed, LORD, Your enemies—
   indeed, Your enemies will perish;
   all evildoers will be scattered.
10 You have lifted up my •horn [h] like that
     of a wild ox;
   I have been anointed with oil.
11 My eyes look down on my enemies;
   my ears hear evildoers when they attack me.
12 The righteous thrive like a palm tree
   and grow like a cedar tree in Lebanon.
13 Planted in the house of the LORD,
   they thrive in the courtyards of our God.

WORD STUDY

Hebrew word:
mizmor [miz MOHR]

HCSB translation:
psalm

Focus passage:
Psalm 92 superscription

Mizmor, related to the verb *zamar* (*to sing*), was used for a type of song most often accompanied by a musical instrument. It is used only in the superscriptions of certain Psalms. The term is so closely identified with the Psalms that it is translated *psalm.* It is a more specific term than *shir,* another Hebrew word for "song," although these two terms often appear together (Ps 30:1).

14 They will still bear fruit in old age,
healthy and green,[a]
15 to declare: "The LORD is just;
He is my rock, and there is no unrighteousness
in Him."[b]

PSALM 93
GOD'S ETERNAL REIGN

1 The LORD reigns! He is robed in majesty;
the LORD is robed, enveloped in strength.
The world is firmly established; it cannot
be shaken.[c]
2 Your throne has been established
from the beginning;[d]
You are from eternity.[e]
3 The floods have lifted up, LORD,
the floods have lifted up their voice;
the floods lift up their pounding waves.
4 Greater than the roar of many waters—
the mighty breakers of the sea—
the LORD on high is majestic.[f]
5 LORD, Your testimonies are completely reliable;[g]
holiness is the beauty of[h] Your house
for all the days to come.

PSALM 94
THE JUST JUDGE

1 LORD, God of vengeance—
God of vengeance, appear.[i]
2 Rise up, Judge of the earth;
repay the proud what they deserve.[j]
3 LORD, how long will the wicked—
how long will the wicked gloat?
4 They pour out arrogant words;
all the evildoers boast.
5 LORD, they crush Your people;
they afflict Your heritage.[k]
6 They kill the widow and the foreigner
and murder the fatherless.[l]
7 They say, "The LORD doesn't see it.
The God of Jacob doesn't pay attention."

NOTES
[a] **92:14** Ps 1:3; Jr 17:8
[b] **92:15** Dt 32:4; 2 Ch 19:7; Zph 3:5
[c] **93:1** Ps 96:10; 1 Ch 16:30-31; Jr 10:12
[d] **93:2** Lit *from then*
[e] **93:2** Ps 9:7; 90:2; 103:19
[f] **93:4** Ezk 1:24; 43:2
[g] **93:5** Ps 19:7
[h] **93:5** Or *holiness characterizes*
[i] **94:1** Ps 18:47-48; 2 Sm 22:48; Jr 46:10
[j] **94:2** Ps 28:4; 98:9; Gn 18:25
[k] **94:4-5** Ps 31:18; 2 Sm 20:19; Jl 2:17
[l] **94:6** Dt 27:19; Jb 22:9; 29:12; Is 10:2

NOTES

a **94:11** Or *futile*
b **94:11** 1 Co 3:20
c **94:12** Ps 25:5,9; 71:17; Is 48:17
d **94:13** Ps 7:15; 9:15; Pr 26:27
e **94:14** 1 Sm 12:22
f **94:15** Or *heart will support*; lit *heart after*
g **94:15** Ps 36:10; 64:10; 97:11
h **94:18** Ps 18:35; 66:9; 121:3;
i **94:19** Ps 139:23
j **94:21** Ps 106:38; 2 Kg 21:16; Jr 26:15
k **94:22** Ps 46:1,7; 62:2,6; 2 Sm 22:3
l **94:23** Ps 73:27; 94:23; 101:5,8
m **95:1** Ps 81:1; 98:4,6; Jb 38:7

8 Pay attention, you stupid people!
Fools, when will you be wise?

9 Can the One who shaped the ear not hear,
the One who formed the eye not see?

10 The One who instructs nations,
the One who teaches man knowledge—
does He not discipline?

11 The LORD knows man's thoughts;
they are meaningless.[a] [b]

12 LORD, happy is the man You discipline
and teach from Your law[c]

13 to give him relief from troubled times
until a pit is dug for the wicked.[d]

14 The LORD will not forsake His people
or abandon His heritage,[e]

15 for justice will again be righteous,
and all the upright in heart will follow[f] it.[g]

16 Who stands up for me against the wicked?
Who takes a stand for me against evildoers?

17 If the LORD had not been my help,
I would soon rest in the silence ⌊of death⌋.

18 If I say, "My foot is slipping,"
Your faithful love will support me, LORD.[h]

19 When I am filled with cares,[i]
Your comfort brings me joy.

20 Can a corrupt throne—
one that creates trouble by law—
become Your ally?

21 They band together against the life
of the righteous
and condemn the innocent to death.[j]

22 But the LORD is my refuge;
my God is the rock of my protection.[k]

23 He will pay them back for their sins
and destroy them for their evil.
The LORD our God will destroy them.[l]

PSALM 95
WORSHIP AND WARNING

1 Come, let us shout joyfully to the LORD,
shout triumphantly to the rock
of our salvation![m]

2 Let us enter His presence with thanksgiving;
let us shout triumphantly to Him in song.

3   For the LORD is a great God,
a great King above all gods.[a]

4   The depths of the earth are in His hand,
and the mountain peaks are His.

5   The sea is His; He made it.
His hands formed the dry land.[b]

6   Come, let us worship and bow down;
let us kneel before the LORD our Maker.[c]

7   For He is our God,
and we are the people of His pasture, the sheep
under His care.[d] [e]
Today, if you hear His voice:[f]

8   "Do not harden your hearts as at Meribah,
as on that day at Massah in the wilderness[g]

9   where your fathers tested Me;
they tried Me, though they had seen what I did.

10   For 40 years I was disgusted with
that generation;
I said, 'They are a people whose hearts go astray;
they do not know My ways.'[h]

11   So I swore in My anger,
'They will not enter My rest.' "[i]

PSALM 96[j]

KING OF THE EARTH

1   Sing a new song to the LORD;
sing to the LORD, all the earth.[k]

2   Sing to the LORD, praise His name;[l]
proclaim His salvation[m] from day to day.

3   Declare His glory among the nations,
His wonderful works among all peoples.[n]

4   For the LORD is great and is highly praised;
He is feared above all gods.[o]

5   For all the gods of the peoples are idols,
but the LORD made the heavens.

6   Splendor and majesty are before Him;
strength and beauty are in His sanctuary.[p]

7   Ascribe to the LORD, families of the peoples,
ascribe to the LORD glory and strength.

8   Ascribe to the LORD the glory of His name;
bring an offering and enter His courts.

9   Worship the LORD in His holy majesty;
tremble before Him, all the earth.[q]

NOTES

[a] **95:3** Ps 47:2; 96:4; Dt 10:17
[b] **95:5** Gn 1:10; Jnh 1:9
[c] **95:6** Ps 22:30; Ezr 9:5; Is 45:23
[d] **95:7** Lit *sheep of His hand*
[e] **95:7** Ps 100:3
[f] **95:7** Dt 13:4; Jos 24:24
[g] **95:8** Ex 17:7; Nm 27:14; Dt 6:16
[h] **95:10** Is 42:16; Jr 5:4
[i] **95:7-11** Heb 3:7-11,15; 4:4-7
[j] 1 Ch 16:23-33
[k] **96:1** Ps 98:1; 1 Ch 16:23; Is 42:10
[l] **96:2** Ps 72:19; 100:4; 145:1
[m] **96:2** Gn 49:18; Ex 14:13; 15:2
[n] **96:3** Ps 40:5; 78:4; 1 Ch 16:9,24
[o] **96:4** Ps 47:2; 48:1; 1 Ch 16:25
[p] **96:6** Ps 104:1; 1 Ch 16:27
[q] **96:7-9** Ps 29:1-2; 1 Ch 26:8-9

WORD STUDY

Hebrew word:
Yahweh [YAH weh]

HCSB translation:
LORD, Yahweh

Focus passage:
Psalm 96:1,2,4,7-10,13

Yahweh is the personal name of the God of the Bible and the specific covenant name of Israel's God, unique among the gods of the nations. A pivotal passage in the name's origination is Exodus 3:14, where God says to Moses, "I *AM WHO I AM*." This statement probably indicated *Yahweh's* commitment to deliver His people from slavery, a redemptive act that would reveal His character. *Yahweh* is particularly associated with situations in which God directly reveals Himself to individuals. In contrast to the more general term for God (*El/Elohim*), *Yahweh* is more personal and relational, focusing on God's unique relationship with His people. In light of this, the Israelites addressed their prayers specifically to *Yahweh* (Ps 12:1).

NOTES

a **96:10** Ps 93:1; 1 Ch 16:30
b **96:10** Ps 9:8; 98:9
c **96:11** Ps 97:1; 98:7; 1 Ch 16:31-32
d **97:2** Ps 97:2; Dt 4:11; 2 Sm 22:10
e **97:5** Mc 1:4
f **97:7** LXX, Syr read *All His angels*; Heb 1:6
g **97:8** Lit *daughters*
h **97:8** Ps 48:11
i **97:9** Ps 95:3; 96:4; 1 Ch 16:25
j **97:10** Am 5:15; Pr 8:13
k **97:11** One Hb ms, LXX, other versions read *rises to shine*
l **97:11** Lit *Light is sown*

10 Say among the nations: "The LORD reigns.
The world is firmly established; it cannot
be shaken. ᵃ
He judges the peoples fairly." ᵇ

11 Let the heavens be glad and the earth rejoice;
let the sea and all that fills it resound. ᶜ

12 Let the fields and everything in them exult.
Then all the trees of the forest will shout for joy

13 before the LORD, for He is coming—
for He is coming to judge the earth.
He will judge the world with righteousness
and the peoples with His faithfulness.

PSALM 97

THE MAJESTIC KING

1 The LORD reigns! Let the earth rejoice;
let the many islands be glad.

2 Clouds and thick darkness surround Him;
righteousness and justice are the foundation
of His throne. ᵈ

3 Fire goes before Him
and burns up His foes on every side.

4 His lightning lights up the world;
the earth sees and trembles.

5 The mountains melt like wax at the presence
of the LORDᵉ—
at the presence of the Lord of all the earth.

6 The heavens proclaim His righteousness;
all the peoples see His glory.

7 All who serve carved images,
those who boast in idols, will be put to shame.
All the godsᶠ will worship Him.

8 Zion hears and is glad,
and the townsᵍ of Judah rejoice
because of Your judgments, ʰ LORD.

9 For You, LORD, are the •Most High over all
the earth;
You are exalted above all the gods. ⁱ

10 You who love the LORD, hate evil!ʲ
He protects the lives of His godly ones;
He rescues them from the hand of the wicked.

11 Light dawnsᵏ ˡ for the righteous,
gladness for the upright in heart.

12 Be glad in the LORD, you righteous ones,^a
and praise His holy name.^b

PSALM 98

PRAISE THE KING

A psalm.

1 Sing a new song to the LORD,^c
for He has performed wonders;
His right hand and holy arm have won Him
victory.^d

2 The LORD has made His victory known;
He has revealed His righteousness in the sight
of the nations.^e

3 He has remembered His love and faithfulness
to the house of Israel;
all the ends of the earth have seen
our God's victory.^f

4 Shout to the LORD, all the earth;^g
be jubilant, shout for joy, and sing.

5 Sing to the LORD with the lyre,
with the lyre and melodious song.^h

6 With trumpets and the blast of the ram's horn
shout triumphantly in the presence of the LORD,
our King.

7 Let the sea and all that fills it,
the world and those who live in it, resound.ⁱ

8 Let the rivers clap their hands;
let the mountains shout together for joy

9 before the LORD, for He is coming to judge
the earth.
He will judge the world righteously
and the peoples fairly.^j

PSALM 99

THE KING IS HOLY

1 The LORD reigns! Let the peoples tremble.
He is enthroned above the cherubim.^k
Let the earth quake.

2 The LORD is great in Zion;
He is exalted above all the peoples.

NOTES

^a **97:12** Ps 32:11; 64:10; Jl 2:23
^b **97:12** Lit *praise the mention,* or
memory, of His holiness
^c **98:1** Ps 96:1; 1 Ch 16:23; Is
42:10
^d **98:1** Ps 20:7; 60:5; Is 52:10
^e **98:2** Is 56:1
^f **98:3** Is 45:22; 52:10
^g **98:4** Ps 100:1
^h **98:5** Is 51:3
ⁱ **98:7** Ps 96:11; 97:1; 1 Ch
16:31-32
^j **98:9** Ps 9:8; 96:13; 98:9
^k **99:1** Ex 25:22; 1 Sm 4:4; Ezk
11:22

NOTES

a 99:3 Ps 44:8; 138:2; Neh 1:5
b 99:4 Ps 37:28; Is 61:8
c 99:5 Ps 132:7; 1 Ch 28:2; Is 66:1
d 99:7 Nm 12:5; 14:14; Dt 31:15-18
e 99:8 Lit *avenged*
f 99:8 Or *but avenged misdeeds done against them*
g 99:8 Lv 26:25; Dt 32:41
h 99:9 Ps 2:6; 48:1; Ezk 20:40
i 100:1-2 Ps 95:1-2; 98:4-6
j 100:3 Alt Hb tradition, other Hb mss, LXX, Syr, Vg read *and not we ourselves*
k 100:3 Gn 1:26-27; Dt 32:6
l 100:3 Ps 79:13
m 100:4 Ps 75:1; 79:13; 119:62
n 100:4-5 Ps 118:1-4; 136; Lm 3:22-23

3 Let them praise Your great and awe-inspiring name. [a]
He is holy.

4 The mighty King loves justice. [b]
You have established fairness;
You have administered justice and righteousness in Jacob.

5 Exalt the LORD our God;
bow in worship at His footstool. [c]
He is holy.

6 Moses and Aaron were among His priests;
Samuel also was among those calling on His name.
They called to the LORD, and He answered them.

7 He spoke to them in a pillar of cloud; [d]
they kept His decrees and the statutes He gave them.

8 O LORD our God, You answered them.
You were a God who forgave them,
but punished [e] their misdeeds. [f] [g]

9 Exalt the LORD our God;
bow in worship at His holy mountain, [h]
for the LORD our God is holy.

PSALM 100

BE THANKFUL

A psalm of thanksgiving.

1 Shout triumphantly to the LORD,
all the earth.

2 Serve the LORD with gladness;
come before Him with joyful songs. [i]

3 Acknowledge that the LORD is God.
He made us, and we are His [j] [k]—
His people, the sheep of His pasture. [l]

4 Enter His gates with thanksgiving
and His courts with praise.
Give thanks to Him and praise His name. [m]

5 For the LORD is good, and His love is eternal;
His faithfulness endures through all generations. [n]

PSALM 101

A VOW OF INTEGRITY

A Davidic psalm.

NOTES

a **101:4** Lit *not know*
b **101:5** Is 5:15
c **101:7** Ps 31:18; 52:3; 63:11
d **101:7** Lit *in front of my eyes*
e **101:8** Ps 119:119

1   I will sing of faithful love and justice;
    I will sing praise to You, LORD.
2   I will pay attention to the way of integrity.
    When will You come to me?
    I will live with integrity of heart in my house.
3   I will not set anything godless before my eyes.
    I hate the doing of transgression;
    it will not cling to me.
4   A devious heart will be far from me;
    I will not be involved with[a] evil.
5   I will destroy anyone who secretly slanders
        his neighbor;
    I cannot tolerate anyone with haughty eyes
        or an arrogant heart.[b]
6   My eyes ⌊favor⌋ the faithful of the land
    so that they may sit down with me.
    The one who follows the way of integrity
        may serve me.
7   No one who acts deceitfully will live in my palace;
    no one who tells lies[c] will remain in
        my presence.[d]
8   Every morning I will destroy all the wicked
        of the land,
    eliminating all evildoers[e] from the LORD's city.

PSALM 102

AFFLICTION IN LIGHT OF ETERNITY

*A prayer of an afflicted person who is weak and pours
out his lament before the LORD.*

1   LORD, hear my prayer;
    let my cry for help come before You.
2   Do not hide Your face from me in my day
        of trouble.
    Listen closely to me;
    answer me quickly when I call.
3   For my days vanish like smoke,
    and my bones burn like a furnace.

^a **102:6** Or *a pelican of the desert*
^b **102:20** Lit *free sons of death*
^c **102:23** Other Hb mss, LXX read *His*

4 My heart is afflicted, withered like grass;
I even forget to eat my food.

5 Because of the sound of my groaning,
my flesh sticks to my bones.

6 I am like a desert owl,^a
like an owl among the ruins.

7 I stay awake;
I am like a solitary bird on a roof.

8 My enemies taunt me all day long;
they ridicule and curse me.

9 I eat ashes like bread
and mingle my drinks with tears

10 because of Your indignation and wrath;
for You have picked me up and thrown me
aside.

11 My days are like a lengthening shadow,
and I wither away like grass.

12 But You, LORD, are enthroned forever;
Your fame ⌊endures⌋ to all generations.

13 You will arise and have compassion on Zion,
for it is time to show favor to her—
the appointed time has come.

14 For Your servants take delight in its stones
and favor its dust.

15 Then the nations will fear the name of the LORD,
and all the kings of the earth Your glory,

16 for the LORD will rebuild Zion;
He will appear in His glory.

17 He will pay attention to the prayer of the destitute
and will not despise their prayer.

18 This will be written for a later generation,
and a newly created people will praise
the LORD:

19 He looked down from His holy heights—
the LORD gazed out from heaven to earth—

20 to hear a prisoner's groaning,
to set free those condemned to die,^b

21 so that they might declare the name of the LORD
in Zion
and His praise in Jerusalem,

22 when peoples and kingdoms are assembled
to serve the LORD.

23 He has broken my^c strength
in midcourse;
He has shortened my days.

NOTES

^a **102:24** Lit *days*
^b **102:25-27** Heb 1:10-12
^c **103:5** Lit *your ornament*; Hb uncertain
^d **103:7** Ex 33:13
^e **103:8** Ex 34:6

24 I say: "My God, do not take me in the middle
of my life!^a
Your years continue through all generations.

25 Long ago You established the earth,
and the heavens are the work of Your hands.

26 They will perish, but You will endure;
all of them will wear out like clothing.
You will change them like a garment, and they
will pass away.

27 But You are the same,
and Your years will never end.^b

28 Your servants' children will dwell ⌊securely⌋,
and their offspring will be established
before You."

PSALM 103

THE FORGIVING GOD

Davidic.

1 My soul, praise the LORD,
and all that is within me, praise His holy name.

2 My soul, praise the LORD,
and do not forget all His benefits.

3 He forgives all your sin;
He heals all your diseases.

4 He redeems your life from the •Pit;
He crowns you with faithful love
and compassion.

5 He satisfies you^c with goodness;
your youth is renewed like the eagle.

6 The LORD executes acts of righteousness
and justice for all the oppressed.

7 He revealed His ways to Moses,^d
His deeds to the people of Israel.

8 The LORD is compassionate and gracious,
slow to anger and full of faithful love.^e

9 He will not always accuse ⌊us⌋
or be angry forever.

10 He has not dealt with us as our sins deserve
or repaid us according to our offenses.

11 For as high as the heavens are above the earth,
so great is His faithful love toward those
who fear Him.

a 103:14 Gn 2:7
b 103:16 Lit *place no longer knows it*
c 104:3 Gn 1:6-7
d 104:4 Or *angels*
e 104:4 Heb 1:7
f 104:5 Ps 93:1; 96:10

12 As far as the east is from the west,
so far has He removed our transgressions
from us.

13 As a father has compassion on his children,
so the LORD has compassion on those who fear
Him.

14 For He knows what we are made of,
remembering that we are dust.[a]

15 As for man, his days are like grass—
he blooms like a flower of the field;

16 when the wind passes over it, it vanishes,
and its place is no longer known.[b]

17 But from eternity to eternity the LORD's
faithful love is toward those who fear Him,
and His righteousness toward the grandchildren

18 of those who keep His covenant,
who remember to observe His instructions.

19 The LORD has established His throne in heaven,
and His kingdom rules over all.

20 Praise the LORD, ⌊all⌋ His angels
of great strength,
who do His word,
obedient to His command.

21 Praise the LORD, all His armies,
His servants who do His will.

22 Praise the LORD, all His works
in all the places where He rules.
My soul, praise the LORD!

PSALM 104
GOD THE CREATOR

1 My soul, praise the LORD!
LORD my God, You are very great;
You are clothed with majesty and splendor.

2 He wraps Himself in light as if it were a robe,
spreading out the sky like a canopy,

3 laying the beams of His palace on the waters
⌊above⌋,[c]
making the clouds His chariot,
walking on the wings of the wind,

4 and making the winds His messengers,[d]
flames of fire His servants.[e]

5 He established the earth on its foundations;
it will never be shaken.[f]

NOTES
^a **104:8** Or *away. They flowed over the mountains and went down valleys*
^b **104:9** Gn 1:9-10
^c **104:16** Lit *are satisfied*
^d **104:19** Lit *moon for*
^e **104:19** Gn 1:14-18
^f **104:24** Lit *possessions*
^g **104:25** Gn 1:21

6 You covered it with the deep as if it were
   a garment;
the waters stood above the mountains.

7 At Your rebuke the waters fled;
at the sound of Your thunder they hurried away—

8 mountains rose and valleys sank^a—
to the place You established for them.

9 You set a boundary they cannot cross;
they will never cover the earth again.^b

10 He causes the springs to gush into the valleys;
they flow between the mountains.

11 They supply water for every wild beast;
the wild donkeys quench their thirst.

12 The birds of the sky live beside ⌊the springs⌋;
they sing among the foliage.

13 He waters the mountains from His palace;
the earth is satisfied by the fruit of Your labor.

14 He causes grass to grow for the livestock
and ⌊provides⌋ crops for man to cultivate,
producing food from the earth,

15 wine that makes man's heart glad—
making his face shine with oil—
and bread that sustains man's heart.

16 The trees of the LORD flourish,^c
the cedars of Lebanon that He planted.

17 There the birds make their nests;
the stork makes its home in the pine trees.

18 The high mountains are for the wild goats;
the cliffs are a refuge for hyraxes.

19 He made the moon to mark the^d seasons;^e
the sun knows when to set.

20 You bring darkness, and it becomes night,
when all the forest animals stir.

21 The young lions roar for their prey
and seek their food from God.

22 The sun rises; they go back
and lie down in their dens.

23 Man goes out to his work
and to his labor until evening.

24 How countless are Your works, LORD!
In wisdom You have made them all;
the earth is full of Your creatures.^f

25 Here is the sea, vast and wide,
teeming with creatures^g beyond number—
living things both large and small.

a **104:26** Ps 74:14; Jb 41:1; Is 27:1
b **104:30** Or *Spirit*
c **105:5** Lit *judgments of His mouth*

26 There the ships move about,
    and Leviathan,[a] which You formed to play there.
27 All of them wait for You
    to give them their food at the right time.
28 When You give it to them, they gather it;
    when You open Your hand, they are satisfied
        with good things.
29 When You hide Your face, they are terrified;
    when You take away their breath, they die
        and return to the dust.
30 When You send Your breath,[b]
        they are created,
    and You renew the face of the earth.
31 May the glory of the LORD endure forever;
    may the LORD rejoice in His works.
32 He looks at the earth, and it trembles;
    He touches the mountains, and they pour out
        smoke.
33 I will sing to the LORD all my life;
    I will sing praise to my God while I live.
34 May my meditation be pleasing to Him;
    I will rejoice in the LORD.
35 May sinners vanish from the earth
    and the wicked be no more.
    My soul, praise the LORD!
    •Hallelujah!

PSALM 105

GOD'S FAITHFULNESS TO HIS PEOPLE

1 Give thanks to the LORD, call on His name;
    proclaim His deeds among the peoples.
2 Sing to Him, sing praise to Him;
    tell about all His wonderful works!
3 Honor His holy name;
    let the hearts of those who seek the LORD
        rejoice.
4 Search for the LORD and for His strength;
    seek His face always.
5 Remember the wonderful works He has done,
    His wonders, and the judgments
        He has pronounced,[c]
6 O offspring of Abraham His servant,
    O descendants of Jacob—His chosen ones.

7 He is the LORD our God;
His judgments ⌊govern⌋ the whole earth.

8 He forever remembers His covenant,
the promise He ordained for a thousand
generations—

9 ⌊the covenant⌋ He made with Abraham,
swore[a] to Isaac,

10 and confirmed to Jacob as a decree
and to Israel as an everlasting covenant:

11 "To you I will give the land of Canaan
as your inherited portion."

12 When they were few in number,
very few indeed, and temporary residents
in ⌊Canaan⌋,

13 wandering from nation to nation,
from one kingdom to another,

14 He allowed no one to oppress them;
He rebuked kings on their behalf:

15 "Do not touch My anointed ones,
or harm My prophets."[b]

16 He called down famine against the land
and destroyed the entire food supply.[c]

17 He had sent a man ahead of them—
Joseph, who was sold as a slave.

18 They hurt his feet with shackles;
his neck was put in an iron collar.

19 Until the time his prediction came true,
the word of the LORD tested him.

20 The king sent ⌊for him⌋ and released him;
the ruler of peoples set him free.

21 He made him master of his household,
ruler over all his possessions—

22 binding[d] his officials at will
and instructing his elders.

23 Then Israel went to Egypt;
Jacob lived as a foreigner in the land of Ham.[e]

24 The LORD[f] made His people very fruitful;
He made them more numerous than their foes,[g]

25 whose hearts He turned to hate His people
and to deal deceptively with His servants.

26 He sent Moses His servant,
and Aaron, whom He had chosen.

27 They performed His miraculous signs
among them,
and wonders in the land of Ham.[h][i]

[a] **105:9** Lit *and His oath*
[b] **105:1-15** 1 Ch 16:8-22
[c] **105:16** Gn 41:53-57
[d] **105:22** LXX, Syr, Vg read *teaching*
[e] **105:23** Egypt
[f] **105:24** Lit *He*
[g] **105:24** Ex 1:7
[h] **105:27** Egypt
[i] **105:27** Ps 78:51; Ex 7:3; 11:9-10

NOTES
a 105:28 Or *for they did . . .* (as a statement)
b 105:28 Ex 10:21-23
c 105:29 Ex 7:15-21
d 105:30 Ex 8:1-6
e 105:31 Ex 8:20-24
f 105:31 Ex 8:16-17
g 105:33 Ex 9:22-26
h 105:34-35 Ex 10:12-15
i 105:36 Ex 12:29-30
j 105:37 Ex 12:35-36
k 105:38 Lit *them*
l 105:38 Ex 12:33
m 105:39 Ex 13:21
n 105:40 Ex 16:13-18
o 105:41 Ex 17:6

28 He sent darkness, and it became dark—
for did they[a] not defy His commands?[b]

29 He turned their waters into blood
and caused their fish to die.[c]

30 Their land was overrun with frogs,
even in their kings' chambers.[d]

31 He spoke, and insects came[e]—
gnats throughout their country.[f]

32 He gave them hail for rain,
and lightning throughout their land.

33 He struck their vines and fig trees
and shattered the trees of their territory.[g]

34 He spoke and locusts came—
young locusts without number.

35 They devoured all the vegetation in their land
and consumed the produce of their soil.[h]

36 He struck all the firstborn in their land,
all their first progeny.[i]

37 Then He brought Israel out with silver and gold,[j]
and no one among His tribes stumbled.

38 Egypt was glad when they left,
for dread of Israel[k] had fallen on them.[l]

39 He spread a cloud as a covering
and ⌊gave⌋ a fire to light up the night.[m]

40 They asked, and He brought quail
and satisfied them with bread from heaven.[n]

41 He opened a rock, and water gushed out;
it flowed like a stream in the desert.[o]

42 For He remembered His holy promise
to Abraham His servant.

43 He brought His people out with rejoicing,
His chosen ones with shouts of joy.

44 He gave them the lands of the nations,
and they inherited what other peoples had
worked for.

45 ⌊All this happened⌋ so that they might keep
His statutes
and obey His laws.
•Hallelujah!

PSALM 106

ISRAEL'S UNFAITHFULNESS TO GOD

1 •Hallelujah!
Give thanks to the LORD, for He is good;

His faithful love endures forever.

2 Who can declare the LORD's mighty acts
or proclaim all the praise due Him?

3 How happy are those who uphold justice,
who practice righteousness at all times.

4 Remember me, LORD, when You show favor
to Your people.
Come to me with Your salvation

5 so that I may enjoy the prosperity
of Your chosen ones,
rejoice in the joy of Your nation,
and boast about Your heritage.[a]

6 Both we and our fathers have sinned;
we have gone astray and have acted wickedly.

7 Our fathers in Egypt did not grasp
⌊the significance of⌋ Your wonderful works
or remember Your many acts of faithful love;
instead, they rebelled by the sea—the °Red Sea.[b]

8 Yet He saved them for His name's sake,
to make His power known.[c]

9 He rebuked the °Red Sea, and it dried up;
He led them through the depths as through
a desert.

10 He saved them from the hand of the adversary;
He redeemed them from the hand of the enemy.

11 Water covered their foes;
not one of them remained.

12 Then they believed His promises
and sang His praise.

13 They soon forgot His works
and would not wait for His counsel.[d]

14 They were seized with craving in the desert
and tested God in the wilderness.

15 He gave them what they asked for,
but sent a wasting disease among them.[e]

16 In the camp they were envious of Moses
and of Aaron, the LORD's holy one.

17 The earth opened up and swallowed Dathan;
it covered the assembly of Abiram.

18 Fire blazed throughout their assembly;
flames consumed the wicked.[f]

19 At Horeb they made a calf
and worshiped the cast metal image.

20 They exchanged their glory[g]
for the image of a grass-eating ox.[h]

NOTES

[a] 106:5 Dt 32:9
[b] 106:7 Ex 14:10-12
[c] 106:8 Ex 9:16
[d] 106:13 Ex 15:22-27
[e] 106:13-15 Ex 16:1-3; 17:1-7;
Nm 11
[f] 106:16-18 Nm 16:1-40
[g] 106:20 God
[h] 106:20 Jr 2:11; Rm 1:23

[a] 106:22 Egypt
[b] 106:23 Ex 32:1-14
[c] 106:25 Dt 1:27
[d] 106:26 Nm 13:32–14:35
[e] 106:27 Lv 26:33; Dt 4:27; 28:64
[f] 106:28 Nm 25:3; Dt 4:3
[g] 106:28 Lit *sacrifices for dead ones*
[h] 106:29-30 Nm 25:1-8
[i] 106:32 Lit *and it was evil for Moses*
[j] 106:33 Some Hb mss, LXX, Syr, Vg; other Hb mss read *they rebelled against His Spirit*
[k] 106:33 Nm 20:2-13
[l] 106:34 Jdg 1:27-36
[m] 106:36 Jdg 2:3
[n] 106:37-38 Dt 12:31; 2 Kg 17:17; Ezk 16:20-21

21 They forgot God their Savior,
who did great things in Egypt,

22 wonderful works in the land of Ham,[a]
awe-inspiring deeds at the •Red Sea.

23 So He said He would have destroyed them—
if Moses His chosen one had not
stood before Him in the breach
to turn His wrath away from destroying ⌊them⌋.[b]

24 They despised the pleasant land
and did not believe His promise.

25 They grumbled in their tents[c]
and did not listen to the LORD's voice.

26 So He raised His hand against them
⌊with an oath⌋
that He would make them fall in the desert[d]

27 and would disperse their descendants
among the nations,
scattering them throughout the lands.[e]

28 They aligned themselves with Baal of Peor[f]
and ate sacrifices offered to lifeless gods.[g]

29 They provoked the LORD with their deeds,
and a plague broke out against them.

30 But Phinehas stood up and intervened,
and the plague was stopped.[h]

31 It was credited to him as righteousness
throughout all generations to come.

32 They angered ⌊the LORD⌋ at the waters
of Meribah,
and Moses suffered[i] because of them;

33 for they embittered his spirit,[j]
and he spoke rashly with his lips.[k]

34 They did not destroy the peoples
as the LORD had commanded them,[l]

35 but mingled with the nations
and adopted their ways.

36 They served their idols,
which became a snare to them.[m]

37 They sacrificed their sons and daughters
to demons.

38 They shed innocent blood—
the blood of their sons and daughters
whom they sacrificed to the idols of Canaan;
so the land became polluted with blood.[n]

39 They defiled themselves by their actions
and prostituted themselves by their deeds.

NOTES
^a **106:43** Jdg 2:11-20; 3:8
^b **106:47-48** 2 Ch 16:35-36
^c **107:1** 1 Ch 16:34
^d **107:4** Lit *They*

40 Therefore the LORD's anger burned against
His people,
and He abhorred His own inheritance.

41 He handed them over to the nations,
those who hated them ruled them.

42 Their enemies oppressed them,
and they were subdued under their power.

43 He rescued them many times,
but they continued to rebel deliberately
and were beaten down by their sin.[a]

44 When He heard their cry,
He took note of their distress,

45 remembered His covenant with them,
and relented according to the abundance
of His faithful love.

46 He caused them to be pitied
before all their captors.

47 Save us, LORD our God,
and gather us from the nations,
so that we may give thanks to Your holy name
and make Your praise our pride.

48 May the LORD, the God of Israel, be praised
from everlasting to everlasting.
Let all the people say, "Amen!"
•Hallelujah![b]

BOOK V
(PSALMS 107–150)
PSALM 107
THANKSGIVING FOR GOD'S DELIVERANCE

1 Give thanks to the LORD, for He is good;
His faithful love endures forever.[c]

2 Let the redeemed of the LORD proclaim
that He has redeemed them from the hand
of the foe

3 and has gathered them from the lands—
from the east and the west,
from the north and the south.

4 Some[d] wandered in the desolate wilderness,
finding no way to a city where
they could live.

NOTES

a **107:5** Lit *their soul fainted*
b **107:9** Ps 34:10; Lk 1:53
c **107:10** Lit *They*
d **107:10** Or *the shadow of death*
e **107:10** Is 42:7; Lk 1:79
f **107:12** Lit *hearts*
g **107:14** Or *the shadow of death*
h **107:16** Is 45:2
i **107:22** Ps 50:14; Lv 7:12; Heb 13:15
j **107:23** Lit *They*
k **107:25** Lit *of it*

WORD STUDY

Hebrew word:
nipla'ot [nih flah OHT] /
pele' [PEH leh]

HCSB translation:
wonderful works, wonders

Focus passage:
Psalm 107:8,15,21,24,31

Nipla'ot and *pele'*, related to the Hebrew verb *pala'* (*to be difficult, extraordinary, wonderful*), indicate a work of God that is beyond human comprehension. The terms primarily describe God's acts—especially during the exodus and the conquest of Canaan—on Israel's behalf. God's *wondrous works* are experienced as redemptive (Ps 98:1) and cause awe and wonder among His people, who usually express these emotions through hymns (Ex 15:11). Each Israelite generation expected to see God work *wonders* (Ps 40:5). His *wondrous acts* were intended to cause other nations to marvel (Ex 3:20) and to realize that He is the true God (Ps 72:18). Israel was to remember God's *wondrous deeds* (Ps 78:11), declare them publicly (Ps 9:1), teach them to their children (Ps 78:4), and give thanks for them (Ps 75:1). God's *wonders* can also refer to heavenly wonders or acts of creation (Ps 136:4).

5 They were hungry and thirsty;
their spirits failed[a] within them.
6 Then they cried out to the LORD in their trouble;
He rescued them from their distress.
7 He led them by the right path
to go to a city where they could live.
8 Let them give thanks to the LORD
for His faithful love
and His wonderful works for the •human race.
9 For He has satisfied the thirsty
and filled the hungry with good things.[b]
10 Others[c] sat in darkness and gloom[d]—
prisoners in cruel chains[e]—
11 because they rebelled against God's commands
and despised the counsel of the •Most High.
12 He broke their spirits[f] with hard labor;
they stumbled, and there was no one to help.
13 Then they cried out to the LORD in their trouble;
He saved them from their distress.
14 He brought them out of darkness and gloom[g]
and broke their chains apart.
15 Let them give thanks to the LORD
for His faithful love
and His wonderful works for the •human race.
16 For He has broken down the bronze gates
and cut through the iron bars.[h]
17 Fools suffered affliction
because of their rebellious ways and their sins.
18 They loathed all food
and came near the gates of death.
19 Then they cried out to the LORD in their trouble;
He saved them from their distress.
20 He sent His word and healed them;
He rescued them from the •Pit.
21 Let them give thanks to the LORD
for His faithful love
and His wonderful works for the •human race.
22 Let them offer sacrifices of thanksgiving[i]
and announce His works with shouts of joy.
23 Others[j] went to sea in ships,
conducting trade on the vast waters.
24 They saw the LORD's works,
His wonderful works in the deep.
25 He spoke and raised a tempest
that stirred up the waves of the sea.[k]

26 Rising up to the sky, sinking down
    to the depths,
their courage^a melting away in anguish,

27 they reeled and staggered like drunken men,
and all their skill was useless.

28 Then they cried out to the LORD
    in their trouble,
and He brought them out of their distress.

29 He stilled the storm to a murmur,
and the waves of the sea^b were hushed.^c

30 They rejoiced when the waves^d grew quiet.
Then He guided them to the harbor
    they longed for.

31 Let them give thanks to the LORD
    for His faithful love
and His wonderful works
    for the •human race.

32 Let them exalt Him in the assembly
    of the people
and praise Him in the council
    of the elders.

33 He turns rivers into desert,
    springs of water into thirsty ground,

34 and fruitful land into salty wasteland,
because of the wickedness of its inhabitants.

35 He turns a desert into a pool of water,
dry land into springs of water.^e

36 He causes the hungry to settle there,
and they establish a city where they can live.

37 They sow fields and plant vineyards
that yield a fruitful harvest.

38 He blesses them, and they multiply greatly;^f
He does not let their livestock decrease.

39 When they are diminished and are humbled
by cruel oppression and sorrow,

40 He pours contempt on nobles^g
and makes them wander
    in trackless wastelands.^h

41 But He lifts the needy out of their suffering
and makes their families ⌊multiply⌋ like flocks.

42 The upright see it and rejoice,ⁱ
and all injustice shuts its mouth.^j

43 Let whoever is wise pay attention
    to these things
and consider^k the LORD's acts of faithful love.^l

^a **107:26** Lit *souls*
^b **107:29** Lit *of them*
^c **107:29** Ps 89:9; Mt 8:26; Lk 8:24
^d **107:30** Lit *when they*
^e **107:35** Ps 114:8; Is 41:17-18
^f **107:38** Gn 1:28
^g **107:40** Jb 12:21
^h **107:40** Jb 12:24
ⁱ **107:42** Ps 64:10; Jb 22:19
^j **107:42** Jb 5:16
^k **107:43** Lit *and let them consider*
^l **107:43** Ps 64:9; Hs 14:9

PSALM 108

A PLEA FOR VICTORY

A song. A Davidic psalm.

1 My heart is confident, God;
  I will sing; I will sing praises with the whole
    of my being.[a]

2 Wake up, harp and lyre!
  I will wake up the dawn.

3 I will praise You, LORD, among the peoples;
  I will sing praises to You among the nations.

4 For Your faithful love is higher than
    the heavens;
  Your faithfulness reaches the clouds.

5 Be exalted above the heavens, God;
  let Your glory be over the whole earth.[b]

6 Save with Your right hand and answer me
  so that those You love may be rescued.

7 God has spoken in His sanctuary:[c]
  "I will triumph!
  I will divide up Shechem.
  I will apportion the Valley of Succoth.

8 Gilead is Mine, Manasseh is Mine,
  and Ephraim is My helmet;
  Judah is My scepter.[d]

9 Moab is My washbasin;
  on Edom I throw My sandal.
  Over Philistia I shout in triumph."

10 Who will bring me to the fortified city?
  Who will lead me to Edom?

11 Have You not rejected us, God?
  God, You do not march out with our armies.

12 Give us aid against the foe,
  for human help is worthless.

13 With God we will perform valiantly;
  He will trample our foes.[e]

PSALM 109

PRAYER AGAINST AN ENEMY

For the choir director. A Davidic psalm.

1 O God of my praise,
  do not be silent.

2   For wicked and deceitful mouths open
      against me;
  they speak against me with lying tongues.

3   They surround me with hateful words
  and attack me without cause.^a

4   In return for my love they accuse me,
  but I continue to pray.^b

5   They repay me evil for good,
  and hatred for my love.^c

6   Set a wicked person over him;
  let an accuser stand at his right hand.^d

7   When he is judged, let him be found guilty,
  and let his prayer be counted as sin.

8   Let his days be few;
  let another take over his position.^e

9   Let his children be fatherless
  and his wife a widow.

10   Let his children wander as beggars,
  searching ⌊for food⌋ far
      from their demolished homes.

11   Let a creditor seize all he has;
  let strangers plunder what he has worked for.

12   Let no one show him kindness,
  and let no one be gracious to his fatherless children.

13   Let the line of his descendants be cut off;
  let their name be blotted out in the next
      generation.^f

14   Let his forefathers' guilt be remembered
      before the LORD,^g
  and do not let his mother's sin be blotted out.

15   Let their sins^h always remain before the LORD,
  and let Him cut off ⌊all⌋ memory of them
      from the earth.

16   For he did not think to show kindness,
  but pursued the wretched poor
      and the brokenhearted
  in order to put them to death.

17   He loved cursing—let it fall on him;
  he took no delight in blessing—let it be far
      from him.

18   He wore cursing like his coat—
  let it enter his body like water
  and go into his bones like oil.

19   Let it be like a robe he wraps around himself,
  like a belt he always wears.

NOTES

^a **109:3** Ps 35:7; 69:4; Jn 15:25
^b **109:4** Lit *but I, prayer*
^c **109:4-5** Ps 35:11-13; 38:20; Pr 17:13
^d **109:6** Zch 3:1
^e **109:8** Ac 1:20
^f **109:13** Jb 18:17,19; Pr 10:7
^g **109:14** Ex 34:7
^h **109:15** Lit *Let them*

WORD STUDY

Hebrew word:
'ebyon [ehv YOHN]

HCSB translation:
needy, poor

Focus passage:
Psalm 109:16,22,31

'Ebyon describes people who lack material goods and must depend on others for daily needs. The Mosaic Law legislates treatment of the *poor* (Ex 23:6), and the Prophets stress the importance of justice for the *poor* (Ez 22:29). The wicked, who do not honor God's covenant, oppose the *needy* (Is 32:7), but Yahweh cares for them (1 Sm 2:8). Defending the cause of the *needy* is the mark of one who knows the Lord (Jr 22:16). Metaphorically, *'ebyon* can refer to those who have a spiritual need for God (Ps 40:17). Often, the physically and the spiritually *needy* are linked, since both must rely daily upon God's provision. The Psalms frequently speak of God's special relationship with the righteous *poor*, who present their requests for justice to Him (Ps 109:31).

NOTES

a 109:23 Ps 102:11
b 109:24 Lit *denied from fat*
c 109:25 Lit *to them*
d 109:29 Ps 35:26; Jb 8:22
e 109:30 Ps 35:18; 111:1
f 110:1 Mt 22:44; Mk 12:36; Lk 20:42-43; Ac 2:34-35; 1 Co 15:25; Heb 1:13
g 110:2 One Hb ms, LXX, Tg read *You will rule*
h 110:2 Lit *Rule in the midst of Your*
i 110:3 Lit *power*
j 110:3 Hb obscure

20 Let this be the LORD's payment to my accusers,
to those who speak evil against me.

21 But You, GOD my Lord,
deal ⌊kindly⌋ with me for Your name's sake;
deliver me because of the goodness
of Your faithful love.

22 For I am poor and needy;
my heart is wounded within me.

23 I fade away like a lengthening shadow;[a]
I am shaken off like a locust.

24 My knees are weak from fasting,
and my body is emaciated.[b]

25 I have become an object of ridicule
to my accusers;[c]
when they see me, they shake their heads
⌊in scorn⌋.

26 Help me, LORD my God;
save me according to Your faithful love

27 so they may know that this is Your hand
and that You, LORD, have done it.

28 Though they curse, You will bless.
When they rise up, they will be put to shame,
but Your servant will rejoice.

29 My accusers will be clothed with disgrace;[d]
they will wear their shame like a cloak.

30 I will fervently thank the LORD with my mouth;
I will praise Him in the presence of many.[e]

31 For He stands at the right hand of the needy,
to save him from those who would condemn him.

PSALM 110

THE PRIESTLY KING

A Davidic psalm.

1 The LORD declared to my Lord:
"Sit at My right hand
until I make Your enemies Your footstool."[f]

2 The LORD will extend Your mighty scepter
from Zion.
Rule[g] over Your surrounding[h] enemies.

3 Your people will volunteer
on Your day of battle.[i]
In holy splendor, from the womb of the dawn,
the dew of Your youth belongs to You.[j]

NOTES

a **110:4** Heb 5:6,10; 7:17,21
b **110:6** Rv 14:20; 19:17-18
c **111:1** The lines of this poem
  form an •acrostic.
d **111:10** Pr 9:10
e **111:10** Lit *follow them*

4 The LORD has sworn an oath and will not take it
     back:
   "Forever, You are a priest
   like Melchizedek."[a]
5 The Lord is at Your right hand;
   He will crush kings on the day of His anger.
6 He will judge the nations, heaping up
     corpses;[b]
   He will crush leaders over the entire world.
7 He will drink from the brook by the road;
   therefore, He will lift up His head.

PSALM 111

PRAISE FOR THE LORD'S WORKS

1 •Hallelujah![c]
   I will praise the LORD with all my heart
   in the assembly of the upright
     and in the congregation.
2 The LORD's works are great,
     studied by all who delight in them.
3 All that He does is splendid and majestic;
   His righteousness endures forever.
4 He has caused His wonderful works
     to be remembered.
   The LORD is gracious and compassionate.
5 He has provided food for those who fear Him;
   He remembers His covenant forever.
6 He has shown His people the power
     of His works
   by giving them the inheritance of the nations.
7 The works of His hands are truth
     and justice;
   all His instructions are trustworthy.
8 They are established forever and ever,
     enacted in truth and uprightness.
9 He has sent redemption to His people.
   He has ordained His covenant forever.
   His name is holy and awe-inspiring.
10 The •fear of the LORD is the beginning
     of wisdom;[d]
   all who follow His instructions[e] have
     good insight.
   His praise endures forever.

NOTES

a **112:1** The lines of this poem form an •acrostic.
b **112:9** 2 Co 9:9

WORD STUDY

Hebrew word:
'olam [oh LAHM]

HCSB translation:
everlasting, forever

Focus passage:
Psalm 112:6

The noun *'olam* speaks of past or future time. While it occasionally refers to time during one's life span, *'olam* usually speaks of people, events, and things beyond one's earthly existence, often indicating a vast time span between the reader or audience and the concept referred to (Is 58:12). Regarding the past, *'olam* speaks of antiquity (Is 63:9). Regarding the future, *'olam* usually speaks of the future beyond one's lifetime. Thus, plundered cities, lands, and nations would remain destitute and barren into the distant future (Ps 81:15). The heavens (Ps 148:6) and the earth (Ps 78:69) are expected to exist *forever*. In reference to God's existence, *'olam* speaks of His eternality. He existed before creation, and He will exist without end.

PSALM 112

THE TRAITS OF THE RIGHTEOUS

1 •Hallelujah!a
Happy is the man who •fears the LORD,
taking great delight in His commandments.

2 His descendants will be powerful in the land;
the generation of the upright will be blessed.

3 Wealth and riches are in his house,
and his righteousness endures forever.

4 Light shines in the darkness for the upright.
He is gracious, compassionate, and righteous.

5 Good will come to a man who lends generously
and conducts his business fairly.

6 He will never be shaken.
The righteous will be remembered forever.

7 He will not fear bad news;
his heart is confident, trusting in the LORD.

8 His heart is assured; he will not fear.
In the end he will look in triumph on his foes.

9 He distributes freely to the poor;
his righteousness endures forever.b
His •horn will be exalted in honor.

10 The wicked man will see ⌊it⌋ and be angry;
he will gnash his teeth in despair.
The desire of the wicked will come to nothing.

PSALM 113

PRAISE TO THE MERCIFUL GOD

1 •Hallelujah!
Give praise, servants of the LORD;
praise the name of the LORD.

2 Let the name of the LORD be praised
both now and forever.

3 From the rising of the sun to its setting,
let the name of the LORD be praised.

4 The LORD is exalted above all the nations,
His glory above the heavens.

5 Who is like the LORD our God—
the One enthroned on high,

6 who stoops down to look
on the heavens and the earth?

7　He raises the poor from the dust
　　and lifts the needy from the garbage heap

8　in order to seat them with nobles—
　　with the nobles of His people.

9　He gives the childless woman a household,
　　⌊making her⌋ the joyful mother of children.
　　*Hallelujah!

PSALM 114

GOD'S DELIVERANCE OF ISRAEL

1　When Israel came out of Egypt—
　　the house of Jacob from a people
　　who spoke a foreign language—

2　Judah became His sanctuary,
　　Israel, His dominion.

3　The sea looked and fled;ᵃ
　　the Jordan turned back.ᵇ

4　The mountains skipped like rams,
　　the hills, like lambs.

5　Why was it, sea, that you fled?
　　Jordan, that you turned back?

6　Mountains, that you skipped like rams?
　　Hills, like lambs?

7　Tremble, earth, at the presence of the Lord,
　　at the presence of the God of Jacob,

8　who turned the rock into a pool of water,
　　the flint into a spring of water.ᶜ

PSALM 115

GLORY TO GOD ALONE

1　Not to us, LORD, not to us,
　　but to Your name give glory
　　because of Your faithful love, because of Your truth.

2　Why should the nations say,
　　"Where is their God?"

3　Our God is in heaven
　　and does whatever He pleases.

4　Their idols are silver and gold,
　　made by human hands.

5　They have mouths, but cannot speak,
　　eyes, but cannot see.

NOTES

a 115:8 Or *May those who make them become*
b 115:4-8 Ps 135:15-18
c 115:9 Other Hb mss, LXX, Syr read *House of Israel*
d 115:16 Lit LORD's *heavens*

6 They have ears, but cannot hear,
noses, but cannot smell.

7 They have hands, but cannot feel,
feet, but cannot walk.
They cannot make a sound with their throats.

8 Those who make them are[a] just like them,
as are all who trust in them.[b]

9 Israel,[c] trust in the LORD!
He is their help and shield.

10 House of Aaron, trust in the LORD!
He is their help and shield.

11 You who •fear the LORD, trust in the LORD!
He is their help and shield.

12 The LORD remembers us and will bless ⌊us⌋.
He will bless the house of Israel;
He will bless the house of Aaron;

13 He will bless those who •fear the LORD—
small and great alike.

14 May the LORD add to ⌊your numbers⌋,
both yours and your children's.

15 May you be blessed by the LORD,
the Maker of heaven and earth.

16 The heavens are the LORD's,[d]
but the earth He has given to the •human race.

17 It is not the dead who praise the LORD,
nor any of those descending into the silence
⌊of death⌋.

18 But we will praise the LORD,
both now and forever.
•Hallelujah!

PSALM 116

THANKS TO GOD FOR DELIVERANCE

1 I love the LORD because He has heard
my appeal for mercy.

2 Because He has turned His ear to me,
I will call ⌊out to Him⌋ as long as I live.

3 The ropes of death were wrapped
around me,
and the torments of •Sheol overcame me;
I encountered trouble and sorrow.

4 Then I called on the name of the LORD:
"LORD, save me!"

NOTES
^a **116:13** Rm 3:4
^b **116:13** Or *proclaim* or *invoke the name of*; lit *call on the name of*
^c **116:15** Or *valuable*
^d **116:17** Or *proclaim* or *invoke the name of*; lit *call on the name of*
^e **117:1** Rm 15:11

5 The LORD is gracious and righteous;
our God is compassionate.

6 The LORD guards the inexperienced;
I was helpless, and He saved me.

7 Return to your rest, my soul,
for the LORD has been good to you.

8 For You, ⌊LORD,⌋ rescued me
from death,
my eyes from tears,
my feet from stumbling.

9 I will walk before the LORD
in the land of the living.

10 I believed, even when I said,
"I am severely afflicted."

11 In my alarm I said,
"Everyone is a liar."^a

12 How can I repay the LORD
all the good He has done for me?

13 I will take the cup of salvation
and worship^b the LORD.

14 I will fulfill my vows to the LORD
in the presence of all His people.

15 In the sight of the LORD
the death of His faithful ones is costly.^c

16 LORD, I am indeed Your servant;
I am Your servant, the son
of Your female servant.
You have loosened my bonds.

17 I will offer You a sacrifice of thanksgiving
and will worship^d the LORD.

18 I will fulfill my vows to the LORD,
in the very presence of all
His people,

19 in the courts of the LORD's house—
within you, Jerusalem.
•Hallelujah!

PSALM 117

UNIVERSAL CALL TO PRAISE

1 Praise the LORD, all nations!
Glorify Him, all peoples!^e

2 For great is His faithful love to us;
the LORD's faithfulness endures forever.
•Hallelujah!

PSALM 118

THANKSGIVING FOR VICTORY

1 Give thanks to the LORD, for He is good;
His faithful love endures forever.

2 Let Israel say,
"His faithful love endures forever."

3 Let the house of Aaron say,
"His faithful love endures forever."

4 Let those who fear the LORD say,
"His faithful love endures forever."

5 I called to the LORD in distress;
the LORD answered me ⌊and put me⌋
in a spacious place. a

6 The LORD is for me; I will not be afraid.
What can man do to me? b

7 With the LORD for me as my helper,
I will look in triumph on those who hate me.

8 It is better to take refuge in the LORD
than to trust in man.

9 It is better to take refuge in the LORD
than to trust in nobles.

10 All the nations surrounded me;
in the name of the LORD I destroyed them.

11 They surrounded me, yes, they surrounded me;
in the name of the LORD I destroyed them.

12 They surrounded me like bees; c
they were extinguished like a fire among thorns;
in the name of the LORD I destroyed them.

13 You d pushed me e hard to make me fall,
but the LORD helped me.

14 The LORD is my strength and my song;
He has become my salvation. f

15 There are shouts of joy and victory
in the tents of the righteous:
"The LORD's right hand strikes with power!

16 The LORD's right hand is raised!
The LORD's right hand strikes with power!"

17 I will not die, but I will live
and proclaim what the LORD has done.

18 The LORD disciplined me severely
but did not give me over to death.

19 Open the gates of righteousness for me;
I will enter through them and give thanks
to the LORD.

20   This is the gate of the LORD;
      the righteous will enter through it.

21   I will give thanks to You because You have
            answered me
      and have become my salvation.

22   The stone that the builders rejected
      has become the cornerstone.[a]

23   This came from the LORD;
      it is wonderful in our eyes.[b]

24   This is the day the LORD has made;
      let us rejoice and be glad in it.

25   LORD, save us!
      LORD, please grant us success!

26   Blessed is he who comes in the name
            of the LORD.[c]
      From the house of the LORD we bless you.

27   The LORD is God and has given us light.
      Bind the festival sacrifice with cords to the horns
            of the altar.

28   You are my God, and I will give You thanks.
      ⌊You are⌋ my God; I will exalt You.

29   Give thanks to the LORD, for He is good;
      His faithful love endures forever.

[a] **118:22** Lk 20:17; Ac 4:11; 1 Pt 2:4,7
[b] **118:23** Mt 21:42; Mk 12:11
[c] **118:25-26** Mt 21:9; Mk 11:9-10; Lk 13:35; Jn 12:13
[d] **119:1** The stanzas of this poem form an •acrostic.

PSALM 119

DELIGHT IN GOD'S WORD

א *Alef*

1   How[d] happy are those whose way
            is blameless,
      who live according to the law
            of the LORD!

2   Happy are those who keep His decrees
      and seek Him with all their heart.

3   They do nothing wrong;
      they follow His ways.

4   You have commanded that Your precepts
      be diligently kept.

5   If only my ways were committed
      to keeping Your statutes!

6   Then I would not be ashamed
      when I think about all Your commands.

7   I will praise You with a sincere heart
      when I learn Your righteous judgments.

WORD STUDY

Hebrew word:
torah [toh RAH]

HCSB translation:
law, instruction

Focus passage:
Psalm 119:1

Torah refers primarily to *instruction*, either a single *instruction* or a collection of *instructions*. *Torah* can be either general (Pr 3:1) or specific (Ex 16:4) *instruction*. In the OT, *torah* was first associated with the *instructions* that God revealed to Moses and that Israel was to follow. These *instructions* included civil laws (Ex 18:16) and religious laws (Lv 6:9). The OT uses *torah* flexibly to refer to the book of Deuteronomy (Dt 1:5), all of Moses' writings (Jos 8:31), the prophets (Dn 9:10), or the Word of God (Ps 19:7). The focus of *torah* is not its specific form but its divine authority. Anything referred to as *torah* in the OT is understood to be authoritative because it comes from God. That is why the godly person delights in God's *torah* and meditates on it continuously (Ps 1:2).

NOTES

a **119:9** Or *keeping it according to Your*

8 I will keep Your statutes;
   never abandon me.

ב *Bet*

9 How can a young man keep his way pure?
   By keeping Your[a] word.

10 I have sought You with all my heart;
   don't let me wander from Your commands.

11 I have treasured Your word in my heart
   so that I may not sin against You.

12 LORD, may You be praised;
   teach me Your statutes.

13 With my lips I proclaim
   all the judgments from Your mouth.

14 I rejoice in the way ⌊revealed by⌋ Your decrees
   as much as in all riches.

15 I will meditate on Your precepts
   and think about Your ways.

16 I will delight in Your statutes;
   I will not forget Your word.

ג *Gimel*

17 Deal generously with Your servant so that
       I might live;
   then I will keep Your word.

18 Open my eyes so that I may see
   wonderful things in Your law.

19 I am a stranger on earth;
   do not hide Your commands from me.

20 I am continually overcome
   by longing for Your judgments.

21 You rebuke the proud, the accursed,
   who wander from Your commands.

22 Take insult and contempt away from me,
   for I have kept Your decrees.

23 Though princes sit together speaking against me,
   Your servant will think about Your statutes;

24 Your decrees are my delight
   and my counselors.

ד *Dalet*

25 My life is down in the dust;
   give me life through Your word.

26 I told You about my life, and You listened to me;
   teach me Your statutes.

NOTES

a **119:28** Or *My soul weeps*
b **119:32** Lit *You enlarge my heart*
c **119:33** Or *will keep it as my reward*
d **119:37** Other Hb mss, Tg read *word*

27 Help me understand the meaning
  of Your precepts
so that I can meditate on Your wonders.
28 I am weary[a] from grief;
strengthen me through Your word.
29 Keep me from the way of deceit,
and graciously give me Your instruction.
30 I have chosen the way of truth;
I have set Your ordinances ⌊before me⌋.
31 I cling to Your decrees;
LORD, do not put me to shame.
32 I pursue the way of Your commands,
for You broaden my understanding.[b]

ה *He*

33 Teach me, LORD, the meaning of Your statutes,
and I will always keep them.[c]
34 Help me understand Your instruction, and I will
  obey it
and follow it with all my heart.
35 Help me stay on the path of Your commands,
for I take pleasure in it.
36 Turn my heart to Your decrees
and not to material gain.
37 Turn my eyes from looking at
  what is worthless;
give me life in Your ways.[d]
38 Confirm what You said to Your servant,
for it produces reverence for You.
39 Turn away the disgrace I dread;
indeed, Your judgments are good.
40 How I long for Your precepts!
Give me life through Your righteousness.

ו *Vav*

41 Let Your faithful love come to me, LORD,
Your salvation, as You promised.
42 Then I can answer the one who taunts me,
for I trust in Your word.
43 Never take the word of truth from my mouth,
for I hope in Your judgments.
44 I will always keep Your law,
forever and ever.
45 I will walk freely in an open place
because I seek Your precepts.

46 I will speak of Your decrees before kings
and not be ashamed.

47 I delight in Your commands,
which I love.

48 I will lift up my hands[a] to Your commands,
which I love,
and will meditate on Your statutes.

ז *Zayin*

49 Remember ⌊Your⌋ word to Your servant,
through which You have given me hope.

50 This is my comfort in my affliction:
Your promise has given me life.

51 The arrogant constantly ridicule me,
but I do not turn away from Your instruction.

52 LORD, I remember Your judgments from long ago
and find comfort.

53 Rage seizes me because of the wicked
who reject Your instruction.

54 Your statutes are ⌊the theme of⌋ my song
during my earthly life.[b]

55 I remember Your name in the night, LORD,
and I keep Your law.

56 This is my ⌊practice⌋:
I obey Your precepts.

ח *Khet*

57 The LORD is my portion;[c]
I have promised to keep Your words.

58 I have sought Your favor with all my heart;
be gracious to me according to Your promise.

59 I thought about my ways
and turned my steps back to Your decrees.

60 I hurried, not hesitating
to keep Your commands.

61 Though the ropes of the wicked were wrapped
around me,
I did not forget Your law.

62 I rise at midnight to thank You
for Your righteous judgments.

63 I am a friend to all who •fear You,
to those who keep Your precepts.

64 LORD, the earth is filled with
Your faithful love;
teach me Your statutes.

ת *Tet*

65 LORD, You have treated Your servant well,
just as You promised.

66 Teach me good judgment and discernment,
for I rely on Your commands.

67 Before I was afflicted I went astray,
but now I keep Your word.

68 You are good, and You do what is good;
teach me Your statutes.

69 The arrogant have smeared me with lies,
but I obey Your precepts with all my heart.

70 Their hearts are hard and insensitive,
but I delight in Your instruction.

71 It was good for me to be afflicted
so that I could learn Your statutes.

72 Instruction from Your lips is better for me
than thousands of gold and silver pieces.

י *Yod*

73 Your hands made me and formed me;
give me understanding so that I can learn
Your commands.

74 Those who •fear You will see me and rejoice,
for I hope in Your word.

75 I know, LORD, that Your judgments are just
and that You have afflicted me fairly.

76 May Your faithful love comfort me,
as You promised Your servant.

77 May Your compassion come to me so that
I may live,
for Your instruction is my delight.

78 Let the arrogant be put to shame for slandering
me with lies;
I will meditate on Your precepts.

79 Let those who •fear You,
those who know Your decrees, turn to me.

80 May my heart be blameless regarding
Your statutes
so that I will not be put to shame.

כ *Kaf*

81 I long for Your salvation;
I hope in Your word.

82 My eyes grow weary ⌊looking⌋ for what
You have promised;

I ask, "When will You comfort me?"

83 Though I have become like a wineskin ⌊dried⌋
by smoke,
I do not forget Your statutes.

84 How many days ⌊must⌋ Your servant ⌊wait⌋?
When will You execute judgment
on my persecutors?

85 The arrogant have dug pits for me;
they violate Your instruction.

86 All Your commands are true;
people persecute me with lies—help me!

87 They almost ended my life on earth,
but I did not abandon Your precepts.

88 Give me life in accordance with
Your faithful love,
and I will obey the decree You have spoken.

ל *Lamed*

89 LORD, Your word is forever;
it is firmly fixed in heaven.

90 Your faithfulness is for all generations;
You established the earth, and it stands firm.

91 They stand today in accordance with
Your judgments,
for all things are Your servants.

92 If Your instruction had not been my delight,
I would have died in my affliction.

93 I will never forget Your precepts,
for You have given me life through them.

94 I am Yours; save me,
for I have sought Your precepts.

95 The wicked hope to destroy me,
but I contemplate Your decrees.

96 I have seen a limit to all perfection,
but Your command is without limit.

מ *Mem*

97 How I love Your teaching!
It is my meditation all day long.

98 Your command makes me wiser than my enemies,
for it is always with me.

99 I have more insight than all my teachers
because Your decrees are my meditation.

100 I understand more than the elders
because I obey Your precepts.

101   I have kept my feet from every evil path
to follow Your word.

102   I have not turned from Your judgments,
for You Yourself have instructed me.

103   How sweet Your word is to my taste—
⌊sweeter⌋ than honey to my mouth.

104   I gain understanding from Your precepts;
therefore I hate every false way.

]   Nun

105   Your word is a lamp for my feet
and a light on my path.

106   I have solemnly sworn
to keep Your righteous judgments.

107   I am severely afflicted;
LORD, give me life through Your word.

108   LORD, please accept my willing offerings
of praise,
and teach me Your judgments.

109   My life is constantly in danger,[a]
yet I do not forget Your instruction.

110   The wicked have set a trap for me,
but I have not wandered from Your precepts.

111   I have Your decrees as a heritage forever;
indeed, they are the joy of my heart.

112   I am resolved to obey Your statutes
to the very end.[b]

ם   Samek

113   I hate the double-minded,
but I love Your instruction.

114   You are my shelter and my shield;
I hope in Your word.

115   Depart from me, you evil ones,
so that I may obey my God's commands.

116   Sustain me as You promised, and I will live;
do not let me be ashamed of my hope.

117   Sustain me so that I can be safe
and be concerned with Your statutes
continually.

118   You reject all who stray from Your statutes,
for their deceit is a lie.

119   You remove all the wicked on earth as if
they were[c] dross;
therefore, I love Your decrees.

[a] **119:109** Lit *my hand*
[b] **119:112** Or *statutes; the reward is eternal*
[c] **119:119** Other Hb mss, DSS, LXX, Aq, Sym, Jer read *All the wicked of the earth You count as*

NOTES
a **119:120** Lit *My flesh shudders*
b **119:128** Lit *I therefore follow carefully*

120 I shudder[a] in awe of You;
I fear Your judgments.

ע   *Ayin*

121 I have done what is just and right;
do not leave me to my oppressors.

122 Guarantee Your servant's well-being;
do not let the arrogant oppress me.

123 My eyes grow weary ⌊looking for⌋
Your salvation
and for Your righteous promise.

124 Deal with Your servant based on
Your faithful love;
teach me Your statutes.

125 I am Your servant; give me understanding
so that I may know Your decrees.

126 It is time for the LORD to act,
⌊for⌋ they have broken Your law.

127 Since I love Your commandments
more than gold, even the purest gold,

128 I carefully follow[b] all Your precepts
and hate every false way.

פ   *Pe*

129 Your decrees are wonderful;
therefore I obey them.

130 The revelation of Your words brings light
and gives understanding to the inexperienced.

131 I pant with open mouth
because I long for Your commands.

132 Turn to me and be gracious to me,
as is ⌊Your⌋ practice toward those who love
Your name.

133 Make my steps steady through Your promise;
don't let sin dominate me.

134 Redeem me from human oppression,
and I will keep Your precepts.

135 Show favor to Your servant,
and teach me Your statutes.

136 My eyes pour out streams of tears
because people do not follow Your instruction.

צ   *Tsade*

137 You are righteous, LORD,
and Your judgments are just.

NOTES

a **119:150** Some Hb mss, LXX, Sym, Jer read *who maliciously persecute me*

138 The decrees You issue are righteous
and altogether trustworthy.
139 My anger overwhelms me
because my foes forget Your words.
140 Your word is completely pure,
and Your servant loves it.
141 I am insignificant and despised,
but I do not forget Your precepts.
142 Your righteousness is an everlasting
righteousness,
and Your instruction is true.
143 Trouble and distress have overtaken me,
but Your commands are my delight.
144 Your decrees are righteous forever.
Give me understanding, and I will live.

ק *Qof*

145 I call with all my heart; answer me, LORD.
I will obey Your statutes.
146 I call to You; save me,
and I will keep Your decrees.
147 I rise before dawn and cry out for help;
I hope in Your word.
148 I am awake through each watch of the night
to meditate on Your promise.
149 In keeping with Your faithful love, hear my voice.
LORD, give me life, in keeping with Your justice.
150 Those who pursue evil plans[a] come near;
they are far from Your instruction.
151 You are near, LORD,
and all Your commands are true.
152 Long ago I learned from Your decrees
that You have established them forever.

ר *Resh*

153 Consider my affliction and rescue me,
for I have not forgotten Your instruction.
154 Defend my cause, and redeem me;
give me life, as You promised.
155 Salvation is far from the wicked
because they do not seek Your statutes.
156 Your compassions are many, LORD;
give me life, according to Your judgments.
157 My persecutors and foes are many.
I have not turned from Your decrees.

158 I have seen the disloyal and feel disgust
   because they do not keep Your word.

159 Consider how I love Your precepts;
   LORD, give me life, according to
    Your faithful love.

160 The entirety of Your word is truth,
   and all Your righteous judgments endure forever.

ש *Sin* / ש *Shin*

161 Princes have persecuted me without cause,
   but my heart fears ⌊only⌋ Your word.

162 I rejoice over Your promise
   like one who finds vast treasure.

163 I hate and abhor falsehood,
   ⌊but⌋ I love Your instruction.

164 I praise You seven times a day
   for Your righteous judgments.

165 Abundant peace belongs to those who love
    Your instruction;
   nothing makes them stumble.

166 LORD, I hope for Your salvation
   and carry out Your commands.

167 I obey Your decrees
   and love them greatly.

168 I obey Your precepts and decrees,
   for all my ways are before You.

ת *Tav*

169 Let my cry reach You, LORD;
   give me understanding according to Your word.

170 Let my plea reach You;
   rescue me according to Your promise.

171 My lips pour out praise,
   for You teach me Your statutes.

172 My tongue sings about Your promise,
   for all Your commandments are righteous.

173 May Your hand be ready to help me,
   for I have chosen Your precepts.

174 I long for Your salvation, LORD,
   and Your instruction is my delight.

175 Let me live, and I will praise You;
   may Your judgments help me.

176 I wander like a lost sheep;
   seek Your servant,
   for I do not forget Your commands.

PSALM 120

A CRY FOR TRUTH AND PEACE

A •song of ascents.

1 In my distress I called to the LORD,
and He answered me:

2 "LORD, deliver me from lying lips
and a deceitful tongue."

3 What will He give you,
and what will He do to you,
you deceitful tongue?

4 A warrior's sharp arrows,
with burning charcoal![a]

5 What misery that I have stayed in Meshech,
that I have lived among the tents of Kedar![b]

6 I have lived too long
with those who hate peace.

7 I am for peace; but when I speak,
they are for war.

PSALM 121

THE LORD OUR PROTECTOR

A •song of ascents.

1 I raise my eyes toward the mountains.
Where will my help come from?

2 My help comes from the LORD,
the Maker of heaven and earth.[c]

3 He will not allow your foot to slip;
your Protector will not slumber.

4 Indeed, the Protector of Israel
does not slumber or sleep.

5 The LORD protects you;
the LORD is a shelter right by your side.[d]

6 The sun will not strike you by day,
or the moon by night.

7 The LORD will protect you from all harm;
He will protect your life.

8 The LORD will protect your coming and going
both now and forever.

NOTES

[a] **120:4** Lit *with coals of the broom bush*

[b] **120:5** *Meshech*: a people far to the north of Palestine; *Kedar*: a nomadic people of the desert to the southeast

[c] **121:2** Ps 124:8

[d] **121:5** Lit *is your shelter at your right hand*

WORD STUDY

Hebrew word:
ma'alah [ma ah LAH]

HCSB translation:
ascents

Focus passages:
Psalms 120-134 superscriptions

The noun *ma'alah*, related to the verb *'alah* (*to go up*), appears in the titles of Psalms 120-134, The Songs of Ascents. Since *ma'alah* can refer to a journey, many scholars believe The Songs of Ascents were used as "Pilgrimage Psalms" sung during journeys to Jerusalem for religious festivals. Others believe they were psalms sung by Jewish exiles on their journey from Babylon back to Jerusalem. A third theory is that the Levites performed these Songs of Ascents on the temple steps during religious ceremonies. Support for this third view comes from the term's common reference to a structure, such as a ramp or set of steps, that provides an ascent. The Mishnah, a collection of Jewish oral laws, also supports this view.

PSALM 122

A PRAYER FOR JERUSALEM

A Davidic •song of ascents.

1 I rejoiced with those who said to me,
"Let us go to the house of the LORD."

2 Our feet are standing
within your gates, Jerusalem—

3 Jerusalem, built as a city ⌊should be⌋,
solidly joined together,

4 where the tribes, the tribes of the LORD, go up
to give thanks to the name of the LORD.
(This is an ordinance for Israel.)

5 There, thrones for judgment are placed,
thrones of the house of David.

6 Pray for the peace of Jerusalem:
"May those who love you prosper;

7 may there be peace within your walls,
prosperity within your fortresses."

8 For the sake of my brothers and friends,
I will say, "Peace be with you."

9 For the sake of the house of the LORD our God,
I will seek your good.

PSALM 123

LOOKING FOR GOD'S FAVOR

A •song of ascents.

1 I lift my eyes to You,
the One enthroned in heaven.

2 Like a servant's eyes on His master's hand,
like a servant girl's eyes on her mistress's hand,
so our eyes are on the LORD our God
until He shows us favor.

3 Show us favor, LORD, show us favor,
for we've had more than enough contempt.

4 We've had more than enough
scorn from the arrogant
⌊and⌋ contempt from the proud.

PSALM 124

THE LORD IS ON OUR SIDE

A Davidic •song of ascents.

1   If the LORD had not been on our side—
    let Israel say—
2   If the LORD had not been on our side
    when men attacked us,
3   then they would have swallowed us alive
    in their burning anger against us.
4   Then the waters would have engulfed us;
    the torrent would have swept over us;
5   the raging waters would have swept over us.
6   Praise the LORD,
    who has not let us be ripped apart by their teeth.
7   We have escaped like a bird
        from the hunter's net;
    the net is torn, and we have escaped.
8   Our help is in the name of the LORD,
    the Maker of heaven and earth.[a]

PSALM 125

ISRAEL'S STABILITY

A •song of ascents.

1   Those who trust in the LORD are
        like Mount Zion.
    It cannot be shaken; it remains forever.
2   Jerusalem—the mountains surround her.
    And the LORD surrounds His people,
    both now and forever.
3   The scepter of the wicked will not remain
    over the land allotted to the righteous,
    so that the righteous will not apply their hands
        to injustice.
4   Do good, LORD, to the good,
    to those whose hearts are upright.
5   But as for those who turn aside
        to crooked ways,
    the LORD will banish them with the evildoers.
    Peace be with Israel.[b]

NOTES

^a **126:1** Or LORD *returned those of Zion who had been captives*
^b **126:4** Or *Return our captives*
^c **126:4** Seasonal streams in the arid south country
^d **127:2** Or *work; He gives such things to His loved ones while [they] sleep*

PSALM 126

ZION'S RESTORATION

A •song of ascents.

1 When the LORD restored the fortunes of Zion, ^a
we were like those who dream.

2 Our mouths were filled with laughter then,
and our tongues with shouts of joy.
Then they said among the nations,
"The LORD has done great things for them."

3 The LORD had done great things for us;
we were joyful.

4 Restore our fortunes, ^b LORD,
like watercourses in the Negev. ^c

5 Those who sow in tears
will reap with shouts of joy.

6 Though one goes along weeping,
carrying the bag of seed,
he will surely come back with shouts of joy,
carrying his sheaves.

PSALM 127

THE BLESSING OF THE LORD

A Solomonic •song of ascents.

1 Unless the LORD builds a house,
its builders labor over it in vain;
unless the LORD watches over a city,
the watchman stays alert in vain.

2 In vain you get up early and stay up late,
eating food earned by hard work;
certainly He gives sleep to the one He loves. ^d

3 Sons are indeed a heritage from the LORD,
children, a reward.

4 Like arrows in the hand of a warrior
are the sons born in one's youth.

5 Happy is the man who has filled his quiver
with them.
Such men will never be put to shame
when they speak with ⌊their⌋ enemies
at the city gate.

PSALM 128

BLESSINGS FOR THOSE WHO FEAR GOD

A •song of ascents.

1 How happy is everyone who •fears the LORD,
who walks in His ways!

2 You will surely eat what your hands
have worked for.
You will be happy, and it will go well for you.

3 Your wife will be like a fruitful vine
within your house,
your sons, like young olive trees
around your table.

4 In this very way the man who •fears the LORD
will be blessed.

5 May the LORD bless you from Zion,
so that you will see the prosperity of Jerusalem
all the days of your life,

6 and will see your children's children!
Peace be with Israel.ᵃ

PSALM 129

PROTECTION OF THE OPPRESSED

A •song of ascents.

1 Since my youth they have often attacked me—
let Israel say—

2 Since my youth they have often attacked me,
but they have not prevailed against me.

3 Plowmen plowed over my back;
they made their furrows long.

4 The LORD is righteous;
He has cut the ropes of the wicked.

5 Let all who hate Zion
be driven back in disgrace.

6 Let them be like grass on the rooftops,
which withers before it grows upᵇ

7 and can't even fill the hands of the reaper
or the arms of the one who binds sheaves.

8 Then none who pass by will say,
"May the LORD's blessing be on you."
We bless you in the name of the LORD.

NOTES

a 130:7 Ps 131:3
b 131:3 Ps 130:7

PSALM 130

AWAITING REDEMPTION

A •song of ascents.

1   Out of the depths I call to You, LORD!
2   Lord, listen to my voice;
let Your ears be attentive
to my cry for help.
3   LORD, if You considered sins,
Lord, who could stand?
4   But with You there is forgiveness,
so that You may be revered.
5   I wait for the LORD; I wait,
and put my hope in His word.
6   I ⌊wait⌋ for the Lord
more than watchmen for the morning—
more than watchmen for the morning.
7   Israel, hope in the LORD.[a]
For there is faithful love with the LORD,
and with Him is redemption in abundance.
8   And He will redeem Israel
from all its sins.

PSALM 131

A CHILDLIKE SPIRIT

A Davidic •song of ascents.

1   LORD, my heart is not proud; my eyes are not
haughty.
I do not get involved with things too great
or too difficult for me.
2   Instead, I have calmed and quieted myself
like a little weaned child with its mother;
I am like a little child.
3   Israel, hope in the LORD,[b]
both now and forever.

WORD STUDY

Hebrew word:
'awon [ah VOHN]

HCSB translation:
sins, iniquity, guilt

Focus passage:
Psalm 130:3,8

The Hebrew noun *'awon* is related to the verb *'awah* (*to bend, twist, distort*), suggesting that *iniquity* involves a distortion or twisting. *'Awon* can refer to an act of *iniquity* as well as the responsibility and punishment for that act. To the Hebrew mind, these three aspects were not strictly separated. *'Awon* may refer to violations of religious (1 Sm 3:13-14) or civil law (Hs 7:1), whether committed intentionally (Jos 22:20) or unintentionally (Nm 15:31). Scripture teaches that God may choose to forgive a person who has committed *iniquity* (Ps 103:3).

PSALM 132

DAVID AND ZION CHOSEN

A •song of ascents.

1 LORD, remember David
and all the hardships he endured,[a]

2 and how he swore an oath to the LORD,
making a vow to the Mighty One of Jacob:

3 "I will not enter my house[b]
or get into my bed,[c]

4 I will not allow my eyes to sleep
or my eyelids to slumber

5 until I find a place for the LORD,
a dwelling for the Mighty One of Jacob."[d]

6 We heard of ⌊the ark⌋ in Ephrathah;[e]
we found it in the fields of Jaar.[f]

7 Let us go to His dwelling place;
let us worship at His footstool.[g]

8 Arise, LORD, come to Your resting place,
You and the ark ⌊that shows⌋ Your strength.

9 May Your priests be clothed with righteousness,
and may Your godly people shout for joy.

10 Because of Your servant David,
do not reject Your anointed one.[h] [i]

11 The LORD swore an oath to David,
a promise He will not abandon:
"I will set one of your descendants[j]
on your throne.[k]

12 If your sons keep My covenant
and My decrees that I will teach them,
their sons will also sit on your throne, forever."[l]

13 For the LORD has chosen Zion;
He has desired it for His home:[m]

14 "This is My resting place forever;
I will make My home here because I have
desired it.

15 I will abundantly bless its food;
I will satisfy its needy with bread.

16 I will clothe its priests with salvation,
and its godly people will shout for joy.

17 There I will make a •horn grow for David;[n]
I have prepared a lamp for My anointed one.[o]

18 I will clothe his enemies with shame,
but the crown he wears[p] will be glorious."

NOTES

[a] **132:1** 1 Ch 22:14
[b] **132:3** Lit *enter the tent of my house*
[c] **132:3** Lit *into the couch of my bed*
[d] **132:5** 2 Sm 7:1-13
[e] **132:6** Bethlehem or the district around it; Gn 35:19
[f] **132:6** Kiriath-jearim; 1 Sm 7:1-2
[g] **132:7** 1 Ch 28:2
[h] **132:10** The king
[i] **132:8-10** 2 Ch 6:41-42
[j] **132:11** Lit *set the fruit of your body*
[k] **132:11** Ac 2:30
[l] **132:11-12** Ps 89:3-4,35; 2 Sm 7:12-16; Ac 2:30
[m] **132:13** Ps 78:68; Dt 12:5; Zch 2:12
[n] **132:17** 2 Sm 23:5; Lk 1:69
[o] **132:17** 1 Kg 11:36
[p] **132:18** Lit *but on him his crown*

WORD STUDY

Hebrew word:
ranan [rah NAHN]

HCSB translation:
shout for joy

Focus passage:
Psalm 132:9,16

Ranan speaks of the act of shouting emotionally. *Ranan* usually speaks of joyous *shouting* directed toward God and connected with a specific reason for praise. Though used primarily in formal religious contexts (Ps 95:1), *ranan* also occurs in non-liturgical settings (Is 16:10). God is praised with joyful *shouting* because of His redemption (Ps 51:16), military victories (Zch 2:10), creation (Jb 38:7), provision (Jr 31:12), and coming righteous rule (Ps 96:12). Joyful shouting is occasioned by God's attributes of greatness (Is 12:6), righteousness (Ps 51:14), and by His name (Ps 89:12).

a 133:2 Ex 30:22-33
b 133:3 The tallest mountain in the region, noted for its abundant precipitation
c 134:1 1 Ch 9:23-27; Is 30:29
d 134:2 Ps 28:2; 141:2; 1 Tm 2:8
e 134:3 Ps 115:15; Gn 2:4; Ac 14:15

PSALM 133

LIVING IN HARMONY

A Davidic •song of ascents.

1   How good and pleasant it is
when brothers can live together!

2   It is like fine oil on the head,
running down on the beard,
running down Aaron's beard,
onto his robes.[a]

3   It is like the dew of Hermon[b]
falling on the mountains of Zion.
For there the LORD has appointed the blessing—
life forevermore.

PSALM 134

CALL TO EVENING WORSHIP

A •song of ascents.

1   Now praise the LORD, all you servants
of the LORD
who stand in the LORD's house at night![c]

2   Lift up your hands in the holy place,
and praise the LORD![d]

3   May the LORD, Maker of heaven and earth,
bless you from Zion.[e]

PSALM 135

THE LORD IS GREAT

1   •Hallelujah!
Praise the name of the LORD.
Give praise, you servants of the LORD

2   who stand in the house of the LORD,
in the courts of the house of our God.

3   Praise the LORD, for the LORD is good;
sing praise to His name, for it is delightful.

4   For the LORD has chosen Jacob for Himself,
Israel as His treasured possession.

5   For I know that the LORD is great;
our Lord is greater than all gods.

6 The LORD does whatever He pleases
in heaven and on earth,
in the seas and all the depths.
7 He causes the clouds to rise from the ends
of the earth.
He makes lightning for the rain
and brings the wind from His storehouses.
8 He struck down the firstborn of Egypt,[a]
both people and animals.
9 He sent signs and wonders against you, Egypt,
against Pharaoh and all his officials.
10 He struck down many nations
and slaughtered mighty kings:
11 Sihon king of the Amorites,
Og king of Bashan,[b]
and all the kings of Canaan.
12 He gave their land as an inheritance,
an inheritance to His people Israel.
13 LORD, Your name ⌊endures⌋ forever,
Your reputation, LORD, through all
generations.[c]
14 For the LORD will judge His people
and have compassion on His servants.[d]
15 The idols of the nations are of silver and gold,
the work of human hands.
16 They have mouths, but cannot speak,
eyes, but cannot see.
17 They have ears, but cannot hear;
indeed, there is no breath in their mouths.
18 Those who make them are just like them,
as are all who trust in them.
19 House of Israel, praise the LORD!
House of Aaron, praise the LORD!
20 House of Levi, praise the LORD!
You who revere the LORD, praise the LORD![e]
21 May the LORD be praised from Zion;
He dwells in Jerusalem.
•Hallelujah!

PSALM 136

GOD'S LOVE IS ETERNAL

1 Give thanks to the LORD, for He is good.
His love is eternal.

NOTES
[a] 135:8 Ps 78:51; 105:36
[b] 135:10-11 Nm 21:21-35
[c] 135:13 Ex 3:15
[d] 135:14 Dt 32:36; Heb 10:30
[e] 135:15-20 Ps 115:4-11

NOTES
a 136:5 Gn 1:6-8; Pr 3:19
b 136:6 Gn 1:9-10
c 136:7 Gn 1:14-19
d 136:10 Ps 135:8; Ex 12:29
e 136:12 Ex 6:1,6; Dt 4:34
f 136:13 Ex 14:21
g 136:15 Ex 14:27
h 136:16 Dt 8:2,15
i 136:17-22 Ps 135:10-12; Nm
   21:21-35

2　Give thanks to the God of gods.
His love is eternal.

3　Give thanks to the Lord of lords.
His love is eternal.

4　He alone does great wonders.
His love is eternal.

5　He made the heavens skillfully.[a]
His love is eternal.

6　He spread the land on the waters.[b]
His love is eternal.

7　He made the great lights:[c]
His love is eternal.

8　the sun to rule by day,
His love is eternal.

9　the moon and stars to rule by night.
His love is eternal.

10　He struck the firstborn of the Egyptians[d]
His love is eternal.

11　and brought Israel out from among them
His love is eternal.

12　with a strong hand and outstretched arm.[e]
His love is eternal.

13　He divided the •Red Sea[f]
His love is eternal.

14　and led Israel through,
His love is eternal.

15　but hurled Pharaoh and his army
　　into the •Red Sea.[g]
His love is eternal.

16　He led His people in the wilderness.[h]
His love is eternal.

17　He struck down great kings
His love is eternal.

18　and slaughtered famous kings—
His love is eternal.

19　Sihon king of the Amorites
His love is eternal.

20　and Og king of Bashan—
His love is eternal.

21　and gave their land as an inheritance,
His love is eternal.

22　an inheritance to Israel His servant.[i]
His love is eternal.

23　He remembered us in our humiliation
His love is eternal.

24 and rescued us from our foes.
His love is eternal.
25 He gives food to every creature.[a]
His love is eternal.
26 Give thanks to the God of heaven!
His love is eternal.

PSALM 137
LAMENT OF THE EXILES

1 By the rivers of Babylon—
there we sat down and wept
when we remembered Zion.
2 There we hung up our lyres
on the poplar trees,
3 for our captors there asked us for songs,
and our tormentors, for rejoicing:
"Sing us one of the songs of Zion."
4 How can we sing the LORD's song
on foreign soil?
5 If I forget you, Jerusalem,
may my right hand forget ⌊its skill⌋.
6 May my tongue stick to the roof
of my mouth
if I do not remember you,
if I do not exalt Jerusalem as my greatest joy!
7 Remember, LORD, ⌊what⌋ the Edomites said
that day[b] at Jerusalem:
"Destroy it! Destroy it
down to its foundations!"[c]
8 Daughter Babylon, doomed to destruction,
happy is the one who pays you back
what you have done to us.
9 Happy is he who takes your little ones
and dashes them against the rocks.[d]

PSALM 138
A THANKFUL HEART

Davidic.

1 I will give You thanks with all my heart;
I will sing Your praise before
the heavenly beings.[e]

NOTES
[a] **136:25** Ps 104:27; 145:15; 147:9
[b] **137:7** The day Jerusalem fell to the Babylonians in 586 B.C.
[c] **137:7** Ob 10-14
[d] **137:9** Is 13:16
[e] **138:1** Or *the gods* (Jb 1:6; 2:1), or *before judges* or *kings* (Ps 82:1,6-7; Ex 21:6; 22:7-8)

WORD STUDY

Hebrew word:
shir [SHEER]

HCSB translation:
song

Focus passage:
Psalms 137:3-4

Shir probably indicated a song that could be sung with or without instrumental accompaniment. Songs were important in the cultural life of Israel and addressed a wide variety of subjects, such as love (Sg 1:1), victory (Jdg 5:12), and departure (Gn 31:27). *Shir* most often occurs in formal religious contexts, usually indicating an expression of praise to God. Singing a "new *song*" is the appropriate response to a new work of God (Ps 33:3). The community sang religious festival *songs* (Is 30:29) or dedicatory *songs* (Ps 30) during celebrations. *Shir* occurs in 30 Psalm titles and often appears in conjunction with *mizmor,* the Hebrew word for psalm.

[a] **138:2** 2 Sm 7
[b] **138:3** Hb obscure
[c] **138:4** Lit *hear the words of Your mouth*
[d] **139:8** Jb 17:13; Is 14:11

2 I will bow down toward Your holy temple
and give thanks to Your name
for Your constant love and faithfulness.
You have exalted Your name and Your promise
above everything else.[a]

3 On the day I called, You answered me;
You increased strength within me.[b]

4 All the kings on earth will give You thanks,
LORD,
when they hear what You have promised.[c]

5 They will sing of the LORD's ways,
for the LORD's glory is great.

6 Though the LORD is exalted,
He takes note of the humble;
but He knows the haughty from afar.

7 If I walk in the thick of danger,
You will preserve my life from the anger
of my enemies.
You will extend Your hand;
Your right hand will save me.

8 The LORD will fulfill ⌊His purpose⌋ for me.
LORD, Your love is eternal;
do not abandon the work of Your hands.

PSALM 139

THE ALL-KNOWING, EVER-PRESENT GOD

For the choir director. A Davidic psalm.

1 LORD, You have searched me and known me.

2 You know when I sit down and when I stand up;
You understand my thoughts from far away.

3 You observe my travels and my rest;
You are aware of all my ways.

4 Before a word is on my tongue,
You know all about it, LORD.

5 You have encircled me;
You have placed Your hand on me.

6 ⌊This⌋ extraordinary knowledge is beyond me.
It is lofty; I am unable to ⌊reach⌋ it.

7 Where can I go to escape Your Spirit?
Where can I flee from Your presence?

8 If I go up to heaven, You are there;
if I make my bed in •Sheol,[d] You are there.

9   If I live at the eastern horizon
⌊or⌋ settle at the western limits,[a]

10 even there Your hand will lead me;
Your right hand will hold on to me.

11 If I say, "Surely the darkness will hide me,
and the light around me will become night"—

12 even the darkness is not too dark for You.
The night shines like the day;
darkness and light are alike to You.

13 For it was You who created my inward parts;[b]
You knit me together in my mother's womb.

14 I will praise You
because I am[c] unique in remarkable ways.
Your works are wonderful,
and I know ⌊this⌋ very well.

15 My bones were not hidden from You
when I was made in secret,
when I was formed in the depths of the earth.

16 Your eyes saw me when I was formless;
all ⌊my⌋ days were written in Your book
and planned
before a single one of them began.[d]

17 God, how difficult[e] Your thoughts are for me
⌊to comprehend⌋;
how vast their sum is!

18 If I counted them, they would outnumber
the grains of sand;
when I wake up,[f] I am still with You.

19 God, if only You would kill the wicked
(stay away from me, you bloodthirsty men)

20 who invoke You deceitfully.
Your enemies swear ⌊by You⌋ falsely.

21 LORD, don't I hate those who hate You,
and detest those who rebel against You?

22 I hate them with extreme hatred;
I consider them my enemies.

23 Search me, God, and know my heart;
test me and know my concerns.

24 See if there is any offensive[g] way in me;
lead me in the everlasting way.

[a] **139:9** Lit *I take up the wings of the dawn; I dwell at the end of the sea*
[b] **139:13** Lit *my kidneys*
[c] **139:14** DSS, some LXX mss, Syr, Jer read *because You are*
[d] **139:16** Ps 69:28; Ex 32:32; Jb 14:5
[e] **139:17** Or *precious*
[f] **139:18** Other Hb mss read *I come to an end*
[g] **139:24** Or *idolatrous*

NOTES
^a **140:1** Ps 18:48; 2 Sm 22:49
^b **140:2** Ps 21:11; 35:4; 41:7
^c **140:3** Rm 3:13
^d **140:4** Ps 71:4; 82:4; 97:10
^e **140:4** Lit *to trip up my steps*
^f **140:5** Ps 142:3; Jr 18:22
^g **140:6** Ps 22:10; 63:1; 118:28
^h **140:11** Hb obscure
ⁱ **140:12** Alt Hb tradition reads *You*
^j **140:12** Pr 31:9; Jr 22:16
^k **141:1** Ps 17:6; 31:17; 88:9

PSALM 140

PRAYER FOR RESCUE

For the choir director. A Davidic psalm.

1 Rescue me, LORD, from evil men.
Keep me safe from violent men[a]
2 who plan evil[b] in their hearts.
They stir up wars all day long.
3 They make their tongues as sharp as a snake's bite;
viper's venom is under their lips.[c] •*Selah*
4 Protect me, LORD, from the clutches
of the wicked.[d]
Keep me safe from violent men
who plan to make me stumble.[e]
5 The proud hide a trap with ropes for me;[f]
they spread a net along the path
and set snares for me. •*Selah*
6 I say to the LORD, "You are my God."[g]
Listen, LORD, to my cry for help.
7 Lord, GOD, my strong Savior,
You shield my head on the day of battle.
8 LORD, do not grant the desires of the wicked;
do not let them achieve their goals.
⌊Otherwise,⌋ they will become proud. •*Selah*
9 As for the heads of those who surround me,
let the trouble their lips cause overwhelm ⌊them⌋.
10 Let hot coals fall on them.
Let them be thrown into the fire,
into the abyss, never again to rise.
11 Do not let a slanderer stay in the land.
Let evil relentlessly[h] hunt down a violent man.
12 I[i] know that the LORD upholds the just cause
of the poor,
justice for the needy.[j]
13 Surely the righteous will praise Your name;
the upright will live in Your presence.

PSALM 141

PROTECTION FROM SIN AND SINNERS

A Davidic psalm.

1 LORD, I call on You;[k] hurry to ⌊help⌋ me.
Listen to my voice when I call on You.

154

2   May my prayer be set before You as incense,
the raising of my hands as the evening offering.

3   LORD, set up a guard for my mouth;
keep watch at the door of my lips.

4   Do not let my heart turn to any evil thing
or wickedly perform reckless acts
with men who commit sin.[a]
Do not let me feast on their delicacies.

5   Let the righteous one strike me—it is ⌊an act of⌋
faithful love;
let him rebuke me—it is oil for my head;
let me[b] not refuse it.
Even now my prayer is against the evil acts
of the wicked.[c]

6   When their rulers[d] will be thrown off the sides
of a cliff,[e]
the people[f] will listen to my words, for they are
pleasing.

7   As when one plows and breaks up the soil,
⌊turning up rocks⌋,
so our[g] bones have been scattered at the mouth
of •Sheol.

8   But my eyes ⌊look⌋ to You, Lord GOD.
I seek refuge in You;[h] do not let me die.[i]

9   Protect me from[j] the trap they have set for me,
and from the snares of evildoers.

10   Let the wicked fall into their own nets,
while I pass ⌊safely⌋ by.

PSALM 142

A CRY OF DISTRESS

A Davidic •Maskil. When he was in the cave.[k]
A prayer.

1   I cry aloud to the LORD;
I plead aloud to the LORD for mercy.

2   I pour out my complaint before Him;
I reveal my trouble to Him.

3   Although my spirit is weak within me,[l]
You know my way.
Along this path I travel
they have hidden a trap for me.

4   Look to the right and see:[m]
no one stands up for me;

NOTES

a **141:4** Ps 6:8; Jb 34:8-10
b **141:5** Lit *my head*
c **141:5** Lit *of them*
d **141:6** Or *judges*
e **141:6** 2 Ch 25:12
f **141:6** Lit *cliff, and they*
g **141:7** DSS reads *my*; some
  LXX mss, Syr read *their*
h **141:8** Ps 7:1; 57:1; 144:2
i **141:8** Or *not pour out my life*
j **141:9** Lit *from the hands of*
k 1 Sm 22:1-4; 24:3; 2 Sm 23:14
l **142:3** Ps 61:2; Jnh 2:7
m **142:4** DSS, LXX, Syr, Vg, Tg
  read *I look to the right and I*
  see

WORD STUDY

Hebrew word:
nepesh [NEH fehsh]
HCSB translation:
life, self, appetite, soul, mind
Focus passage:
Psalm 141:8

Nepesh literally means "throat." Since the throat is the organ of eating and consumption, *nepesh* became associated with appetites and longings, including hunger and desire (Ps 35:25). *Nepesh* can refer to that part of a person that expresses appetites (Pr 16:26), human emotions, and spiritual expressions (Jb 19:2). Because the throat is the organ of breathing, *nepesh* is associated with breath (Gn 1:30) and with life itself (Ps 30:3). This connection with life led to *nepesh's* also being associated with blood (Gn 9:4-5). *Nepesh* can refer to all living beings—those "who have the breath of life in them" (Gn 1:20-21). The term is so closely associated with the life of a person that it is frequently used as a personal pronoun. "My *nepesh*" is another way of saying "me" or "I."

a 142:5 Ps 116:9; Is 38:11
b 142:6 Ps 17:1; 88:2; 2 Ch 6:19
c 142:6 Ps 18:17; 2 Sm 22:18
d 142:7 Ps 13:6; 116:7; 119:74
e 143:2 Jb 14:3; Ec 12:14
f 143:2 Rm 3:23
g 143:3 Lm 3:6
h 143:5 Ps 77:12; 119:15; 145:5
i 143:7 Ps 69:17; 102:2
j 143:7 Ps 28:1; 30:3; Is 38:18
k 143:8 Ps 59:16; 119:147-149

there is no refuge for me;
no one cares about me.

5 I cry to You, LORD;
I say, "You are my shelter,
my portion in the land of the living." [a]

6 Listen to my cry, [b]
for I am very weak.
Rescue me from those who pursue me,
for they are too strong for me. [c]

7 Free me from prison
so that I can praise Your name.
The righteous will gather around me
because You deal generously with me. [d]

PSALM 143
A CRY FOR HELP

A Davidic psalm.

1 LORD, hear my prayer.
In Your faithfulness listen to my plea,
and in Your righteousness answer me.

2 Do not bring Your servant into judgment, [e]
for no one alive is righteous in Your sight. [f]

3 For the enemy has pursued me,
crushing me to the ground,
making me live in darkness
like those long dead. [g]

4 My spirit is weak within me;
my heart is overcome with dismay.

5 I remember the days of old;
I meditate on all You have done;
I reflect on the work of Your hands. [h]

6 I spread out my hands to You;
I am like parched land before You. •Selah

7 Answer me quickly, LORD;
my spirit fails. [i]
Don't hide Your face from me,
or I will be like those going down to the •Pit. [j]

8 Let me experience Your faithful love
in the morning, [k]
for I trust in You.
Reveal to me the way I should go,
because I long for You.

9 Rescue me from my enemies, LORD;
I come to You for protection.[a]

10 Teach me to do Your will, for You are my God.[b]
May Your gracious Spirit lead me
on level ground.[c]

11 For Your name's sake, LORD, let me live.
In Your righteousness deliver me from trouble,[d]

12 and in Your faithful love destroy my enemies.
Wipe out all those who attack me,[e]
for I am Your servant.

PSALM 144

A KING'S PRAYER

Davidic.

1 May the LORD my rock be praised,
who trains my hands for battle
and my fingers for warfare.

2 He is my faithful love and my fortress,
my stronghold and my deliverer.
He is my shield, and I take refuge in Him;[f]
He subdues my people[g] under me.

3 LORD, what is man, that You care for him,
the son of man, that You think of him?[h]

4 Man is like a breath;
his days are like a passing shadow.

5 LORD, part Your heavens and come down.[i]
Touch the mountains, and they will smoke.[j]

6 Flash ⌊Your⌋ lightning and scatter the foe;[k]
shoot Your arrows and rout them.

7 Reach down[l] from on high;
rescue me from deep water,[m] and set me free
from the grasp of foreigners

8 whose mouths speak lies,
whose right hands are deceptive.

9 God, I will sing a new song to You;
I will play on a ten-stringed harp[n] for You—

10 the One who gives victory to kings,
who frees His servant David
from the deadly sword.

11 Set me free and rescue me from the grasp
of foreigners
whose mouths speak lies,
whose right hands are deceptive.

NOTES

[a] **143:9** Lit *I cover myself to You*
[b] **143:10** Ps 25:5; 31:14
[c] **143:10** Ps 26:12; 27:11
[d] **143:11** Ps 23:3; 106:8; 109:21
[e] **143:12** Ps 54:5; 73:27; 101:8
[f] **144:1-2** Ps 18:2; 71:1-3; 2 Sm 22:2-3
[g] **144:2** Other Hb mss, DSS, Aq, Syr, Tg, Jer read *subdues peoples*; Ps 18:47; 2 Sm 22:48
[h] **144:3** Ps 8:4
[i] **144:5** Ps 18:9-10; 2 Sm 22:10
[j] **144:5** Ps 104:32
[k] **144:6** Lit *scatter them*
[l] **144:7** Lit *down Your hands*
[m] **144:7** Ps 18:16; 2 Sm 22:17
[n] **144:9** Ps 33:3; 40:3; 98:1

Notes

a **144:14** Or *will bear heavy loads*, or *will be pregnant*

b **144:14** Or *be no plague, no miscarriage*

c **145:1** The lines of this poem form an •acrostic.

d **145:1** Ps 30:1; 118:28; Is 25:1

e **145:1-2** Ps 63:4; 96:2; 100:4

f **145:3** Ps 48:1; 96:4; 1 Ch 16:25

g **145:3** Jb 5:9; 9:10; Is 40:28

h **145:5** LXX, Syr read *They*

i **145:5** Ps 96:6; 104:1; 1 Ch 16:27; Jb 37:22

j **145:5** LXX, Syr read *and they will tell of*

k **145:6** Alt Hb tradition, Jer read *great deeds*

l **145:6** Ps 106:2; Dt 10:21; 1 Ch 17:19-21

m **145:8** Ps 86:15; 103:8; Ex 34:6; Nm 14:18

n **145:8-9** Ex 34:6; Neh 9:17; Jnh 4:2

o **145:10** Lit *Your*

p **145:11** Ps 21:13; 1 Ch 29:11-12; 2 Ch 20:6

Word Study

Hebrew word:
ma'aseh [mah ah SEH]

HCSB translation:
work, deed

Focus passage:
Psalm 145:4,9-10,17

Ma'aseh is related to the verb *'asah* (*to do, make, accomplish, fashion*). It can refer to human work or labor (Gn 5:29) or to general human activities and deeds, which are judged to be either good (1 Sm 19:4) or bad (Neh 6:14). *Ma'aseh* can also refer to a product of human labor (Gn 40:17). This could include an idol, "the *work* of man's hands" (Jr 25:6-7). In reference to God, *ma'aseh* can refer to the products of God's creative activity (Ps 8:6) and to His saving *works* (Dt 3:24). God's *deeds* always reveal His moral and ethical perfection.

12 Then our sons will be like plants nurtured
in their youth,
our daughters, like corner pillars that are carved
in the palace style.

13 Our storehouses will be full, supplying all kinds
of produce;
our flocks will increase by thousands
and tens of thousands in our open fields.

14 Our cattle will be well fed.ᵃ
There will be no breach ⌊in the walls,⌋ no going
⌊into captivity,⌋ᵇ
and no cry of lament in our public squares.

15 Happy are the people with such ⌊blessings⌋.
Happy are the people whose God is the LORD.

PSALM 145

PRAISING GOD'S GREATNESS

A Davidic hymn.

1 Iᶜ exalt You, my Godᵈ the King,
and praise Your name forever and ever.

2 I will praise You every day;
I will honor Your name forever and ever.ᵉ

3 The LORD is great and is highly praised;ᶠ
His greatness is unsearchable.ᵍ

4 One generation will declare Your works to the next
and will proclaim Your mighty acts.

5 Iʰ will speak of Your glorious splendorⁱ
andʲ Your wonderful works.

6 They will proclaim the power of
Your awesome works,
and I will declare Your greatness.ᵏ ˡ

7 They will give a testimony of
Your great goodness
and will joyfully sing of Your righteousness.

8 The LORD is gracious and compassionate,
slow to anger and great in faithful love.ᵐ

9 The LORD is good to everyone;
His compassion ⌊rests⌋ on all He has made.ⁿ

10 All You have made will praise You, LORD;
theᵒ godly will bless You.

11 They will speak of the glory of Your kingdom
and will declare Your might,ᵖ

12 informing ⌊all⌋ people[a] of Your mighty acts
and of the glorious splendor of Your[b] kingdom.

13 Your kingdom is an everlasting kingdom;
Your rule is for all generations.[c] [d]

14 The LORD helps all who fall;
He raises up all who are oppressed.[e] [f]

15 All eyes look to You,
and You give them their food in due time.[g]

16 You open Your hand
and satisfy the desire of every living thing.

17 The LORD is righteous in all His ways[h]
and gracious in all His acts.

18 The LORD is near all who call out to Him,[i]
all who call out to Him with integrity.

19 He fulfills the desires of those who •fear Him;
He hears their cry for help and saves them.[j]

20 The LORD guards all those who love Him,
but He destroys all the wicked.

21 My mouth will declare the LORD's praise;
let every living thing praise His holy name
forever and ever.

PSALM 146
THE GOD OF COMPASSION

1 •Hallelujah!
My soul, praise the LORD.

2 I will praise the LORD all my life;
I will sing to the LORD as long as I live.[k]

3 Do not trust in nobles,
in man, who cannot save.

4 When his breath[l] leaves him, he returns
to the ground;[m]
on that day his plans die.

5 Happy is the one whose help is the God of Jacob,
whose hope is in the LORD his God,

6 the Maker of heaven and earth,[n]
the sea and everything in them.
He remains faithful forever,

7 executing justice for the exploited[o]
and giving food to the hungry.
The LORD frees prisoners.

8 The LORD opens ⌊the eyes of⌋ the blind.[p]
The LORD raises up those who are oppressed.[q]
The LORD loves the righteous.[r]

NOTES

[a] **145:12** Lit *informing the sons of man*
[b] **145:12** Lit *His*
[c] **145:13** One Hb ms, LXX, Syr add *The LORD is faithful in His words and gracious in all His actions.*
[d] **145:13** Dn 4:3
[e] **145:14** Lit *bowed down*
[f] **145:14** Ps 37:24; 119:116; 146:8
[g] **145:15** Ps 104:27
[h] **145:17** Ps 11:7; Dn 9:14; Zph 3:5
[i] **145:18** Ps 34:18; 86:5; Dt 4:7; Jr 23:23
[j] **145:19** Ps 18:6; Ex 2:23-24; 2 Ch 20:9
[k] **146:2** Ps 63:4; 104:33
[l] **146:4** Or *spirit*
[m] **146:4** Gn 2:7; 3:19
[n] **146:5-6** Ps 115:15; 121:2; 124:8
[o] **146:7** Ps 103:6; Ex 22:22-24; Dt 10:18
[p] **146:8** Is 35:5; Mt 9:27-30; 11:5
[q] **146:8** Lit *bowed down*
[r] **146:8** Ps 37:28

NOTES

a 146:9 Ex 22:22-23; Dt 10:18
b 146:9 Ps 1:6; Pr 4:19; Jr 12:1
c 146:10 Ex 15:18; Is 24:23; Mc 4:7
d 147:1 Ps 33:1; 135:3
e 147:2 Ps 51:18; Ezr 6:3; Neh 2:17; Dn 9:25
f 147:2 Dt 30:4; Neh 1:9; Is 11:12
g 147:3 Ps 34:18; Is 61:1
h 147:5 Lit *understanding has no number*
i 147:5 Ps 147:5; Jb 12:13; Is 40:14,28
j 147:7 Ps 149:3
k 147:10 Lit *legs*
l 147:11 Ps 33:18; 149:4; Dt 5:29
m 147:14 Ps 81:16

9 The LORD protects foreigners
and helps the fatherless and the widow,[a]
but He frustrates the ways of the wicked.[b]

10 The LORD reigns forever;[c]
your God, O Zion, ⌊reigns⌋ for all generations.
•Hallelujah!

PSALM 147

GOD RESTORES JERUSALEM

1 •Hallelujah!
How good it is to sing to our God,
for praise is pleasant and lovely.[d]

2 The LORD rebuilds Jerusalem;[e]
He gathers Israel's exiled people.[f]

3 He heals the brokenhearted
and binds up their wounds.[g]

4 He counts the number of the stars;
He gives names to all of them.

5 Our Lord is great, vast in power;
His understanding is infinite.[h] [i]

6 The LORD helps the afflicted
but brings the wicked to the ground.

7 Sing to the LORD with thanksgiving;
play the lyre to our God,[j]

8 who covers the sky with clouds,
prepares rain for the earth,
and causes grass to grow on the hills.

9 He provides the animals with their food,
and the young ravens, what they cry for.

10 He is not impressed by the strength of a horse;
He does not value the power[k] of a man.

11 The LORD values those who fear Him,
those who hope in His faithful love.[l]

12 Exalt the LORD, Jerusalem;
praise your God, Zion!

13 For He strengthens the bars of your gates
and blesses your children within you.

14 He endows your territory with prosperity;
He satisfies you with the finest wheat.[m]

15 He sends His command throughout the earth;
His word runs swiftly.

16 He spreads snow like wool;
He scatters frost like ashes;

17 He throws His hailstones like crumbs.
Who can withstand His cold?

18 He sends His word and melts them;
He unleashes His winds,^a and the waters flow.

19 He declares His word to Jacob,
His statutes and judgments to Israel.

20 He has not done this for any nation;
they do not know^b ⌊His⌋ judgments.
•Hallelujah!

PSALM 148
CREATION'S PRAISE OF THE LORD

1 •Hallelujah!
Praise the LORD from the heavens;
praise Him in the heights.

2 Praise Him, all His angels;
praise Him, all His •hosts.

3 Praise Him, sun and moon;
praise Him, all you shining stars.

4 Praise Him, highest heavens,
and you waters above the heavens.

5 Let them praise the name of the LORD,^c
for He commanded, and they were created.

6 He set them in position forever and ever;
He gave an order that will never pass away.

7 Praise the LORD from the earth,
all sea monsters^d and ocean depths,^e

8 lightning^f and hail, snow and cloud,
powerful wind that executes His command,

9 mountains and all hills,
fruit trees and all cedars,

10 wild animals and all cattle,
creatures that crawl and flying birds,

11 kings of the earth and all peoples,
princes and all judges of the earth,

12 young men as well as young women,
old and young together.

13 Let them praise the name of the LORD,
for His name alone is exalted.
His majesty covers heaven and earth.

14 He has raised up a •horn for His people,^g
praise from all His godly ones,
from the Israelites, the people close to Him.
•Hallelujah!

NOTES

^a **147:18** Or *breath*
^b **147:20** DSS, LXX, Syr, Tg read
He has not made known to
them
^c **148:5** Ps 113:1; 135:1; Jl 2:26
^d **148:7** Ps 74:13; Gn 1:21; Jb
7:12
^e **148:7** Gn 1:2; 7:11; Jnh 2:5
^f **148:8** Or *fire*
^g **148:14** Ps 89:17,24; 1 Sm 2:10;
Lk 1:69

NOTES

[a] **149:1** Ps 96:1; 98:1; Is 42:10

[b] **149:2** Jl 2:23

[c] **149:3** Ps 30:11; Jb 21:12; Jr 31:4,13

[d] **149:6** Lit *throat*

[e] **149:7** Ezk 25:16-17; Mc 5:15

[f] **150:1** Ps 19:1

[g] **150:3** 1 Ch 15:28; 2 Ch 5:12-14

[h] **150:4-5** 2 Sm 6:5; 1 Ch 13:8; Jb 21:12

PSALM 149

PRAISE FOR GOD'S TRIUMPH

1 •Hallelujah!
Sing to the LORD a new song, [a]
His praise in the assembly of the godly.

2 Let Israel celebrate its Maker;
let the children of Zion rejoice [b] in their King.

3 Let them praise His name with dancing
and make music to Him with tambourine
and lyre. [c]

4 For the LORD takes pleasure in His people;
He adorns the humble with salvation.

5 Let the godly celebrate in triumphal glory;
let them shout for joy on their beds.

6 Let the exaltation of God be in their mouths [d]
and a two-edged sword in their hands,

7 inflicting vengeance on the nations [e]
and punishment on the peoples,

8 binding their kings with chains
and their dignitaries with iron shackles,

9 carrying out the judgment decreed against them.
This honor is for all His godly people.
•Hallelujah!

PSALM 150

PRAISE THE LORD

1 •Hallelujah!
Praise God in His sanctuary.
Praise Him in His mighty heavens. [f]

2 Praise Him for His powerful acts;
praise Him for His abundant greatness.

3 Praise Him with trumpet blast;
praise Him with harp and lyre. [g]

4 Praise Him with tambourine and dance;
praise Him with flute and strings.

5 Praise Him with resounding cymbals;
praise Him with clashing cymbals. [h]

6 Let everything that breathes praise the LORD.
•Hallelujah!

Proverbs

PROVERBS 1

THE PURPOSE OF PROVERBS

NOTES

a 1:3 Pr 2:9
b 1:4 Or *simple*, or *gullible*
c 1:5 Pr 9:9; 16:21,23
d 1:6 Or *an enigma*
e 1:6 Hab 2:6
f 1:7 Pr 9:10; 15:33; Jb 28:28
g 1:7 This verse states the theme of Proverbs.
h 1:7 Eph 5:17
i 1:8 Pr 6:20; 31:1
j 1:8-9 Pr 6:20-21
k 1:10 Ps 141:4
l 1:11 Lit *Let's ambush for blood*
m 1:11 Lit *person for no reason*
n 1:13 Pr 24:4
o 1:14 Lit *us; one bag will be for all of us*

1 The proverbs of Solomon son of David,
  king of Israel:
2 For gaining wisdom and being instructed;
  for understanding insightful sayings;
3 for receiving wise instruction
  ⌊in⌋ righteousness, justice, and integrity;[a]
4 for teaching shrewdness to the inexperienced,[b]
  knowledge and discretion to a young man—
5 a wise man will listen and increase his learning,[c]
  and a discerning man will obtain guidance—
6 for understanding a proverb or a parable,[d]
  the words of the wise, and their riddles.[e]
7 The •fear of the LORD is the beginning
    of knowledge;[f]
  fools despise wisdom and instruction.[g] [h]

AVOID THE PATH OF THE VIOLENT

8 Listen, my son, to your father's instruction,
  and don't reject your mother's teaching,[i]
9 for they will be a garland of grace on your head
  and a ⌊gold⌋ chain around your neck.[j]
10 My son, if sinners entice you, don't be persuaded.[k]
11 If they say—"Come with us!
  Let's set an ambush and kill someone.[l]
  Let's attack some innocent person just for fun![m]
12 Let's swallow them alive, like •Sheol,
  still healthy as they go down to the •Pit.
13 We'll find all kinds of valuable property
  and fill our houses with plunder.[n]
14 Throw in your lot with us,
  and we'll all share our money"[o]—

NOTES

a 1:15 Pr 16:19
b 1:16 Lit to shed blood
c 1:16 Pr 6:17; Is 59:7
d 1:18 Lit they ambush for their blood
e 1:19 Pr 11:16-18; Ezk 22:27; Hab 2:6-12
f 1:19 Lit takes the life of its masters
g 1:20 Pr 8:1; 9:3
h 1:21 Lit at the head of
i 1:23 Lit back to my reprimands
j 1:23 Pr 1:23; 3:11; 15:5,31-32
k 1:24 Is 65:2
l 1:29 Pr 1:7
m 1:30 Pr 5:12; 15:5
n 1:31 Pr 14:14; 28:19

WORD STUDY

Hebrew word:
mashal [mah SHAHL]

HCSB translation:
oracle, proverb

Focus passage:
Proverbs 1:1,6

Mashal is used of several related literary forms. It may refer to a short, popular saying or maxim. In Proverbs the *mashal* is often a single sentence designed to give wise instruction (Pr 1:1-6), and may compare or contrast two items (Pr 15:2). It may also refer to a longer statement or discourse that employs metaphor or simile (Pr 26:17-19), or to a prediction that is hard to understand (Ezk 17:2). Additionally, *mashal* may refer to something that serves as an illustrative story or example (Pr 7:6-23). The expression "become a *mashal*" speaks of God's punishment of His people as an example to others (Ps 44:14).

15 my son, don't travel that road with them
or set foot on their path, [a]

16 because their feet run toward trouble
and they hurry to commit murder. [b] [c]

17 It is foolish to spread a net
where any bird can see it,

18 but they set an ambush to kill themselves; [d]
they attack their own lives.

19 Such are the paths of all who pursue gain dishonestly; [e]
it takes the lives of those who profit from it. [f]

WISDOM'S PLEA

20 Wisdom calls out in the street;
she raises her voice in the public squares. [g]

21 She cries out above [h] the commotion;
she speaks at the entrance of the city •gates:

22 "How long, foolish ones, will you love ignorance?
⌊How long⌋ will ⌊you⌋ mockers enjoy mocking
and ⌊you⌋ fools hate knowledge?

23 If you turn to my discipline, [i] [j]
then I will pour out my spirit on you
and teach you my words.

24 Since I called out and you refused,
extended my hand and no one paid attention, [k]

25 since you neglected all my counsel
and did not accept my correction,

26 I, in turn, will laugh at your calamity.
I will mock when terror strikes you,

27 when terror strikes you like a storm
and your calamity comes like a whirlwind,
when trouble and stress overcome you.

28 Then they will call me, but I won't answer;
they will search for me, but won't find me.

29 Because they hated knowledge,
didn't choose to •fear the LORD, [l]

30 were not interested in my counsel,
and rejected all my correction, [m]

31 they will eat the fruit of their way
and be glutted with their own schemes. [n]

32 For the waywardness of the inexperienced will kill them,
and the complacency of fools will destroy them.

33 But whoever listens to me will live securely
and be free from the fear of danger."

PROVERBS 2
WISDOM'S WORTH

1 My son, if you accept my words
and store up my commands within you,

2 listening closely[a] to wisdom
and directing your heart to understanding;

3 furthermore, if you call out to insight
and lift your voice to understanding,

4 if you seek it like silver
and search for it like hidden treasure,

5 then you will understand the •fear of the LORD
and discover the knowledge of God.

6 For the LORD gives wisdom;
from His mouth come knowledge
and understanding.

7 He stores up success[b] for the upright;
He is a shield for those who live with integrity[c]

8 so that He may guard the paths of justice
and protect the way of His loyal followers.

9 Then you will understand righteousness,
justice,
and integrity—every good path.

10 For wisdom will enter your heart,
and knowledge will delight your soul.

11 Discretion will watch over you,
and understanding will guard you,

12 rescuing you from the way of evil—
from the one who says perverse things,

13 ⌊from⌋ those who abandon the right paths
to walk in ways of darkness,[d]

14 ⌊from⌋ those who enjoy doing evil
and celebrate perversity,

15 whose paths are crooked,
and whose ways are devious.

16 It will rescue you from a forbidden woman,[e]
from a stranger[f] with her flattering talk,[g]

17 who abandons the companion of her youth
and forgets the covenant of her God;[h]

18 for her house sinks down to death
and her ways to the land of the departed spirits.[i]

NOTES

a **2:2** Lit *you, stretching out your ear*

b **2:7** Or *resourcefulness*

c **2:7** Pr 10:9; 20:7; 28:18

d **2:11-13** Pr 16:17; 15:19

e **2:16** Pr 9:13-18

f **2:16** Or *foreign woman*

g **2:16** Pr 5:3,20; 6:24; 7:5,21

h **2:17** Mal 2:14

i **2:18** Pr 9:18; 21:16

WORD STUDY

Hebrew word:
tebunah [teh voo NAH]

HCSB translation:
understanding

Focus passage:
Proverbs 2:2,3,6,11

Tebunah refers to the *understanding* needed to live successfully. *Tebunah* does not refer to intellectual understanding, but to good craftsmanship (Ex 31:3), business savvy (Ez 28:4), and speaking ability (Jb 32:11). It may refer to ability in discerning God's purposes (Dt 32:28) and in discerning earthly (Ob 1:7) and spiritual (Is 44:19) realities. *Understanding*, a gift of God (1 Kgs 4:29), may be acquired during a long life (Jb 12:12). Proverbs describes the man who acquires *understanding* as happy (3:13), quiet (11:12), patient (14:29), humble (18:2), and successful (19:8). He enjoys acting wisely (10:23), walks the straight path (15:21), draws out the thoughts of others (20:5), and administers family matters wisely (24:3). Proverbs uses *understanding* as another name for Lady Wisdom (8:1).

NOTES

a 2:16-19 Pr 7:5,21-27; 23:27-28
b 2:21 Mt 5:5-6
c 3:2 Lit *days, years of life*
d 3:1-2 Pr 4:1-4; 6:20-23; 7:1-3
e 3:3 Pr 6:21; 7:3
f 3:4 Dt 4:6; Lk 2:52
g 3:6 Pr 11:5
h 3:7 Pr 26:5,12; 28:11,26
i 3:7 Pr 16:6; Jb 1:1; Ps 37:27
j 3:8 Lit *navel*
k 3:9 Lv 23:9-14
l 3:10 Mal 3:10
m 3:11 Pr 5:11-13; 15:5,31-33
n 3:12 Pr 13:24; Jb 5:17-18; Heb 12:5-7
o 3:14 Pr 8:10,19; 16:16; 22:1

19 None return who go to her;
none reach the paths of life.[a]

20 So follow the way of good people,
and keep to the paths of the righteous.

21 For the upright will inhabit the land,
and those of integrity will remain in it;[b]

22 but the wicked will be cut off from the land,
and the treacherous uprooted from it.

PROVERBS 3

TRUST THE LORD

1 My son, don't forget my teaching,
but let your heart keep my commands;

2 for they will bring you
many days, a full life,[c] and well-being.[d]

3 Never let loyalty and faithfulness leave you.
Tie them around your neck;
write them on the tablet of your heart.[e]

4 Then you will find favor and high regard
in the sight of God and man.[f]

5 Trust in the LORD with all your heart,
and do not rely on your own understanding;

6 think about Him in all your ways,
and He will guide you on the right paths.[g]

7 Don't consider yourself to be wise;[h]
•fear the LORD and turn away from evil.[i]

8 This will be healing for your body[j]
and strengthening for your bones.

9 Honor the LORD with your possessions
and with the first produce of your entire harvest;[k]

10 then your barns will be completely filled,
and your vats will overflow with new wine.[l]

11 Do not despise the LORD's instruction, my son,
and do not loathe His discipline;[m]

12 for the LORD disciplines the one He loves,
just as a father, the son he delights in.[n]

WISDOM BRINGS HAPPINESS

13 Happy is a man who finds wisdom
and who acquires understanding,

14 for she is more profitable than silver,
and her revenue is better than gold.[o]

15 She is more precious than jewels;
    nothing you desire compares with her. [a]

16 Long life [b] is in her right hand;
    in her left, riches and honor. [c]

17 Her ways are pleasant,
    and all her paths, peaceful.

18 She is a tree of life to those who embrace her,
    and those who hold on to her are happy.

19 The LORD founded the earth by wisdom
    and established the heavens by understanding.

20 By His knowledge the watery depths broke open, [d]
    and the clouds dripped with dew.

21 Maintain ⌊your⌋ competence and discretion.
    My son, don't lose sight of them.

22 They will be life for you [e]
    and adornment [f] for your neck.

23 Then you will go safely on your way;
    your foot will not stumble.

24 When you lie down, you will not be afraid;
    you will lie down, and your sleep will be pleasant.

25 Don't fear sudden danger
    or the ruin of the wicked when it comes,

26 for the LORD will be your confidence [g]
    and will keep your foot from a snare.

TREAT OTHERS FAIRLY

27 When it is in your power, [h]
    don't withhold good from the one to whom
        it is due.

28 Don't say to your neighbor, "Go away!
        Come back later.
    I'll give it tomorrow"—when it is there
        with you.

29 Don't plan any harm against your neighbor,
    for he trusts you and lives near you.

30 Don't accuse anyone without cause, [i]
    when he has done you no harm.

31 Don't envy a violent man [j]
    or choose any of his ways;

32 for the devious are detestable to the LORD,
    but He is a friend [k] to the upright. [l]

33 The LORD's curse is on the household
        of the wicked,
    but He blesses the home of the righteous;

[a] **3:15** Pr 8:11; 20:15
[b] **3:16** Lit *Length of days*
[c] **3:16** Pr 8:18; 21:21; 22:4
[d] **3:20** Gn 7:11
[e] **3:22** Or *your throat*; Hb *nephesh* can mean *throat*, *soul*, or *life*.
[f] **3:22** Or *grace*
[g] **3:26** Or *be at your side*
[h] **3:27** Lit *in the power of your hands*
[i] **3:30** Pr 24:28
[j] **3:31** Pr 23:17; 24:1,19; Ps 37:1
[k] **3:32** Or *confidential counsel*
[l] **3:32** Pr 11:20; 12:22; 15:8-9

NOTES

a 3:34 Jms 4:6; 1 Pt 5:5
b 3:35 Or *but haughty fools dishonor*, or *but fools exalt dishonor*
c 4:4 Pr 3:1-2; 6:20-23; 7:1-2
d 4:5 Pr 16:16
e 4:7 Pr 16:16
f 4:9 Pr 16:31

34 He mocks those who mock,
but gives grace to the humble. [a]

35 The wise will inherit honor,
but He holds up fools to dishonor. [b]

PROVERBS 4

A FATHER'S EXAMPLE

1 Listen, ⌊my⌋ sons, to a father's discipline,
and pay attention so that you may gain
understanding,

2 for I am giving you good instruction.
Don't abandon my teaching.

3 When I was a son with my father,
tender and precious to my mother,

4 he taught me and said:
"Your heart must hold on to my words.
Keep my commands and live. [c]

5 Get wisdom, get understanding; [d]
don't forget or turn away from the words
of my mouth.

6 Don't abandon wisdom, and she will watch over
you;
love her, and she will guard you.

7 Wisdom is supreme—so get wisdom.
And whatever else you get, get understanding. [e]

8 Cherish her, and she will exalt you;
if you embrace her, she will honor you.

9 She will place a garland of grace on your head;
she will give you a crown of beauty." [f]

TWO WAYS OF LIFE

10 Listen, my son. Accept my words,
and you will live many years.

11 I am teaching you the way of wisdom;
I am guiding you on straight paths.

12 When you walk, your steps will not
be hindered;
when you run, you will not stumble.

13 Hold on to instruction; don't let go.
Guard it, for it is your life.

14 Don't set foot on the path of the wicked;
don't proceed in the way of evil ones.

15   Avoid it; don't travel on it.
      Turn away from it, and pass it by.
16   For they can't sleep unless they have done evil;
      they are robbed of sleep unless they make
        someone stumble.
17   They eat the bread of wickedness
      and drink the wine of violence.
18   The path of the righteous is like the light of dawn,
      shining brighter and brighter until midday.
19   But the way of the wicked is like
       the darkest gloom;
      they don't know what makes them stumble.[a]

THE STRAIGHT PATH

20   My son, pay attention to my words;
      listen closely to my sayings.
21   Don't lose sight of them;
      keep them within your heart.
22   For they are life to those who find them,
      and health to one's whole body.
23   Guard your heart above all else,[b]
      for it is the source of life.[c]
24   Don't let your mouth speak dishonestly,
      and don't let your lips talk deviously.
25   Let your eyes look forward;
      fix your gaze[d] straight ahead.
26   Carefully consider the path[e] for your feet,
      and all your ways will be established.[f]
27   Don't turn to the right or to the left;[g]
      keep your feet away from evil.

PROVERBS 5

AVOID SEDUCTION

1   My son, pay attention to my wisdom;
      listen closely[h] to my understanding
2   so that ⌊you⌋ may maintain discretion
      and your lips safeguard knowledge.
3   Though the lips of the forbidden woman drip
       honey
      and her words are[i] smoother than oil,
4   in the end she's as bitter as •wormwood[j]
      and as sharp as a double-edged sword. [k]

[a] **4:19** Pr 24:16
[b] **4:23** Or *heart with all diligence*
[c] **4:23** Mt 15:19; Mk 7:18-23
[d] **4:25** Lit *eyelids*
[e] **4:26** Or *Clear a path*
[f] **4:26** Pr 5:21
[g] **4:27** Dt 5:32-33; 28:13-14; Jos 23:6
[h] **5:1** Lit *wisdom; stretch out your ear*
[i] **5:3** Lit *her palate is*
[j] **5:4** Pr 5:8-11; 6:32-33
[k] **5:4** Ps 55:21

NOTES

a 5:5 Pr 7:27; 9:18
b 5:8 Pr 2:18; 7:8; 9:14
c 5:12 Pr 1:28-31; 12:1; 13:18
d 5:13 Lit or turn my ear
e 5:15 Sg 4:12,15
f 5:16 Pr 7:12
g 5:18 Mal 2:14
h 5:21 Pr 4:25-26
i 5:22 Pr 11:6

5 Her feet go down to death;
  her steps head straight for •Sheol. a

6 She doesn't consider the path of life;
  she doesn't know that her ways are unstable.

7 So now, ⌊my⌋ sons, listen to me,
  and don't turn away from the words of my mouth.

8 Keep your way far from her.
  Don't go near the door of her house. b

9 Otherwise, you will give up your vitality
    to others
  and your years to someone cruel;

10 strangers will drain your resources,
  and your earnings will end up
    in a foreigner's house.

11 At the end of your life, you will lament
  when your physical body has been consumed,

12 and you will say, "How I hated discipline,
  and how my heart despised correction. c

13 I didn't obey my teachers
  or listen closely d to my mentors.

14 I was on the verge of complete ruin
  before the entire community."

ENJOY MARRIAGE

15 Drink water from your own cistern,
  water flowing from your own well. e

16 Should your springs flow in the streets,
  streams of water in the public squares? f

17 They should be for you alone
  and not for you ⌊to share⌋ with strangers.

18 Let your fountain be blessed,
  and take pleasure in the wife of your youth. g

19 A loving doe, a graceful fawn—
  let her breasts always satisfy you;
  be lost in her love forever.

20 Why, my son, would you be infatuated with
    a forbidden woman
  or embrace the breast of a stranger?

21 For a man's ways are before the LORD's eyes,
  and He considers all his paths. h

22 A wicked man's iniquities entrap him;
  he is entangled in the ropes of his own sin. i

23 He will die because there is no instruction,
  and be lost because of his great stupidity.

PROVERBS 6

FINANCIAL ENTANGLEMENTS

1 My son, if you have put up security
  for your neighbor[a]
  or entered into an agreement
  with[b] a stranger,[c] [d]

2 you have been trapped by the words
  of your lips—
  ensnared by the words of your mouth.

3 Do this, then, my son, and free yourself,
  for you have put yourself
    in your neighbor's power:
  Go, humble yourself, and plead
    with your neighbor.

4 Don't give sleep to your eyes
  or slumber to your eyelids.

5 Escape like a gazelle from a hunter,[e]
  like a bird from a fowler's trap.[f] [g]

LAZINESS

6 Go to the ant, you slacker!
  Observe its ways and become wise.

7 Without leader, administrator, or ruler,

8 it prepares its provisions in summer;
  it gathers its food during harvest.[h]

9 How long will you stay in bed, you slacker?
  When will you get up from your sleep?

10 A little sleep, a little slumber,
   a little folding of the arms to rest,[i]

11 and your poverty will come like a robber,
   your need, like a bandit.[j]

THE MALICIOUS MAN

12 A worthless person,[k] a wicked man,
   who goes around speaking dishonestly,[l]

13 who winks[m] his eyes, signals with his feet,
   and gestures with his fingers,

14 who plots evil with perversity in his heart—
   he stirs up trouble constantly.[n]

15 Therefore calamity will strike him suddenly;
   he will be shattered instantly—
     beyond recovery.[o]

NOTES

[a] 6:1 Or *friend*
[b] 6:1 Lit *or shaken hands for* or *with*
[c] 6:1 The Hb word for *stranger* can refer to a foreigner, an Israelite outside one's family, or simply to another person.
[d] 6:1 Pr 11:15; 17:18; 22:26
[e] 6:5 Lit *hand*
[f] 6:5 Lit *hand*
[g] 6:1-5 Pr 11:15; 17:18; 22:26
[h] 6:8 Pr 10:5; 30:25
[i] 6:10 Pr 26:14; Ec 4:5
[j] 6:10-11 Pr 20:13; 24:33-34; Ec 4:5
[k] 6:12 Pr 16:27; 19:28
[l] 6:12 Pr 4:24
[m] 6:13 Pr 10:10; 16:30; Ps 35:19
[n] 6:14 Pr 6:19; 16:27-28; 28:25
[o] 6:15 Pr 24:22; 29:1

WORD STUDY

Hebrew word:
to'ebah [toh ay VAH]

HCSB translation:
detestable thing, abomination

Focus passage:
Proverbs 6:16

To'ebah describes something that is culturally, ethically, or religiously offensive to a particular group. In order to maintain distinctiveness and safety, families and tribes would exclude objects, practices, and persons considered *detestable* by the community. On an ethical basis, the wicked and the righteous each detest the other's value system (Pr 29:27). Many Proverbs deal with *detestable* moral vices (Pr 12:22). Religiously, Yahweh detests pagan practices and attitudes such as prostitution (Dt 23:18), transvestitism (Dt 22:5), homosexuality (Lv 18:22), child sacrifice (Dt 12:31), and idolatry (Dt 27:15). However, it is equally *detestable* to Yahweh when those who are considered His people try to manipulate Him through hypocritical religious ritualism (Is 1:13).

WHAT THE LORD HATES

16 Six things the LORD hates;
in fact, seven are detestable to Him:
17 arrogant eyes,[a] a lying tongue,
hands that shed innocent blood,[b]
18 a heart that plots wicked schemes,
feet eager to run to evil,
19 a lying witness who gives false testimony,[c]
and one who stirs up trouble among brothers.[d]

WARNING AGAINST ADULTERY

20 My son, keep your father's command,
and don't reject your mother's teaching.[e]
21 Always bind them to your heart;
tie them around your neck.[f]
22 When you walk here and there, they will guide
you;
when you lie down, they will watch over you;
when you wake up, they will talk to you.
23 For a commandment is a lamp, teaching is
a light,[g]
and corrective instructions are the way to life.[h]
24 They will protect you from an evil woman,[i]
from the flattering[j] tongue of a stranger.[k]
25 Don't lust in your heart for her beauty
or let her captivate you with her eyelashes.
26 For a prostitute's fee is only a loaf of bread,
but an adulteress[l] goes after ⌊your⌋ very life.[m]
27 Can a man embrace fire[n]
and his clothes not be burned?
28 Can a man walk on coals
without scorching his feet?
29 So it is with the one who sleeps with another
man's wife;
no one who touches her will go unpunished.
30 People don't despise the thief if he steals
to satisfy himself when he is hungry.
31 Still, if caught, he must pay seven times as much;
he must give up all the wealth in his house.[o]
32 The one who commits adultery[p] lacks sense;
whoever does so destroys himself.
33 He will get a beating[q] and dishonor,
and his disgrace will never be removed.

NOTES

[a] **6:17** Pr 21:4; 30:13; Ps 18:27
[b] **6:17** Pr 1:16; Is 59:7
[c] **6:19** Pr 12:17; 14:5,25
[d] **6:19** Pr 6:14; 16:27-28; 28:25
[e] **6:20** Pr 1:8; 31:1
[f] **6:21** Pr 1:9; 3:3; 7:3
[g] **6:23** Ps 119:105
[h] **6:23** Pr 3:1-2; 4:4; 7:2; 19:16
[i] **6:24** LXX reads *from a married woman*
[j] **6:24** Lit *smooth*
[k] **6:24** Pr 7:5
[l] **6:26** Lit *but a wife of a man*
[m] **6:26** Pr 2:18-19; 7:21-23,27; 23:27-28
[n] **6:27** Lit *man take fire to his bosom*
[o] **6:31** Sg 8:7
[p] **6:32** Lit *commits adultery with a woman*
[q] **6:33** Or *plague*

WORD STUDY

Hebrew word:
musar [moo SAHR]
HCSB translation:
instruction, discipline
Focus passage:
Proverbs 6:23

Musar includes both teaching proper standards of behavior and administering the penalty when those standards are disobeyed. *Musar* is an activity of both God (Dt 11:2) and man—typically parents (Pr 4:1) or teachers (Pr 8:10). The term appears most frequently in poetic and prophetic texts. The topic of *instruction* is prominent in Proverbs, where the student of wisdom is exhorted to listen to *instruction* (Pr 1:2). A student who fails to learn from *instruction* will receive *discipline* or *correction* aimed at restoring the disobedient to right living (Pr 13:24). This restorative function is clearly seen in the death of the Suffering Servant who received divine punishment in order to heal the disobedient condition of those for whom He died (Is 53:5).

34 For jealousy enrages a husband,
   and he will show no mercy when he takes
      revenge.[a]

35 He will not be appeased by anything
   or be persuaded by lavish gifts.

PROVERBS 7

1 My son, obey my words,
   and treasure my commands.

2 Keep my commands and live;[b]
   protect my teachings as you would the pupil
      of your eye.[c]

3 Tie them to your fingers;
   write them on the tablet of your heart.[d]

4 Say to wisdom, "You are my sister,"
   and call understanding ⌊your⌋ relative.

5 She will keep you from a forbidden woman,
   a stranger with her flattering talk.[e]

A STORY OF SEDUCTION

6 At the window of my house
   I looked through my lattice.

7 I saw among the inexperienced,[f]
   I noticed among the youths,
   a young man lacking sense.

8 Crossing the street near her corner,
   he strolled down the road to her house

9 at twilight, in the evening,
   in the dark of the night.

10 A woman came to meet him,
   dressed like a prostitute, having a hidden agenda.[g]

11 She is loud and defiant;
   her feet do not stay at home.

12 Now in the street, now in the squares,[h]
   she lurks at every corner.

13 She grabs him and kisses him;
   she brazenly says[i] [j] to him,

14 "I've made fellowship offerings;[k]
   today I've fulfilled my vows.[l]

15 So I came out to meet you,
   to search for you, and I've found you.

16 I've spread coverings on my bed—
   richly colored linen from Egypt.

NOTES

[a] **6:34** Pr 27:4
[b] **7:2** Pr 3:1-2; 4:4; 6:23; 19:16
[c] **7:2** Dt 32:10; Ps 17:8
[d] **7:3** Pr 3:3; 6:21; Dt 6:6,8
[e] **7:5** Pr 5:3,20; 6:24; 7:5,21
[f] **7:7** Or *simple*, or *gullible*, or *naïve*
[g] **7:10** Or *prostitute, with a guarded heart*
[h] **7:12** Pr 5:16
[i] **7:13** Lit *she makes her face strong and says*
[j] **7:13** Pr 21:29
[k] **7:14** Meat from a fellowship offering had to be eaten on the day it was offered; therefore she is inviting him to a feast at her house.
[l] **7:14** Lv 7:11-18; Dt 23:18-19; Ps 56:12

17 I've perfumed my bed
  with myrrh, aloes, and cinnamon.

18 Come, let's drink deeply of lovemaking
    until morning.
  Let's feast on each other's love!

19 My husband isn't home;
  he went on a long journey.

20 He took a bag of money with him
  and will come home at the time
    of the full moon."

21 She seduces him with her persistent pleading;
  she lures with her flattering^a talk.

22 He follows her impulsively
  like an ox going to the slaughter,
  like a deer bounding toward a trap^b

23 until an arrow pierces its^c liver,^d
  like a bird darting into a snare—
  he doesn't know it will cost him his life.

24 Now, ⌊my⌋ sons, listen to me,
  and pay attention to the words of my mouth.

25 Don't let your heart turn aside to her ways;
  don't stray onto her paths.

26 For she has brought many down to death;
  her victims are countless.^e

27 Her house is the road to •Sheol,
  descending to the chambers of death.^f

PROVERBS 8

WISDOM'S APPEAL

1 Doesn't Wisdom call out?
  Doesn't Understanding make her voice heard?

2 At the heights overlooking the road,
  at the crossroads, she takes her stand.

3 Beside the gates at the entry to^g the city,
  at the main entrance, she cries out:^h

4 "People, I call out to you;
  my cry is to mankind.

5 Learn to be shrewd, you who are inexperienced;
  develop common sense, you who are foolish.

6 Listen, for I speak of noble things,
  and what my lips say is right.

7 For my mouth tells the truth,
  and wickedness is detestable to my lips.

8 All the words of my mouth are righteous;
 none of them are deceptive or perverse.

9 All of them are clear to the perceptive,
 and right to those who discover knowledge.

10 Accept my instruction instead of silver,
 and knowledge rather than pure gold.[a]

11 For wisdom is better than precious stones,
 and nothing desirable can compare with it.[b]

12 I, Wisdom, share a home with shrewdness
 and have knowledge and discretion.

13 To •fear the LORD is to hate evil.
 I hate arrogant pride, evil conduct,
  and perverse speech.

14 I possess good advice and competence;[c]
 I have understanding and strength.

15 It is by me that kings reign
 and rulers enact just law;

16 by me, princes lead,
 as do nobles ⌊and⌋ all righteous judges.

17 I love those who love me,
 and those who search for me find me.

18 With me are riches and honor,
 lasting wealth and righteousness.[d]

19 My fruit is better than solid gold,
 and my harvest than pure silver.[e]

20 I walk in the way of righteousness,
 along the paths of justice,

21 giving wealth as an inheritance to those
  who love me,
 and filling their treasuries.

22 The LORD made[f] me at the beginning
  of His creation,
 before His works of long ago.[g]

23 I was formed before ancient times,
 from the beginning, before the earth began.

24 I was brought forth when there were no
  watery depths
 and no springs filled with water.

25 I was brought forth
 before the mountains and hills were established,

26 before He made the land, the fields,
 or the first soil on earth.

27 I was there when He established the heavens,
 when He laid out the horizon on the surface
  of the ocean,

NOTES
a **8:10** Pr 3:14; 8:10,19; 16:16
b **8:11** Pr 3:15; 20:15
c **8:14** Or *resourcefulness*
d **8:18** Pr 3:16; 21:21; 22:4
e **8:19** Pr 3:14; 8:10,19; 16:16
f **8:22** Or *possessed*, or *begot*
g **8:22** Gn 1:1

WORD STUDY

Hebrew word:
da'at [DAH aht]

HCSB translation:
knowledge

Focus passage:
Proverbs 8:9-10,12

Da'at most often speaks of an awareness of people or objects gained through practical interaction with them. *Knowledge* may refer to technical skill (Ex 31:3) or to perception (Dt 4:42). Proverbs 1–9 focuses on *knowledge* as insight gained through theological reflection (Pr 2:10). In chapters 10–29 *knowledge* is primarily the ability to handle relationships (Pr 10:14). *Knowledge* may also refer to the ability to grasp visionary prophetic messages (Nm 24:16) or to use moral discernment (Gn 2:9). In theological contexts God possesses *knowledge*, and He disseminates it to men (Pr 2:6). The fear of the Lord is the beginning of *knowledge* (Pr 1:7), and the perception of His plans and purposes through relationship with Him is referred to as *knowledge* (Is 5:13). The phrase "*knowledge* of God" means to be in right relationship to God, expressed through moral obedience (Jr 22:16).

a 8:29 Jb 38:8-11
b 8:29 Jb 38:4-5
c 8:30 Or *a confidante,* or *a child*
d 8:30 Jb 38-39; Jr 10:12; 51:15
e 8:30 LXX; Hb omits *His*
f 8:30 Pr 3:19-20; Jb 28:20-27
g 8:31 Jb 38:4-7
h 8:31 Heb 2:6-8
i 8:35 Pr 4:4; 7:2; 9:11; 12:28
j 8:35 Pr 3:4; 13:13
k 8:36 Pr 11:19
l 9:1 Pr 14:1
m 9:3 Pr 8:2-3; 9:14-15
n 9:7 Lit *man his blemish*

28 when He placed the skies above,
when the fountains of the ocean gushed forth,

29 when He set a limit for the sea
so that the waters would not violate
His command,[a]
when He laid out the foundations of the earth.[b]

30 I was a skilled craftsman[c] beside Him.[d]
I was His[e] delight every day,[f]
always rejoicing before Him.

31 I was rejoicing in His inhabited world,[g]
delighting in the human race.[h]

32 And now, ⌊my⌋ sons, listen to me;
those who keep my ways are happy.

33 Listen to instruction and be wise;
don't ignore it.

34 Anyone who listens to me is happy,
watching at my doors every day,
waiting by the posts of my doorway.

35 For the one who finds me finds life[i]
and obtains favor from the LORD,[j]

36 but the one who sins against me harms himself;
all who hate me love death."[k]

PROVERBS 9

WISDOM VERSUS FOOLISHNESS

1 Wisdom has built her house;[l]
she has carved out her seven pillars.

2 She has prepared her meat; she has mixed
her wine;
she has also set her table.

3 She has sent out her servants;
she calls out from the highest points
of the city:[m]

4 "Whoever is inexperienced, enter here!"
To the one who lacks sense, she says,

5 "Come, eat my bread,
and drink the wine I have mixed.

6 Leave inexperience behind, and you will live;
pursue the way of understanding.

7 The one who corrects a mocker will bring
dishonor on himself;
the one who rebukes a wicked man
will get hurt.[n]

8 Don't rebuke a mocker, or he will hate you;[a]
  rebuke a wise man, and he will love you.

9 Instruct a wise man, and he will be wiser still;
  teach a righteous man, and he will learn more.[b]

10 The •fear of the LORD is the beginning
    of wisdom,[c]
  and the knowledge of the Holy One[d] is
    understanding.

11 For by Wisdom your days will be many,
  and years will be added to your life.

12 If you are wise, you are wise for
    your own benefit;
  if you mock, you alone will bear
    ⌊the consequences⌋."

13 The woman Folly is rowdy;
  she is gullible and knows nothing.

14 She sits by the doorway of her house,
  on a seat at the highest point of the city,

15 calling to those who pass by,
  who go straight ahead on their paths:[e]

16 "Whoever is inexperienced, enter here!"
  To the one who lacks sense, she says,

17 "Stolen water is sweet,
  and bread ⌊eaten⌋ secretly is tasty!"

18 But he doesn't know that the departed spirits
    are there,[f]
  that her guests are in the depths of •Sheol.[g]

PROVERBS 10

A COLLECTION OF SOLOMON'S PROVERBS

1 Solomon's proverbs:
  A wise son brings joy to his father,
  but a foolish son, heartache to his mother.[h]

2 Ill-gotten gains do not profit anyone,
  but righteousness rescues from death.[i]

3 The LORD will not let the righteous go hungry,[j]
  but He denies the wicked what they crave.

4 Idle hands make one poor,
  but diligent hands bring riches.[k]

5 The son who gathers during summer is prudent;
  the son who sleeps during harvest is disgraceful.[l]

6 Blessings are on the head of the righteous,
  but the mouth of the wicked conceals violence.[m]

a **9:8** Pr 15:12
b **9:9** Pr 1:5; 16:21,23
c **9:10** Pr 9:10; 15:33; Jb 28:28
d **9:10** Pr 30:3; Hs 11:12; Rv 16:5
e **9:14-15** Pr 7:11-12; 9:3-4
f **9:18** Pr 2:18; 21:16
g **9:18** Pr 5:5; 7:27
h **10:1** Pr 15:20; 17:25; 23:24-25; 29:3,15
i **10:2** Pr 11:4,18; 12:28
j **10:3** Ps 37:25
k **10:4** Pr 12:24,27; 13:4,11; 19:15
l **10:5** Pr 6:6-11; 30:25
m **10:6** Pr 10:11

a **10:8** Pr 10:10,17; Hs 4:6

b **10:9** Pr 2:7; 19:1; 20:7; 28:6,18

c **10:10** Pr 6:13; 16:30; Ps 35:19

d **10:10** Pr 10:8

e **10:11** Pr 13:14; 14:27; 16:22

f **10:11** Pr 10:6

g **10:12** Pr 17:9; Jms 5:20; 1 Pt 4:8

h **10:13** Pr 19:29; 26:3

i **10:14** Pr 12:13; 13:3; 18:7

j **10:15** Pr 18:11

k **10:17** Pr 5:12-13,22-23; 13:13-14

l **10:18** Pr 11:13

m **10:19** Pr 17:27-28; Jms 1:19; 3:2

n **10:20** Pr 10:32

o **10:22** Jms 1:17

p **10:22** Or *and He adds no trouble to it*

q **10:23** Pr 15:21

r **10:24** Pr 1:26-27; Is 66:4

s **10:24** Pr 10:28; 11:23; Ps 37:4

t **10:25** Is 29:5-7

u **10:25** Pr 10:30; 12:3,7; Mt 7:24-27

v **10:26** Pr 26:6

WORD STUDY

Hebrew word:
'ewil [eh VEEL]

HCSB translation:
fool

Focus passage:
Proverbs 10:8,10,14,21

'Ewil refers to one who willfully refuses to make moral choices, neither choosing good nor rejecting evil. While the *fool* is primarily depicted as *morally stupid*, he can also be considered *mentally stupid* because he refuses to receive moral instruction and to learn from his mistakes (Pr 12:15). He is characterized by *foolishness* (*'iwwelet*), a moral corruption that leaves him unable to make reasonable moral judgments (Pr 15:21).

---

7 The remembrance of the righteous is a blessing,
but the name of the wicked will rot.

8 A wise heart accepts commands,
but foolish lips will be destroyed.[a]

9 The one who lives with integrity lives securely,[b]
but whoever perverts his ways will be found out.

10 A sly wink of the eye[c] causes grief,
and foolish lips will be destroyed.[d]

11 The mouth of the righteous is a fountain of life,[e]
but the mouth of the wicked conceals violence.[f]

12 Hatred stirs up conflicts,
but love covers all offenses.[g]

13 Wisdom is found on the lips of the discerning,
but a rod is for the back of the one
who lacks sense.[h]

14 The wise store up knowledge,
but the mouth of the fool hastens destruction.[i]

15 A rich man's wealth is his fortified city;[j]
the poverty of the poor is their destruction.

16 The labor of the righteous leads to life;
the activity of the wicked leads to sin.

17 The one who follows instruction is on the path
to life,
but the one who rejects correction goes astray.[k]

18 The one who conceals hatred has lying lips,
and whoever spreads slander is a fool.[l]

19 When there are many words, sin is unavoidable,
but the one who controls his lips is wise.[m]

20 The tongue of the righteous is pure silver;
the heart of the wicked is of little value.[n]

21 The lips of the righteous feed many,
but fools die for lack of sense.

22 The LORD's blessing enriches,[o]
and toil adds nothing to it.[p]

23 As shameful conduct is pleasure for a fool,
so wisdom is for a man of understanding.[q]

24 What the wicked dreads will come upon him,[r]
but what the righteous desires will be given
to him.[s]

25 When the whirlwind passes, the wicked are
no more,[t]
but the righteous are secure forever.[u]

26 Like vinegar to the teeth and smoke to the eyes,[v]
so the slacker is to the one who sends him
⌊on an errand⌋.

27 The •fear of the LORD prolongs life,[a]
   but the years of the wicked are cut short.[b]

28 The hope of the righteous is joy,
   but the expectation of the wicked comes
      to nothing.[c]

29 The way of the LORD is a stronghold
      for the honorable,
   but destruction awaits the malicious.[d]

30 The righteous will never be shaken,
   but the wicked will not remain on the earth.[e]

31 The mouth of the righteous produces wisdom,
   but a perverse tongue will be cut out.[f]

32 The lips of the righteous know
      what is appropriate,
   but the mouth of the wicked, ⌊only⌋
      what is perverse.[g]

PROVERBS 11

1 Dishonest scales are detestable to the LORD,[h]
   but an accurate weight is His delight.[i]

2 When pride comes, disgrace follows,
   but with humility comes wisdom.[j]

3 The integrity of the upright guides them,
   but the perversity of the treacherous destroys
      them.[k]

4 Wealth is not profitable on a day of wrath,
   but righteousness rescues from death.[l]

5 The righteousness of the blameless clears
      his path,
   but the wicked person will fall because of
      his wickedness.

6 The righteousness of the upright rescues them,
   but the treacherous are trapped by
      their own desires.[m]

7 When the wicked dies, his expectation comes
      to nothing,
   and hope placed in wealth[n] [o] vanishes.[p]

8 The righteous is rescued from trouble;
   in his place, the wicked goes in.[q]

9 With his mouth the ungodly destroys his neighbor,
   but through knowledge the righteous are rescued.

10 When the righteous thrive, a city rejoices,
   and when the wicked die, there is
      joyful shouting.

NOTES

a **11:11** Pr 14:34
b **11:11** Pr 14:1; 29:4
c **11:12** Pr 14:21
d **11:13** Pr 10:18; 20:19; Lv 19:16
e **11:14** Pr 15:22; 20:18; 24:6
f **11:15** Pr 6:1-2; 17:18; 22:26
g **11:16** Or *ruthless*
h **11:17** Pr 11:3
i **11:18** Pr 10:2-3
j **11:19** Pr 10:16-17; 19:23
k **11:20** Pr 3:32; 12:22; 15:8-9,26
l **11:21** Lit *Hand to hand*
m **11:21** Pr 16:5
n **11:23** Pr 10:24; Ps 37:4-5; Jr 29:11
o **11:23** Pr 10:28; 11:7
p **11:24** Pr 11:25; 21:26; Ps 112:9
q **11:24** Pr 13:7; 22:16; 28:27
r **11:25** Pr 3:9-10; 11:25; Mt 10:42
s **11:27** Php 4:8

11 A city is exalted by the blessing of the upright,[a]
but it is overthrown by the mouth
   of the wicked.[b]

12 Whoever shows contempt for his neighbor lacks
   sense,
but a man with understanding keeps silent.[c]

13 A gossip goes around revealing a secret,
but the trustworthy keeps a confidence.[d]

14 Without guidance, people fall,
but with many counselors there is deliverance.[e]

15 If someone puts up security for a stranger,
   he will suffer for it,[f]
but the one who hates such agreements
   is protected.

16 A gracious woman gains honor,
but violent[g] men gain ⌊only⌋ riches.

17 A kind man benefits himself,
but a cruel man brings disaster on himself.[h]

18 The wicked man earns an empty wage,
but the one who sows righteousness,
   a true reward.[i]

19 Genuine righteousness ⌊leads⌋ to life,[j]
but pursuing evil ⌊leads⌋ to death.

20 Those with twisted minds are detestable
   to the LORD,
but those with blameless conduct are His delight.[k]

21 Be assured[l] that the wicked will not go
   unpunished,[m]
but the offspring of the righteous will escape.

22 A beautiful woman who rejects good sense
is like a gold ring in a pig's snout.

23 The desire of the righteous ⌊turns out⌋ well,[n]
but the hope of the wicked ⌊leads to⌋ wrath.[o]

24 One person gives freely, yet gains more;[p]
another withholds what is right, only to become
   poor.[q]

25 A generous person will be enriched,
and the one who gives a drink of water
   will receive water.[r]

26 People will curse anyone who hoards grain,
but a blessing will come to the one who sells it.

27 The one who searches for what is good[s] finds
   favor,
but if someone looks for trouble, it will come
   to him.

28 Anyone trusting in his riches will fall,
but the righteous will flourish like foliage. ^a

29 The one who brings ruin on his household
will inherit the wind,
and a fool will be a slave to someone
whose heart is wise.

30 The fruit of the righteous is a tree of life,
but violence ^b takes lives. ^c

31 If the righteous will be repaid on earth,
how much more the wicked and sinful.

PROVERBS 12

1 Whoever loves instruction loves knowledge,
but one who hates correction is stupid. ^d

2 The good obtain favor from the LORD,
but He condemns a man who schemes. ^e

3 Man cannot be made secure by wickedness,
but the root of the righteous is immovable. ^f

4 A capable wife ^g is her husband's crown, ^h
but a wife who causes shame is like rottenness
in his bones. ⁱ

5 The thoughts of the righteous ⌊are⌋ just,
but guidance from the wicked ⌊leads to⌋ deceit.

6 The words of the wicked are a deadly ambush,
but the speech of the upright rescues them.

7 The wicked are overthrown and perish,
but the house of the righteous will stand. ^j

8 A man is praised for his insight,
but a twisted mind is despised.

9 Better to be dishonored, yet have a servant,
than to act important but have no food. ^k

10 A righteous man cares about his animal's health, ^l
but ⌊even⌋ the merciful acts of the wicked
are cruel.

11 The one who works his land will have plenty
of food,
but whoever chases fantasies lacks sense. ^m

12 The wicked desire what evil men have, ⁿ
but the root of the righteous produces ⌊fruit⌋.

13 An evil man is trapped by
⌊his⌋ rebellious speech, ^o
but the righteous escapes from trouble. ^p

14 A man will be satisfied with good by the words
of his mouth,

NOTES

^a **11:28** Pr 11:4; 14:11

^b **11:30** LXX, Syr; Hb reads *but a wise one*

^c **11:30** Pr 13:2; 15:4

^d **12:1** Pr 3:11; 5:11-13; 15:5,31-32

^e **12:2** Pr 14:17; 24:8

^f **12:3** Pr 10:30; Ps 16:8; 21:7

^g **12:4** Or *A wife of quality*, or *A wife of good character*

^h **12:4** Pr 18:22; 19:14; 31:10

ⁱ **12:4** Pr 14:30

^j **12:7** Pr 10:25; Ps 103:17-18; Mt 7:24-27

^k **12:9** Pr 11:24; 13:7

^l **12:10** Pr 27:23

^m **12:11** Pr 28:19

ⁿ **12:12** Or *desire a stronghold of evil*

^o **12:13** Pr 10:14; 13:3; 18:7

^p **12:13** Pr 21:23; 29:6

WORD STUDY

Hebrew word:
tahbulah [tahch boo LAH]

HCSB translation:
counsel, guidance

Focus passage:
Proverbs 12:5

Tahbulah is probably related to the noun *hobel* (*sailor*) and may originally have meant "the skill of steering a boat." Later, *tahbulah* was used figuratively to mean "the skill of steering or guiding actions." In the OT, *tahbulah* is used only in Job and Proverbs, always in its plural form. *Tahbulah* usually refers to the body of *guidance*, *counsel*, or *strategy* offered by a group of skilled counselors. The Hebrew wisdom tradition taught that the discerning man acquires wise counsel from skilled advisors (Pr 1:5). Wars should be fought only after seeking *sound guidance* from wise political advisors (Pr 20:18). Without skillful *guidance* a nation will perish (Pr 11:14). *Tahbulah* is not necessarily moral, for even the wicked can provide helpful counsel for evil purposes (Pr 12:5).

NOTES

a **12:14** Pr 1:31; 18:20; 28:19
b **12:15** Pr 16:2; 21:2
c **12:16** Pr 11:13; 12:23; 17:9
d **12:17** Pr 6:19; 14:5,25
e **12:18** Lv 5:4
f **12:20** Pr 14:22
g **12:22** Pr 3:32; 11:20; 15:8-9,26
h **12:23** Pr 11:13; 12:16
i **12:24** Pr 10:4; 13:4; 19:15
j **12:25** Pr 16:24; Ps 94:19; Mt 6:25-34
k **12:26** Or *man guides his neighbor*
l **12:26** Pr 14:22
m **12:27** Pr 19:15,24; 26:15
n **12:27** Pr 10:4; 13:4; 19:15
o **12:28** Or *righteousness, and in its path there is no death*
p **12:28** Pr 10:2; 13:14; 14:27
q **13:2** Pr 1:10-12; 18:20-21; Is 32:6-8
r **13:3** Pr 10:14; 12:13; 18:7
s **13:4** Pr 10:4; 12:24,27; 19:15

and the work of a man's hands
> will reward him. [a]

15 A fool's way is right in his own eyes, [b]
> but whoever listens to counsel is wise.

16 A fool's displeasure is known at once,
> but whoever ignores an insult is sensible. [c]

17 Whoever speaks the truth declares what is right,
> but a false witness, deceit. [d]

18 There is one who speaks rashly, [e]
> like a piercing sword;
> but the tongue of the wise ⌊brings⌋ healing.

19 Truthful lips endure forever,
> but a lying tongue, only a moment.

20 Deceit is in the hearts of those who plot evil,
> but those who promote peace have joy. [f]

21 No disaster ⌊overcomes⌋ the righteous,
> but the wicked are full of misery.

22 Lying lips are detestable to the LORD,
> but faithful people are His delight. [g]

23 A shrewd person conceals knowledge,
> but a foolish heart publicizes stupidity. [h]

24 The diligent hand will rule,
> but laziness will lead to forced labor. [i]

25 Anxiety in a man's heart weighs it down,
> but a good word cheers it up. [j]

26 A righteous man is careful in dealing
> with his neighbor, [k]
> but the ways of wicked men lead them astray. [l]

27 A lazy man doesn't roast his game, [m]
> but to a diligent man, his wealth is precious. [n]

28 There is life in the path of righteousness,
> but another path leads to death. [o] [p]

PROVERBS 13

1 A wise son ⌊hears his⌋ father's instruction,
> but a mocker doesn't listen to rebuke.

2 From the words of his mouth, a man will enjoy
> good things,
> but treacherous people have an appetite
> for violence. [q]

3 The one who guards his mouth protects his life;
> the one who opens his lips invites his own ruin. [r]

4 The slacker craves, yet has nothing,
> but the diligent is fully satisfied. [s]

5   The righteous hate lying,
    but the wicked act disgustingly
        and disgracefully.
6   Righteousness guards people of integrity,[a]
    but wickedness undermines the sinner.[b]
7   One man pretends to be rich but has nothing;
    another pretends to be poor but has
        great wealth.[c]
8   Riches are a ransom for a man's life,[d]
    but a poor man hears no threat.
9   The light of the righteous shines brightly,[e]
    but the lamp of the wicked is extinguished.[f]
10 Arrogance leads to nothing but strife,[g]
    but wisdom is gained by those who take advice.
11 Wealth obtained by fraud will dwindle,[h]
    but whoever earns it through labor[i]
        will multiply it.[j]
12 Delayed hope makes the heart sick,
    but fulfilled desire is a tree of life.[k]
13 The one who has contempt for instruction
        will pay the penalty,
    but the one who respects a command will be
        rewarded.[l]
14 A wise man's instruction is a fountain of life,
    turning people away from the snares of death.[m]
15 Good sense wins favor,
    but the way of the treacherous never changes.
16 Every sensible person acts knowledgeably,
    but a fool displays his stupidity.
17 A wicked messenger falls into trouble,
    but a trustworthy courier ⌊brings⌋ healing.[n]
18 Poverty and disgrace ⌊come to⌋ those who ignore
        instruction,
    but the one who accepts rebuke will be honored.[o]
19 Desire fulfilled is sweet to the taste,
    but fools hate to turn from evil.[p]
20 The one who walks with the wise will become
        wise,
    but a companion of fools will suffer harm.
21 Disaster pursues sinners,
    but good rewards the righteous.
22 A good man leaves an inheritance
        to his[q] grandchildren,
    but the sinner's wealth is stored up
        for the righteous.[r]

a **13:6** Lit *guards integrity of way*
b **13:6** Pr 10:29
c **13:7** Pr 11:24; 1 Tm 6:17-19; Rv 3:17-18
d **13:8** Pr 10:15; Jb 2:4
e **13:9** Pr 4:18
f **13:9** Pr 20:20; 24:20; Jb 18:5-6
g **13:10** Pr 17:19
h **13:11** Pr 10:2; 20:21; 23:5
i **13:11** Lit *whoever gathers upon (his) hand*
j **13:11** Pr 10:4; 21:5-6
k **13:12** Pr 11:30; 15:4
l **13:13** Pr 3:1-2; 4:4; 6:23
m **13:14** Pr 10:11; 14:27; Ps 116:3
n **13:17** Pr 25:13
o **13:18** Pr 5:12-14; 12:1; 15:31-33
p **13:19** Pr 16:22; 29:27
q **13:22** Or *inheritance: his*
r **13:22** Pr 28:8; Jb 27:13-17; Ec 2:26

NOTES

a **13:24** Pr 22:15; 23:13-14; Heb 12:5-7

b **14:1** Pr 9:1; 24:3

c **14:1** Pr 11:11; 29:4

d **14:2** Pr 3:32

e **14:3** Or *In the mouth of a fool is a rod for his back*, if text is emended

f **14:4** Or *clean*

g **14:5** Pr 6:19; 12:17; 14:25

h **14:7** Pr 20:15

i **14:9** Or *at guilt offerings*

j **14:11** Lit *flourish*

k **14:11** Pr 10:25; 11:28; 12:7; Mt 7:24-27

l **14:12** Lit *ways*

m **14:12** Pr 5:4; 16:25

n **14:14** Pr 1:31; 12:14; 18:20; 28:19

WORD STUDY

Hebrew word:
hakam [khah KHAN]

HCSB translation:
wise, skillful

Focus passage:
Proverbs 14:1,3,16,24

Hakam, related to the noun *hok-mah* (*wisdom*), describes a high level of skill in a particular area. *Hakam* can describe skill in a profession (Ex 28:3), in using good judgment in relationships (Gn 41:33), or in devising schemes or plans (2 Sm 13:3). It may refer to skill in using knowledge acquired through books and other means and, by extension, to a guild of learned advisors skilled in wisdom and prophecy. *Hakam* does not necessarily connote moral virtue. However, in Proverbs and Ecclesiastes, *hakam* does connote virtue and describes skill in right living. The wise consider the consequences of their behavior and change it accordingly. They obey the Lord (Ps 107:43), use discernment (Pr 16:21), turn from evil (Pr 14:16), heed instruction and advice (Pr 9:8), provide instruction and knowledge (Pr 13:14), and promote peace (Pr 16:14).

184

23 The field of the poor yields abundant food,
but without justice, it is swept away.

24 The one who will not use the rod hates his son,
but the one who loves him disciplines him diligently. [a]

25 A righteous man eats until he is satisfied,
but the stomach of the wicked is empty.

PROVERBS 14

1 Every wise woman builds her house, [b]
but a foolish one tears it down
with her own hands. [c]

2 Whoever lives with integrity •fears the LORD,
but the one who is devious in his ways despises Him. [d]

3 The proud speech of a fool ⌊brings⌋ a rod ⌊of discipline⌋, [e]
but the lips of the wise protect them.

4 Where there are no oxen, the feed-trough is empty, [f]
but an abundant harvest ⌊comes⌋
through the strength of an ox.

5 An honest witness does not deceive,
but a dishonest witness utters lies. [g]

6 A mocker seeks wisdom and doesn't find it,
but knowledge ⌊comes⌋ easily to the perceptive.

7 Stay away from a foolish man;
you will gain no knowledge from his speech. [h]

8 The sensible man's wisdom is to consider his way,
but the stupidity of fools deceives ⌊them⌋.

9 Fools mock at making restitution, [i]
but there is goodwill among the upright.

10 The heart knows its own bitterness,
and no outsider shares in its joy.

11 The house of the wicked will be destroyed,
but the tent of the upright will stand. [j] [k]

12 There is a way that seems right to a man,
but its end is the way [l] to death. [m]

13 Even in laughter a heart may be sad,
and joy may end in grief.

14 The disloyal will get what their conduct deserves,
and a good man, what his ⌊deeds deserve⌋. [n]

15 The inexperienced believe anything,
but the sensible watch^a their steps.^b

16 A wise man is cautious and turns from evil,
but a fool is easily angered and is careless.^c

17 A quick-tempered man acts foolishly,
and a man who schemes is hated.^d

18 The gullible inherit foolishness,
but the sensible are crowned with knowledge.

19 The evil bow before those who are good,
the wicked, at the gates of the righteous.

20 A poor man is hated even by his neighbor,
but there are many who love the rich.^e

21 The one who despises his neighbor sins,^f
but whoever shows kindness to the poor
will be happy.

22 Don't those who plan evil go astray?^g
But those who plan good find loyalty and
faithfulness.^h

23 There is profit in all hard work,
but endless talkⁱ leads only to poverty.^j

24 The crown of the wise is their wealth,
but the foolishness of fools produces foolishness.

25 A truthful witness rescues lives,
but one who utters lies is deceitful.^k

26 In the •fear of the LORD one has strong confidence
and his children have a refuge.^l

27 The •fear of the LORD is a fountain of life,
turning people from the snares of death.^m

28 A large population is a king's splendor,
but a shortage of people is a ruler's devastation.

29 A patient person ⌊shows⌋ great understanding,
but a quick-tempered one promotes foolishness.

30 A tranquil heart is life to the body,ⁿ
but jealousy is rottenness to the bones.^o

31 The one who oppresses the poor insults
their Maker,^p
but one who is kind to the needy honors Him.^q

32 The wicked are thrown down by their own sin,
but the righteous have a refuge when they die.^r

33 Wisdom resides in the heart of the discerning;^s
she is known^t even among fools.

34 Righteousness exalts a nation,
but sin is a disgrace to any people.^u

35 A king favors a wise servant,^v
but his anger falls on a disgraceful one.

^a **14:15** Lit *the prudent understand*
^b **14:15** Jms 1:5-8
^c **14:16** Or *and falls*
^d **14:17** Pr 12:2; 24:8
^e **14:20** Pr 19:4,6
^f **14:21** Pr 11:12
^g **14:22** Pr 6:14-15; 12:26
^h **14:22** Pr 12:20
ⁱ **14:23** Lit *but word of lips*
^j **14:23** Pr 21:5
^k **14:25** Pr 6:19; 12:17; 14:5
^l **14:26** Pr 29:25
^m **14:27** Pr 13:14; 16:22; 19:23
ⁿ **14:30** Pr 3:8; 4:22; 16:24
^o **14:30** Pr 12:4; 27:4; Jms 3:16
^p **14:31** Pr 17:5; 21:13
^q **14:31** Pr 3:9; 14:21; 19:17
^r **14:32** Pr 10:25
^s **14:33** Pr 15:14; 18:15
^t **14:33** LXX reads *unknown*
^u **14:34** Pr 11:11
^v **14:35** Pr 22:29

PROVERBS 15

NOTES

a 15:1 Pr 25:15; Ec 10:4
b 15:2 Pr 15:28
c 15:3 2 Ch 16:9; Zch 4:10
d 15:8 Pr 15:29; 21:27; 28:9
e 15:4 Lit *but crookedness in it*
f 15:5 Pr 3:11; 12:1; 15:5,31-33
g 15:8 Pr 15:29; 21:27; 28:9
h 15:9 Pr 3:32; 11:20; 12:22
i 15:11 Jb 26:6
j 15:12 Pr 9:8
k 15:13 Pr 14:30; 15:30; 17:22; 18:14
l 15:14 Pr 14:33; 18:15; Mt 12:34
m 15:16-17 Ps 37:16; 16:8,19; 17:1
n 15:18 Pr 19:19; 22:24-25; 29:22
o 15:19 Pr 16:17,31; 22:5-6

1 A gentle answer turns away anger,[a]
but a harsh word stirs up wrath.

2 The tongue of the wise makes knowledge
attractive,
but the mouth of fools blurts out foolishness.[b]

3 The eyes of the LORD are everywhere,
observing the wicked and the good.[c]

4 The tongue that heals is a tree of life,[d]
but a devious tongue[e] breaks the spirit.

5 A fool despises his father's instruction,
but a person who heeds correction is sensible.[f]

6 The house of the righteous has great wealth,
but trouble accompanies the income
of the wicked.

7 The lips of the wise broadcast knowledge,
but not so the heart of fools.

8 The sacrifice of the wicked is detestable
to the LORD,
but the prayer of the upright is His delight.[g]

9 The LORD detests the way of the wicked,
but He loves the one who pursues righteousness.[h]

10 Discipline is harsh for the one who leaves
the path;
the one who hates correction will die.

11 •Sheol and •Abaddon lie open
before the LORD[i]—
how much more, human hearts.

12 A mocker doesn't love one who corrects him;[j]
he will not consult the wise.

13 A joyful heart makes a face cheerful,
but a sad heart ⌊produces⌋ a broken spirit.[k]

14 A discerning mind seeks knowledge,
but the mouth of fools feeds on foolishness.[l]

15 All the days of the oppressed are miserable,
but a cheerful heart has a continual feast.

16 Better a little with the •fear of the LORD
than great treasure with turmoil.

17 Better a meal of vegetables where there is love
than a fattened calf with hatred.[m]

18 A hot-tempered man stirs up conflict,
but a man slow to anger calms strife.[n]

19 A slacker's way is like a thorny hedge,
but the path of the upright is a highway.[o]

20 A wise son brings joy to his father,
but a foolish one despises his mother.[a]

21 Foolishness brings joy to one without sense,
but a man with understanding walks
a straight path.[b]

22 Plans fail when there is no counsel,
but with many advisers they succeed.[c]

23 A man takes joy in giving an answer;[d]
and a timely word—how good that is!

24 For the discerning the path of life leads upward,
so that he may avoid going down to •Sheol.

25 The LORD destroys the house of the proud,
but He protects the widow's territory.

26 The LORD detests the plans of an evil man,
but pleasant words are pure.[e]

27 The one who profits dishonestly troubles
his household,
but the one who hates bribes will live.[f]

28 The mind of the righteous person thinks
before answering,
but the mouth of the wicked blurts out
evil things.[g]

29 The LORD is far from the wicked,
but He hears the prayer of the righteous.[h]

30 Bright eyes cheer the heart;
good news strengthens[i] the bones.[j]

31 An ear that listens to life-giving rebukes
will be at home among the wise.

32 Anyone who ignores instruction despises himself,
but whoever listens to correction acquires
good sense.[k] [l]

33 The •fear of the LORD is wisdom's instruction,
and humility comes before honor.[m]

PROVERBS 16

1 The reflections of the heart belong to man,
but the answer of the tongue is from the LORD.[n]

2 All a man's ways seem right in his own eyes,
but the LORD weighs the motives.[o] [p]

3 Commit your activities to the LORD
and your plans will be achieved.[q]

4 The LORD has prepared everything
for His purpose—
even the wicked for the day of disaster.[r]

[a] **15:20** Pr 10:1; 23:24-25; 29:3,15
[b] **15:21** Pr 4:11,25; 10:23
[c] **15:22** Pr 8:14-16; 11:14; 24:6
[d] **15:23** Lit *in an answer of his mouth*
[e] **15:26** Pr 11:20; 15:8-9; 16:24
[f] **15:27** Pr 1:19; 17:23; 28:16; Ps 15:5
[g] **15:28** Pr 15:2; 18:13
[h] **15:29** Pr 15:8; 28:9
[i] **15:30** Lit *makes fat*
[j] **15:30** Pr 14:30; 15:13; 17:22
[k] **15:32** Lit *acquires a heart*
[l] **15:31-32** Pr 3:11; 5:12-14; 12:1
[m] **15:33** Pr 18:12; 22:4; 29:23
[n] **16:1** Pr 16:9; 19:21
[o] **16:2** Lit *weighs spirits*
[p] **16:2** Pr 17:3; 19:21; 21:2
[q] **16:3** Ps 37:4-5
[r] **16:4** Rm 9:21-22

NOTES

a **16:5** Pr 6:16-17; 8:13; 2 Ch 32:25

b **16:5** Lit *hand to hand*

c **16:5** Pr 11:21; 16:18; Ps 101:5

d **16:6** Jb 28:28; Pr 3:7

e **16:7** Or *he*

f **16:8** Pr 15:16-17; 16:19; 28:6; Ps 37:16

g **16:9** Pr 16:1; 19:21; 20:24

h **16:10** Or *A divination is on the lips of a king*

i **16:10** 2 Sm 14:17,20

j **16:10** Pr 18:14-15; 2 Sm 23:2-3

k **16:11** Merchants kept the stones for their balance scales in a bag.

l **16:11** Pr 11:1; Lv 19:36; Ezk 45:10; Mc 6:11

m **16:12** Whether the wicked behavior is on the part of the king or someone else is ambiguous in Hb.

n **16:12** Pr 25:5; Ps 101

o **16:14** Ec 10:4

p **16:16** Pr 3:14; 8:10,19; 22:1

q **16:17** Pr 2:11-13; 15:19

r **16:18** Pr 16:5; 18:12; 29:23; Dn 4:37

s **16:19** Alt Hb tradition reads *afflicted*

t **16:19** Pr 15:16-17; 16:8; Ps 37:16

u **16:20** Ps 34:8; 40:4; 84:12; 146:5

v **16:21** Lit *and sweetness of lips*

w **16:21** Pr 1:5; 9:9; 16:23

x **16:22** Pr 10:11; 13:14; 14:27

y **16:23** Lit *learning upon his lips*

z **16:23** Pr 1:5; 9:9; 16:21

5 Everyone with a proud heart is detestable
   to the LORD;[a]
be assured,[b] he will not go unpunished.[c]

6 Wickedness is atoned for by loyalty
   and faithfulness,
and one turns from evil by the •fear of the LORD.[d]

7 When a man's ways please the LORD,
He[e] makes even his enemies to be at peace
   with him.

8 Better a little with righteousness
than great income with injustice.[f]

9 A man's heart plans his way,
but the LORD determines his steps.[g]

10 God's verdict is on the lips of a king;[h][i]
his mouth should not err in judgment.[j]

11 Honest balances and scales are the LORD's;
all the weights in the bag[k] are His concern.[l]

12 Wicked behavior[m] is detestable to kings,
since a throne is established through
   righteousness.[n]

13 Righteous lips are a king's delight,
and he loves one who speaks honestly.

14 A king's fury is a messenger of death,
but a wise man appeases it.[o]

15 When a king's face lights up, there is life;
his favor is like a cloud with spring rain.

16 Acquire wisdom—how much better it is
   than gold!
And acquire understanding—it is preferable
   to silver.[p]

17 The highway of the upright avoids evil;
the one who guards his way protects his life.[q]

18 Pride comes before destruction,
and an arrogant spirit before a fall.[r]

19 Better to be lowly of spirit with the humble[s]
than to divide plunder with the proud.[t]

20 The one who understands a matter finds success,
and the one who trusts in the LORD will be
   happy.[u]

21 Anyone with a wise heart is called discerning,
and pleasant speech[v] increases learning.[w]

22 Insight is a fountain of life[x] for its possessor,
but folly is the instruction of fools.

23 A wise heart instructs its mouth
and increases learning with its speech.[y][z]

24 Pleasant words are a honeycomb:
sweet to the soul and healing to the bones. [a]

25 There is a way that seems right to a man,
but in the end it is the way of death. [b]

26 A worker's appetite works for him
because his hunger[c] urges him on.

27 A worthless man digs up evil,
and his speech is like a scorching fire. [d]

28 A contrary man spreads conflict,
and a gossip separates friends. [e]

29 A violent man lures his neighbor,
leading him in a way that is not good. [f]

30 The one who narrows his eyes is planning
deceptions;
the one who compresses his lips brings about
evil. [g]

31 Gray hair is a glorious crown;[h]
it is found in the way of righteousness.

32 Patience is better than power,
and controlling one's temper,[i] than capturing
a city. [j]

33 The lot is cast into the lap,
but its every decision is from the LORD. [k]

PROVERBS 17

1 Better a dry crust with peace
than a house full of feasting with strife. [l]

2 A wise servant will rule over a disgraceful son
and share an inheritance among brothers.

3 A crucible is for silver and a smelter for gold,
but the LORD is a tester of hearts. [m]

4 A wicked person listens to malicious talk;[n]
a liar pays attention to a destructive tongue.

5 The one who mocks the poor insults his Maker,[o]
and one who rejoices over disaster will not go
unpunished. [p]

6 Grandchildren are the crown of the elderly,
and the pride of sons is their fathers.

7 Excessive speech is not appropriate on a fool's lips;
how much worse are lies for a ruler.

8 A bribe seems like a magic stone to its owner;
wherever he turns, he succeeds. [q]

9 Whoever conceals an offense promotes love,
but whoever gossips about it separates friends. [r]

NOTES

[a] **16:24** Pr 15:26,30; 25:13
[b] **16:25** Pr 14:12; 24:20
[c] **16:26** Lit *mouth*
[d] **16:27** Pr 6:12; 19:28; 26:23
[e] **16:28** Pr 6:14,19; 17:9; 26:20-21; 28:25
[f] **16:29** Pr 28:10; 1 Sm 12:23; Ps 36:4
[g] **16:30** Pr 6:12-14; 10:10; Ps 35:19
[h] **16:31** Pr 4:9; 20:29; Lv 19:32
[i] **16:32** Lit *and ruling over one's spirit*
[j] **16:32** Pr 25:15,28; 29:11
[k] **16:33** Pr 16:1; 19:21; 21:31
[l] **17:1** Pr 21:9,19; 25:24
[m] **17:3** Pr 16:2; 21:2; Is 48:10
[n] **17:4** Lit *to lips of iniquity*
[o] **17:5** Pr 14:31; 21:13
[p] **17:5** Lm 1:21-22; Ezk 25:6-7; 35:15
[q] **17:8** Pr 18:16; 19:6; 21:14
[r] **17:9** Pr 11:13; 16:28; Lv 19:16; Ps 101:5; 1 Pt 4:8

WORD STUDY

Hebrew word:
kesil [keh SEEL]

HCSB translation:
fool

Focus passage:
Proverbs 17:10,12,16,21,24,25

Kesil refers to one whose foolishness results from laziness and complacency. The *kesil's* stupidity does not stem from a willful disregard of moral issues, but from apathy toward them. This moral apathy distinguishes the *kesil* from the *'ewil*, a *fool* who is intentionally immoral. The *kesil* is rude, airing his anger freely (Pr 14:16) and speaking without thinking (Pr 15:2). He is amused by purposeless activity (Ec 7:4-6) and is easily provoked when things don't go his way (Ec 7:9). He is self-indulgent (Pr 19:10), and he squanders his resources (Pr 21:20). Like the *'ewil*, he displays his foolishness (Pr 13:16), loves ignorance (Pr 1:22), and repeats his foolish behavior (Pr 26:11). He brings harm to his companions (Pr 13:20) and is self-deceived (Pr 14:8) and self-destructive (Ec 4:5).

10 A rebuke cuts into a perceptive person
more than a hundred lashes into a fool.

11 An evil man seeks only rebellion;
a cruel messenger [a] will be sent against him.

12 Better for a man to meet a bear robbed of her cubs
than a fool in his foolishness.

13 If anyone returns evil for good,
evil will never depart from his house.

14 To start a conflict is to release a flood;
stop the dispute before it breaks out. [b]

15 Acquitting the guilty and condemning the just—
both are detestable to the LORD. [c]

16 Why does a fool have money in his hand
with no intention of buying wisdom? [d]

17 A friend loves at all times,
and a brother is born for a difficult time. [e]

18 One without sense enters an agreement [f]
and puts up security for his friend. [g]

19 One who loves to offend loves strife;
one who builds a high threshold invites injury. [h]

20 One with a twisted mind will not succeed,
and one with deceitful speech will fall into ruin. [i]

21 A man fathers a fool to his own sorrow;
the father of a fool has no joy. [j]

22 A joyful heart is good medicine,
but a broken spirit dries up the bones. [k]

23 A wicked man secretly takes a bribe
to subvert the course of justice. [l]

24 Wisdom is the focus of the perceptive,
but a fool's eyes roam to the ends of the earth.

25 A foolish son is grief to his father
and bitterness to the one who bore him. [m]

26 It is certainly not good to fine an innocent person,
or to beat a noble for his honesty. [n] [o]

27 The intelligent person restrains his words,
and one who keeps a cool head [p] is a man
of understanding.

28 Even a fool is considered wise when he keeps silent,
discerning, when he seals his lips. [q]

PROVERBS 18

1 One who isolates himself pursues
⌊selfish⌋ desires;
he rebels against all sound judgment.

2 A fool does not delight in understanding,
but only wants to show off his opinions.[a]
3 When a wicked man comes, shame does also,
and along with dishonor, disgrace.
4 The words of a man's mouth are deep waters,[b]
a flowing river, a fountain of wisdom.
5 It is not good to show partiality to the guilty
by perverting the justice due the innocent.[c]
6 A fool's lips lead to strife,
and his mouth provokes a beating.
7 A fool's mouth is his devastation,
and his lips are a trap for his life.[d]
8 A gossip's words are like choice food
that goes down to one's innermost being.[e] [f]
9 The one who is truly lazy in his work
is brother to a vandal.[g] [h]
10 The name of the LORD is a strong tower;
the righteous run to it and are protected.[i] [j]
11 A rich man's wealth is his fortified city;
in his imagination it is like a high wall.[k]
12 Before his downfall a man's heart is proud,
but before honor comes humility.[l]
13 The one who gives an answer before he listens—
this is foolishness and disgrace for him.[m]
14 A man's spirit can endure sickness,
but who can survive a broken spirit?[n]
15 The mind of the discerning acquires
knowledge,
and the ear of the wise seeks it.[o]
16 A gift opens doors[p] for a man
and brings him before the great.[q]
17 The first to state his case seems right
until another comes and cross-examines him.[r]
18 ⌊Casting⌋ the lot ends quarrels
and separates powerful opponents.
19 An offended brother is ⌊harder to reach⌋ than
a fortified city,
and quarrels are like the bars of a fortress.
20 From the fruit of his mouth a man's stomach
is satisfied;
he is filled with the product of his lips.[s]
21 Life and death are in the power of the tongue,
and those who love it will eat its fruit.[t]
22 A man who finds a wife finds a good thing
and obtains favor from the LORD.[u]

NOTES

a **18:2** Lit *to uncover his heart*
b **18:4** Pr 20:5
c **18:5** Pr 24:23-24; Lv 19:15; Dt 24:17; Ps 15:5
d **18:7** Pr 10:14; 12:13; 13:3
e **18:8** Lit *to the chambers of the belly*
f **18:8** Pr 26:22
g **18:9** Lit *master of destruction*
h **18:9** Pr 28:24
i **18:10** Lit *raised high*
j **18:10** Pr 29:25
k **18:11** Pr 10:15
l **18:12** Pr 11:2; 16:18; 29:23
m **18:13** Pr 15:28
n **18:14** Pr 15:13; 17:22
o **18:15** Pr 14:33; 15:14
p **18:16** Lit *gift makes room*
q **18:16** Pr 17:8; 19:6; 21:14
r **18:17** 1 Kg 3:16-28
s **18:20** Pr 1:31; 12:14; 14:14
t **18:21** Pr 13:2; Mt 15:11,18-20; Jms 3:8
u **18:22** Pr 19:14; 31:10

WORD STUDY

Hebrew word:
rib [REEV]

HCSB translation:
strife, dispute

Focus passage:
Proverbs 18:6,17

Rib may refer to a *quarrel* or *dispute* between individuals (Dt 25:1) or groups (Gn 13:7) and may describe military conflicts (Ps 18:43). The *dispute* may be settled outside the courtroom (Pr 17:14), or it may escalate into a lawsuit (Ps 55:9). *Rib* may also refer to a formal lawsuit—either to the entire legal process or to various stages or elements of the legal proceedings (Ex 23:3). Theologically, God often entered into lawsuits against His own people (Ps 103:9). He is invoked as arbiter in *disputes* (Ps 35:23). He pleads the case of the underprivileged (Pr 22:23) and defends the cause of His people (Jr 50:34).

NOTES

a **18:24** Some LXX mss, Syr, Tg, Vg read *friends must be friendly*

b **18:24** Pr 17:17; 27:10; Jn 15:13

c **19:1** Pr 10:9; 15:16; 28:6; Ps 37:16

d **19:2** Lit *who is hasty with feet*

e **19:2** Pr 21:5; 28:20; 29:20

f **19:4** Pr 14:20; 19:6

g **19:5** Pr 19:5,9; 21:28

h **19:6** Pr 29:26

i **19:6** Pr 14:20; 17:8; 19:4

j **19:7** Hb uncertain in this line

k **19:8** Lit *acquires a heart*

l **19:9** Pr 19:5,9; 21:28

m **19:10** Pr 26:1

n **19:11** Pr 11:13; 17:9

o **19:12** Pr 20:2; 28:15

p **19:13** Pr 10:1; 17:25; 28:7

q **19:13** Pr 27:15

r **19:15** Pr 10:4; 13:4; 21:25

s **19:16** Or *despises*, or *treats lightly*

t **19:16** Pr 3:1-2; 4:4; 13:13

23 The poor man pleads,
but the rich one answers roughly.

24 A man with many friends may be harmed,[a]
but there is a friend who stays closer
than a brother.[b]

PROVERBS 19

1 Better a poor man who walks in integrity
than someone who has deceitful lips and is
a fool.[c]

2 Even zeal is not good without knowledge,
and the one who acts hastily[d] sins.[e]

3 A man's own foolishness leads him astray,
yet his heart rages against the LORD.

4 Wealth attracts many friends,
but a poor man is separated from his friend.[f]

5 A false witness will not go unpunished,
and one who utters lies will not escape.[g]

6 Many seek the favor of a ruler,[h]
and everyone is a friend of one who gives gifts.[i]

7 All the brothers of a poor man hate him;
how much more do his friends keep
their distance from him!
He may pursue ⌊them with⌋ words, ⌊but⌋ they
are not ⌊there⌋.[j]

8 The one who acquires good sense[k] loves himself;
one who safeguards understanding finds success.

9 A false witness will not go unpunished,
and one who utters lies perishes.[l]

10 Luxury is not appropriate for a fool—
how much less for a slave to rule over princes![m]

11 A person's insight gives him patience,
and his virtue is to overlook an offense.[n]

12 A king's rage is like a lion's roar,
but his favor is like dew on the grass.[o]

13 A foolish son is his father's ruin,[p]
and a wife's nagging is an endless dripping.[q]

14 A house and wealth are inherited from fathers,
but a sensible wife is from the LORD.

15 Laziness induces deep sleep,
and a lazy person will go hungry.[r]

16 The one who keeps commands preserves
himself;
one who disregards[s] his ways will die.[t]

17 Kindness to the poor is a loan to the LORD,
and He will give a reward to the lender. [a]

18 Discipline your son while there is hope;
don't be intent on killing him. [b] [c]

19 A person with great anger bears the penalty;
if you rescue him, you'll have to do it again. [d]

20 Listen to counsel and receive instruction
so that you may be wise in later life. [e] [f]

21 Many plans are in a man's heart,
but the LORD's decree will prevail. [g]

22 A man's desire should be loyalty
to the covenant;
better to be a poor man than a perjurer. [h]

23 The •fear of the LORD leads to life;
one will sleep at night[i] without danger. [j]

24 The slacker buries his hand in the bowl;
he doesn't even bring it back to his mouth. [k]

25 Strike a mocker, and the inexperienced learn
a lesson;
rebuke the discerning, and he gains knowledge. [l]

26 The one who assaults his father and evicts
his mother
is a disgraceful and shameful son.

27 If you stop listening to instruction, my son,
you will stray from the words of knowledge.

28 A worthless witness mocks justice,
and a wicked mouth swallows iniquity.

29 Judgments are prepared for mockers,
and beatings for the backs of fools. [m]

PROVERBS 20

1 Wine is a mocker, beer is a brawler,
and whoever staggers because of them
is not wise.

2 A king's terrible wrath is like the roaring
of a lion;
anyone who provokes him endangers himself. [n]

3 It is honorable for a man to resolve a dispute,
but any fool can get himself into a quarrel. [o]

4 The slacker does not plow during
planting season;[p]
at harvest time he looks, [q] and there is nothing. [r]

5 Counsel in a man's heart is deep water;[s]
but a man of understanding draws it up.

[a] **19:17** Lit *to him*
[b] **19:18** Lit *don't lift up your soul to his death*
[c] **19:18** Pr 23:13-14; 29:17
[d] **19:19** Pr 22:24-25; 29:22
[e] **19:20** Lit *in your end*
[f] **19:20** Pr 12:1; 15:5,31-32
[g] **19:21** Pr 16:1,9,33; 21:31
[h] **19:22** Pr 19:1; 28:6
[i] **19:23** Lit *will spend the night satisfied*
[j] **19:23** Pr 14:26-27
[k] **19:24** Pr 12:27; 26:14-15
[l] **19:25** Pr 21:11
[m] **19:29** Pr 10:13; 26:3
[n] **20:2** Pr 19:12; 28:15
[o] **20:3** Pr 15:18; 18:6; 22:10
[p] **20:4** Lit *plow in winter*
[q] **20:4** Lit *inquires*
[r] **20:4** Pr 24:30-34
[s] **20:5** Pr 18:4

a 20:6 Pr 28:20; Ps 53:2-3
b 20:7 Pr 2:7,20-21; 10:9; 13:6
c 20:7 Lit *sons*
d 20:8 Pr 20:26
e 20:9 Jb 15:15-16; Ps 14:2-3; Rm 3:9-12
f 20:10 Lit *Stone and stone, measure and measure*
g 20:10 Pr 11:1; 20:23; Dt 25:14-15; Mc 6:10-11
h 20:11 Pr 21:8
i 20:12 Pr 22:2; 29:13
j 20:13 Pr 6:10-11; 24:33-34
k 20:15 Pr 3:15; 8:11
l 20:16 A debtor's outer garment held as collateral; Dt 24:12-13,17; Jb 22:6
m 20:16 Pr 6:1-5; 11:15; 27:13
n 20:18 Pr 11:14; 15:22; 24:6
o 20:19 Pr 11:13; Lv 19:16
p 20:20 Pr 24:20; Ex 21:17
q 20:21 Pr 21:5; 23:5; 28:22
r 20:22 Ps 37:7-9
s 20:23 Lit *A stone and a stone*
t 20:23 Pr 11:1; 20:10; Mc 6:11
u 20:24 Pr 16:9,33; 19:21
v 20:25 Nm 30:2; Dt 23:21; Ec 5:4-6

6 Many a man proclaims his own loyalty,
but who can find a trustworthy man?[a]

7 The one who lives with integrity is righteous;[b]
his children[c] who come after him will be happy.

8 A king sitting on a throne to judge
sifts out all evil with his eyes.[d]

9 Who can say, "I have kept my heart pure;
I am cleansed from my sin"?[e]

10 Differing weights and varying measures[f]—
both are detestable to the LORD.[g]

11 Even a young man is known by his actions—
by whether his behavior is pure and upright.[h]

12 The hearing ear and the seeing eye—
the LORD made them both.[i]

13 Don't love sleep, or you will become poor;
open your eyes, and you'll have enough to eat.[j]

14 "It's worthless, it's worthless!" the buyer says,
but after he is on his way, he gloats.

15 There is gold and a multitude of jewels,
but knowledgeable lips are a rare treasure.[k]

16 Take his garment,[l] for he has put up security
for a stranger;
get collateral if it is for foreigners.[m]

17 Food gained by fraud is sweet to a man,
but afterward his mouth is full of gravel.

18 Finalize plans through counsel,
and wage war with sound guidance.[n]

19 The one who reveals secrets is
a constant gossip;
avoid someone with a big mouth.[o]

20 Whoever curses his father or mother—
his lamp will go out in deep darkness.[p]

21 An inheritance gained prematurely
will not be blessed ultimately.[q]

22 Don't say, "I will avenge this evil!"
Wait on the LORD, and He will rescue you.[r]

23 Differing weights[s] are detestable to the LORD,
and dishonest scales are unfair.[t]

24 A man's steps are determined by the LORD,[u]
so how can anyone understand his own way?

25 It is a trap for anyone to dedicate something
rashly
and later to reconsider his vows.[v]

26 A wise king separates out the wicked
and drives the threshing wheel over them.

27 A person's breath is the lamp of the LORD,
searching the innermost parts.[a] [b]

28 Loyalty and faithfulness deliver a king;
through loyalty he maintains his throne.

29 The glory of young men is their strength,
and the splendor of old men is gray hair.[c]

30 Lashes and wounds purge away evil,
and beatings cleanse the innermost parts.[d]

PROVERBS 21

1 A king's heart is a water channel
in the Lord's hand:
He directs it wherever He chooses.

2 All the ways of a man seem right to him,
but the LORD evaluates the motives.[e]

3 Doing what is righteous and just
is more acceptable to the LORD than sacrifice.[f]

4 The lamp[g] that guides the wicked—
haughty eyes and an arrogant heart[h]—is sin.

5 The plans of the diligent certainly lead to profit,
but anyone who is reckless only becomes poor.[i]

6 Making a fortune through a lying tongue
is a vanishing mist,[j] a pursuit of death.[k] [l]

7 The violence of the wicked sweeps them away
because they refuse to act justly.

8 A guilty man's conduct is crooked,
but the behavior of the innocent is upright.[m]

9 Better to live on the corner of a roof
than to share a house with a nagging wife.[n]

10 A wicked person desires evil;
he has no consideration[o] for his neighbor.

11 When a mocker is punished, the inexperienced
become wiser;
when one teaches a wise man, he acquires
knowledge.[p]

12 The Righteous One considers the house
of the wicked;
He brings the wicked to ruin.

13 The one who shuts his ears to the cry of the poor
will himself also call out and not be answered.[q]

14 A secret gift soothes anger,
and a covert bribe,[r] fierce rage.[s]

15 Justice executed is a joy to the righteous
but a terror to those who practice iniquity.[t]

NOTES

a **20:27** Lit *the chambers of the belly*

b **20:27** Pr 20:30; Ps 139:23

c **20:29** Pr 16:31; Lv 19:32

d **20:30** Lit *beatings the chambers of the belly*

e **21:2** Pr 12:15; 16:2; 17:3

f **21:3** 1 Sm 15:22; Hs 6:6; Mt 9:13

g **21:4** Other mss read *tillage*

h **21:4** Pr 6:16-17; 30:13; Ps 101:5

i **21:5** Pr 10:4; 14:23; 21:20

j **21:6** Or *a breath blown away*

k **21:6** Other Hb mss, LXX, Vg read *a snare of death*

l **21:6** Lit *vanity, ones seeking death*

m **21:8** Pr 20:11

n **21:9** Pr 15:16-17; 17:1; 21:19; 25:24

o **21:10** Or *favor*

p **21:11** Pr 19:25

q **21:13** Pr 14:31; 17:5; 19:17

r **21:14** Lit *a bribe in the bosom*

s **21:14** Pr 17:8; 18:16; 19:6

t **21:15** Pr 10:29

WORD STUDY

Hebrew word:
yashar [yah SHAHR]

HCSB translation:
straight, right

Focus passage:
Proverbs 21:2,8,18,29

Yashar refers literally to straightness as opposed to crookedness. In the OT *yashar* is most often used figuratively to describe a person or action as ethically, morally, legally, or religiously *upright* or *straight*. The *upright* person performs righteous acts (Ps 11:7), fears God and turns from evil (Pr 20:11), is opposed by the wicked (Ps 11:2), and is hardworking (Pr 15:19), honest (Jb 1:8), and morally respectable (Ps 32:11). "To do what is *right* in the LORD's sight" refers to covenantal obedience to God's commands (Dt 12:25).

a 21:16 Pr 2:18; 9:18
b 21:17 Ec 2:1-3,10-11
c 21:18 Or *in place of*
d 21:18 Pr 11:8
e 21:19 Pr 15:16-17; 17:1; 21:9; 25:24
f 21:20 Lit *it*
g 21:20 Pr 10:4; 28:20; Mt 25:1-13
h 21:21 Pr 3:16; 8:18; Mt 6:33
i 21:22 Pr 14:26
j 21:23 Pr 12:13; 13:3
k 21:24 Pr 21:11
l 21:25 Pr 10:4; 12:24; 19:15,24
m 21:26 Lit *He craves a craving*
n 21:26 Pr 11:24-25
o 21:27 Pr 15:8; 28:9
p 21:28 Pr 19:5,9
q 21:29 Pr 7:13
r 21:31 Pr 20:18; 23:6; Ps 20:7; 108:10-13
s 22:1 Pr 10:7; 8:10; Ec 7:1
t 22:2 Lit *poor meet*
u 22:2 Lit *all*
v 22:2 Pr 29:13; Jb 31:13,15

16 The man who strays from the way of wisdom
will come to rest in the assembly
of the departed spirits. [a]

17 The one who loves pleasure will become
a poor man;
whoever loves wine and oil will not get rich. [b]

18 The wicked are a ransom for the righteous,
and the treacherous, for [c] the upright. [d]

19 Better to live in a wilderness
than with a nagging and hot-tempered wife. [e]

20 Precious treasure and oil are in the dwelling
of the wise,
but a foolish man consumes them. [f] [g]

21 The one who pursues righteousness
and faithful love
will find life, righteousness, and honor. [h]

22 The wise conquer a city of warriors
and bring down its mighty fortress. [i]

23 The one who guards his mouth and tongue
keeps himself out of trouble. [j]

24 The proud and arrogant person,
named "Mocker,"
acts with excessive pride. [k]

25 A slacker's craving will kill him
because his hands refuse to work. [l]

26 He is filled with craving [m] all day long,
but the righteous give and don't hold back. [n]

27 The sacrifice of a wicked person is detestable—
how much more so when he brings it
with ulterior motives! [o]

28 A lying witness will perish, [p]
but the one who listens will speak successfully.

29 A wicked man puts on a bold face, [q]
but the upright man considers his way.

30 No wisdom, no understanding, and no counsel
⌊will prevail⌋ against the LORD.

31 A horse is prepared for the day of battle,
but victory comes from the LORD. [r]

PROVERBS 22

1 A good name is to be chosen over great wealth;
favor is better than silver and gold. [s]

2 The rich and the poor have this in common: [t]
the LORD made them both. [u] [v]

3   A sensible person sees danger and takes cover,
    but the inexperienced keep going
        and are punished.[a]
4   The result of humility is •fear of the LORD,
    along with wealth, honor, and life.[b]
5   There are thorns and snares on the path
        of the crooked;[c]
    the one who guards himself stays far from them.
6   Teach a youth about the way he should go;
    even when he is old he will not depart from it.
7   The rich rule over the poor,
    and the borrower is a slave to the lender.[d]
8   The one who sows injustice will reap disaster,[e]
    and the rod of his fury will be destroyed.
9   A generous person[f] will be blessed,
    for he shares his food with the poor.
10 Drive out a mocker, and conflict goes too;
    then lawsuits and dishonor will cease.
11 The one who loves a pure heart
    and gracious lips—the king is his friend.
12 The LORD's eyes keep watch over knowledge,
    but He overthrows the words of the treacherous.
13 The slacker says, "There's a lion outside!
    I'll be killed in the streets!"[g]
14 The mouth of the forbidden woman is
        a deep pit;
    a man cursed by the LORD will fall into it.[h]
15 Foolishness is tangled up in the heart of a youth;
    the rod of discipline will drive it away
        from him.[i]
16 Oppressing the poor to enrich oneself,
    and giving to the rich—both lead only
        to poverty.[j]

WORDS OF THE WISE

17 Listen closely,[k] pay attention to the words
        of the wise,
    and apply your mind to my knowledge.
18 For it is pleasing if you keep them within you[l]
    and if they are[m] constantly on your lips.
19 I have instructed you today—even you—
    so that your confidence may be in the LORD.
20 Haven't I written for you previously[n]
    about counsel and knowledge,

NOTES

[a] **22:3** Pr 27:12; Is 26:20
[b] **22:4** Pr 15:33; 21:21; 29:23
[c] **22:5** Pr 7:23
[d] **22:7** Dt 28:12-13
[e] **22:8** Jb 4:8; Hs 10:13-14
[f] **22:9** Lit *Good of eye*
[g] **22:13** Pr 26:13
[h] **22:14** Pr 2:16-19; 7:5,21,27; 23:27-28
[i] **22:15** Pr 13:24; 23:13-14; 29:15
[j] **22:16** Pr 11:24; 22:7; 28:27
[k] **22:17** Lit *Stretch out your ear*
[l] **22:18** Pr 18:8
[m] **22:18** Or *you; let them be,* or *you, so that*
[n] **22:20** Alt Hb tradition reads *excellent things*; LXX, Syr, Tg, Vg read *three times*; some emend to read *30 sayings.*

NOTES

^a **22:21** Lit *give dependable words*
^b **22:21** Pr 10:26; 25:13
^c **22:22** Pr 24:7; Ru 4:11; Zch 8:16.
^d **22:22-23** Pr 23:10-11; Is 3:13-15
^e **22:24** Lit *with a master of anger*
^f **22:24-25** Pr 15:18; 18:7; 19:19
^g **22:26** Lit *who shakes hands*
^h **22:26** Pr 6:1-5; 11:15; 17:18
ⁱ **22:28** Pr 23:10; Dt 19:14; 27:17
^j **22:29** Pr 14:35
^k **23:1** Or *who*
^l **23:2** Lit *you are the master of an*
^m **23:3** Pr 23:6
ⁿ **23:5** Pr 13:11; 20:21; Jr 17:11
^o **23:6** Lit *eat bread of an evil eye*
^p **23:6** Pr 23:3; Gn 27:4
^q **23:7** Mt 6:21; Lk 12:34
^r **23:9** Lit *in the ears of*

21 in order to teach you true and reliable words,
so that you may give a dependable report[a]
to those who sent you?[b]

22 Don't rob a poor man because he is poor,
and don't crush the oppressed at the •gate,[c]

23 for the LORD will take up their case
and will plunder those who plunder them.[d]

24 Don't make friends with an angry man,[e]
and don't be a companion
of a hot-tempered man,

25 or you will learn his ways
and entangle yourself in a snare.[f]

26 Don't be one of those who enter agreements,[g]
who put up security for loans.[h]

27 If you have no money to pay,
even your bed will be taken from under you.

28 Don't move an ancient property line
that your fathers set up.[i]

29 Do you see a man skilled in his work?
He will stand in the presence of kings.
He will not stand in the presence
of unknown men.[j]

PROVERBS 23

1 When you sit down to dine with a ruler,
consider carefully what[k] is before you,

2 and stick a knife in your throat
if you have a big[l] appetite;

3 don't desire his choice food,[m]
for that food is deceptive.

4 Don't wear yourself out to get rich;
stop giving your attention to it.

5 As soon as your eyes fly to it, it disappears,
for it makes wings for itself
and flies like an eagle to the sky.[n]

6 Don't eat a stingy person's bread,[o]
and don't desire his choice food,[p]

7 for as he thinks within himself, so he is.[q]
"Eat and drink," he says to you,
but his heart is not with you.

8 You will vomit the little you've eaten
and waste your pleasant words.

9 Don't speak to[r] a fool,
for he will despise the insight of your words.

10 Don't move an ancient property line,
and don't encroach on the fields
of the fatherless,[a]

11 for their Redeemer is strong,
and He will take up their case against you.[b]

12 Apply yourself to instruction
and listen to words of knowledge.

13 Don't withhold correction from a youth;
if you beat him with a rod, he will not die.

14 Strike him with a rod,
and you will rescue his life from •Sheol.[c]

15 My son, if your heart is wise,
my heart will indeed rejoice.

16 My innermost being will cheer
when your lips say what is right.[d]

17 Don't be jealous of sinners;[e]
instead, always •fear the LORD.

18 For then you will have a future,
and your hope will never fade.[f]

19 Listen, my son, and be wise;
keep your mind on the right course.

20 Don't associate with those who drink too much
wine,
or with those who gorge themselves on meat.

21 For the drunkard and the glutton will become
poor,
and grogginess will clothe ⌊them⌋ in rags.

22 Listen to your father who gave you life,
and don't despise your mother when[g] she is old.

23 Buy—and do not sell—truth,
wisdom, instruction, and understanding.[h]

24 The father of a righteous son will rejoice greatly,
and one who fathers a wise son will delight
in him.

25 Let your father and mother have joy,
and let her who gave birth to you rejoice.[i]

26 My son, give me your heart,
and let your eyes observe my ways.

27 For a prostitute is a deep pit,
and a forbidden woman is a narrow well;

28 indeed, she sets an ambush like a robber
and increases those among men who are
unfaithful.[j]

29 Who has woe? Who has sorrow?
Who has conflicts? Who has complaints?

a **23:10** Pr 22:28; Hs 5:10
b **23:10-11** Pr 22:22-23,28; Dt
19:14; 27:17
c **23:13-14** Pr 13:24; 19:18;
22:15
d **23:15-16** Pr 10:1; 15:20;
23:24-25
e **23:17** Ps 37:1; 73; Pr 24:1,19
f **23:18** Pr 10:28; 24:14; Jr 29:11
g **23:22** Or *because*
h **23:23** Pr 4:5,7; 16:16
i **23:24-25** Pr 10:1; 15:20; 17:21;
23:15-16
j **23:27-28** Pr 6:26; 7:22-23;
22:14

NOTES

a **23:29** Pr 23:35
b **23:30** Is 5:11
c **23:31** Sg 7:9
d **23:33** Or *will speak perversities*
   or *inverted things*
e **23:35** Pr 23:29
f **23:29-35** Eph 5:18
g **24:1** Pr 23:17; 24:19; Ps 37:1;
   73
h **24:3** Pr 14:1
i **24:5** Pr 21:22
j **24:6** Pr 11:14; 15:22; 20:18
k **24:7** Lit *is too high for*
l **24:7** Pr 17:16,24
m **24:12** Pr 21:2; Ps 44:21

Who has wounds for no reason?[a]
Who has red eyes?

30 Those who linger over wine,
those who go looking for mixed wine.[b]

31 Don't gaze at wine when it is red,
when it gleams in the cup
and goes down smoothly.[c]

32 In the end it bites like a snake
and stings like a viper.

33 Your eyes will see strange things,
and you will say absurd things.[d]

34 You'll be like someone sleeping out at sea
or lying down on the top of a ship's mast.

35 "They struck me, but I feel no pain!
They beat me, but I didn't know it![e]
When will I wake up?
I'll look for another ⌊drink⌋."[f]

PROVERBS 24

1 Don't envy evil men [g]
or desire to be with them,

2 for their hearts plan violence,
and their words stir up trouble.

3 A house is built by wisdom,[h]
and it is established by understanding;

4 by knowledge the rooms are filled
with every precious and beautiful treasure.

5 A wise warrior is better than a strong one,
and a man of knowledge than one of strength;[i]

6 for you should wage war with sound guidance—
victory comes with many counselors.[j]

7 Wisdom is inaccessible to[k] a fool;[l]
he does not open his mouth at the •gate.

8 The one who plots evil
will be called a schemer.

9 A foolish scheme is sin,
and a mocker is detestable to people.

10 If you do nothing in a difficult time,
your strength is limited.

11 Rescue those being taken off to death,
and save those stumbling toward slaughter.

12 If you say, "But we didn't know about this,"
won't He who weighs hearts consider it?[m]
Won't He who protects your life know?

Won't He repay a person according to
   his work?[a]

13 Eat honey, my son, for it is good,
   and the honeycomb is sweet to your palate;
14 realize that wisdom is the same for you.
   If you find it, you will have a future,
   and your hope will never fade.[b]
15 Don't set an ambush, wicked man, at the camp[c]
      of the righteous man;
   don't destroy his dwelling.
16 Though a righteous man falls seven times,
      he will get up,
   but the wicked will stumble into ruin.[d]
17 Don't gloat when your enemy falls,
   and don't let your heart rejoice
      when he stumbles,
18 or the LORD will see, be displeased,
   and turn His wrath away from him.
19 Don't worry because of evildoers,
   and don't envy the wicked.[e]
20 For the evil have no future;[f]
   the lamp of the wicked will be put out.[g]
21 My son, •fear the LORD, as well as the king,[h]
   and don't associate with rebels,[i]
22 for their destruction will come suddenly;
   who knows what disaster these two can bring?
23 These ⌊sayings⌋ also belong to the wise:
   It is not good to show partiality in judgment.[j]
24 Whoever says to the guilty,
      "You are innocent"—
   people will curse him, and tribes will denounce
      him;[k]
25 but it will go well with those who convict
      the guilty,
   and a generous blessing will come upon them.
26 He who gives an honest answer
   gives a kiss on the lips.
27 Complete your outdoor work, and prepare
      your field;
   afterwards, build your house.
28 Don't testify against your neighbor
      without cause.
   Don't deceive with your lips.
29 Don't say, "I'll do to him what he did to me;
   I'll repay the man for what he has done."[l]

NOTES
[a] 24:12 Pr 24:29
[b] 24:14 Pr 10:28; 23:18; Jr 29:11
[c] 24:15 A rural encampment or home not under the protection of a city
[d] 24:16 Pr 29:16
[e] 24:19 Pr 23:17; 24:1; Ps 37:1; 73
[f] 24:20 Pr 14:11; 16:25; Ps 37:38
[g] 24:20 Pr 13:9; 20:20; Jb 21:17
[h] 24:21 Mt 22:21; Rm 13:1-4; 1 Pt 2:13-14
[i] 24:21 Or those given to change
[j] 24:23 Pr 28:21; Dt 1:17; 16:19
[k] 24:23-24 Pr 17:15; 18:5
[l] 24:29 Pr 24:12; Rm 12:19

NOTES

a 24:30-34 Pr 6:10-11; 20:4,13
b 25:4 Lit *will come out*; Ex 32:24
c 25:7 Lit *you before a noble whom your eyes see*
d 25:7 Lk 14:7-11
e 25:8 Or *neighbor*
f 25:9 Or *neighbor*
g 25:10 Lit *and your evil report will not turn back*
h 25:9-10 Pr 17:9; Mt 5:25
i 25:11 Or *like apples of gold in settings of silver*
j 25:11 Pr 8:10; 15:23; 16:16

30 I went by the field of a slacker
and by the vineyard of a man lacking sense.

31 Thistles had come up everywhere,
weeds covered the ground,
and the stone wall was ruined.

32 I saw, and took it to heart;
I looked, and received instruction:

33 a little sleep, a little slumber,
a little folding of the arms to rest,

34 and your poverty will come like a robber,
your need, like a bandit.ᵃ

PROVERBS 25

HEZEKIAH'S COLLECTION

1 These too are proverbs of Solomon,
which the men of Hezekiah, king of Judah,
copied.

2 It is the glory of God to conceal a matter
and the glory of kings to investigate a matter.

3 As the heaven is high and the earth is deep,
so the hearts of kings cannot be investigated.

4 Remove impurities from silver,
and a vessel will be producedᵇ
for a silversmith.

5 Remove the wicked from the king's presence,
and his throne will be established
in righteousness.

6 Don't brag about yourself before the king,
and don't stand in the place of the great;

7 for it is better for him to say to you,
"Come up here!"
than to demote you in plain view of a noble.ᶜ ᵈ

8 Don't take a matter to court hastily.
Otherwise, what will you do afterwards
if your opponentᵉ humiliates you?

9 Make your case with your opponentᶠ
without revealing another's secret;

10 otherwise, the one who hears will disgrace you,
and you'll never live it down.ᵍ ʰ

11 A word spoken at the right time
is like golden apples on a silver tray.ⁱ ʲ

12 A wise correction to a receptive ear
is like a gold ring or an ornament of gold.

202

NOTES

a **25:13** Pr 13:17; 16:24; 25:25
b **25:15** Pr 15:1; 16:32; Ec 10:4
c **25:16** Pr 25:27
d **25:21-22** Mt 5:44; Rm 12:20
e **25:24** Pr 15:17; 17:1; 21:9,19
f **25:25** Or *a weary person*
g **25:25** Pr 15:30
h **25:27** Pr 25:16
i **25:28** Pr 16:32; 29:11
j **26:1** Pr 19:10

13 To those who send him,
  a trustworthy messenger
is like the coolness of snow on a harvest day;
he refreshes the life of his masters. ᵃ

14 The man who boasts about a gift that does not
  exist
is like clouds and wind without rain.

15 A ruler can be persuaded through patience,
and a gentle tongue can break a bone. ᵇ

16 If you find honey, eat only what you need;
otherwise, you'll get sick from it and vomit. ᶜ

17 Seldom set foot in your neighbor's house;
otherwise, he'll get sick of you and hate you.

18 A man giving false testimony
  against his neighbor
is like a club, a sword, or a sharp arrow.

19 Trusting an unreliable person in a time
  of trouble
is like a rotten tooth or a faltering foot.

20 Singing songs to a troubled heart
is like taking off clothing on a cold day,
or like ⌊pouring⌋ vinegar on soda.

21 If your enemy is hungry, give him food to eat,
and if he is thirsty, give him water to drink;

22 for you will heap coals on his head,
and the LORD will reward you. ᵈ

23 The north wind produces rain,
and a backbiting tongue, angry looks.

24 Better to live on the corner of a roof
than in a house shared with a nagging wife. ᵉ

25 Good news from a distant land
is like cold water to a parched throat. ᶠ ᵍ

26 A righteous person who yields to the wicked
is like a muddied spring or a polluted well.

27 It is not good to eat too much honey, ʰ
or to seek glory after glory.

28 A man who does not control his temper ⁱ
is like a city whose wall is broken down.

PROVERBS 26

1 Like snow in summer and rain at harvest,
honor is inappropriate for a fool. ʲ

2 Like a flitting sparrow or a fluttering swallow,
an undeserved curse goes nowhere.

ᵃ 26:3 Pr 10:13; 19:29
ᵇ 26:5 Pr 26:12
ᶜ 26:6 Pr 10:26
ᵈ 26:8 A stone bound in a sling would not release and could harm the person using the sling. A modern equivalent is jamming a cork in a gun barrel.
ᵉ 26:9 Lit *thorn that goes up into*
ᶠ 26:12 Pr 3:7; 26:5
ᵍ 26:13 Pr 22:13
ʰ 26:15 Pr 12:27; 19:24
ⁱ 26:16 Pr 26:5,12; 28:11
ʲ 26:20-21 Pr 15:18; 16:28; 22:10
ᵏ 26:22 Lit *to the chambers of the belly*
ˡ 26:22 Pr 18:8
ᵐ 26:23 LXX; Hb reads *Burning*

3 A whip for the horse, a bridle for the donkey,
and a rod for the backs of fools. ᵃ

4 Don't answer a fool according to his foolishness,
or you'll be like him yourself.

5 Answer a fool according to his foolishness,
or he'll become wise in his own eyes. ᵇ

6 The one who sends a message by a fool's hand
cuts off his own feet and drinks violence. ᶜ

7 A proverb in the mouth of a fool
is like lame legs that hang limp.

8 Giving honor to a fool
is like binding a stone in a sling. ᵈ

9 A proverb in the mouth of a fool
is like a stick with thorns, brandished
by ᵉ the hand of a drunkard.

10 The one who hires a fool, or who hires those
passing by,
is like an archer who wounds everyone.

11 As a dog returns to its vomit,
so a fool repeats his foolishness.

12 Do you see a man who is wise in his own eyes?
There is more hope for a fool than for him. ᶠ

13 The slacker says, "There's a lion in the road—
a lion in the public square!" ᵍ

14 A door turns on its hinge,
and a slacker, on his bed.

15 The slacker buries his hand in the bowl;
he is too weary to bring it to his mouth. ʰ

16 In his own eyes, a slacker is wiser ⁱ
than seven men who can answer sensibly.

17 A passer-by who meddles in a quarrel
that's not his
is like one who grabs a dog by the ears.

18 Like a madman who throws flaming darts
and deadly arrows,

19 so is the man who deceives his neighbor
and says, "I was only joking!"

20 Without wood, fire goes out;
without a gossip, conflict dies down.

21 As charcoal for embers and wood for fire,
so is a quarrelsome man for kindling strife. ʲ

22 A gossip's words are like choice food
that goes down to one's innermost being. ᵏ ˡ

23 Smooth ᵐ lips with an evil heart
are like glaze on an earthen vessel.

24 A hateful person disguises himself
  with his speech
and harbors deceit within.

25 When he speaks graciously, don't believe him,
for there are seven abominations in his heart.

26 Though his hatred is concealed by deception,
his evil will be revealed in the assembly.

27 The one who digs a pit will fall into it,
and whoever rolls a stone—it will come back
  on him. [a]

28 A lying tongue hates those it crushes,
and a flattering mouth causes ruin.

Proverbs 27

1 Don't boast about tomorrow,
for you don't know what a day might bring.

2 Let another praise you, and not
  your own mouth—
a stranger, and not your own lips.

3 A stone is heavy and sand, a burden,
but aggravation from a fool outweighs them
  both.

4 Fury is cruel, and anger is a flood,
but who can withstand jealousy?

5 Better an open reprimand
than concealed love.

6 The wounds of a friend are trustworthy,
but the kisses of an enemy are excessive. [b] [c]

7 A person who is full tramples on a honeycomb,
but to a hungry person, any bitter thing is sweet.

8 A man wandering from his home
is like a bird wandering from its nest.

9 Oil and incense bring joy to the heart,
and the sweetness of a friend is better
  than self-counsel. [d]

10 Don't abandon your friend or your father's friend,
and don't go to your brother's house
  in your time of calamity;
better a neighbor nearby than a brother
  far away. [e]

11 Be wise, my son, and bring my heart joy,
so that I can answer anyone who taunts me. [f]

12 The sensible see danger and take cover;
the foolish keep going and are punished. [g]

[a] 26:27 Est 7:10; Jb 4:8; Dn 6:24; Mt 26:52
[b] 27:6 Others emend the text to read *deceitful.*
[c] 27:6 Pr 26:28; 28:23; 29:5
[d] 27:9 LXX reads *heart, but the soul is torn up by affliction*
[e] 27:10 Pr 17:17
[f] 27:11 Pr 10:1; 23:24-25; 29:3
[g] 27:12 Pr 22:3

a **27:13** A debtor's outer garment held as collateral; Dt 24:12-13; Am 2:8
b **27:13** Pr 6:1-5; 11:15; 20:16
c **27:15** Pr 19:13
d **27:17** Lit *and a man sharpens his friend's face*
e **27:20** Pr 30:15-16; Hab 2:5
f **27:21** Lit *The crucible for silver and the smelter for gold, and a man for a mouth of praise.*
g **27:21** Pr 16:2; 17:3
h **27:27** Pr 31:15
i **28:3** LXX reads *A wicked man*

13 Take his garment, [a] for he has put up security
for a stranger;
get collateral if it is for foreigners. [b]

14 If one blesses his neighbor with a loud voice
early in the morning,
it will be counted as a curse to him.

15 An endless dripping on a rainy day
and a nagging wife are alike. [c]

16 The one who controls her controls the wind
and grasps oil with his right hand.

17 Iron sharpens iron,
and one man sharpens another. [d]

18 Whoever tends a fig tree will eat its fruit,
and whoever looks after his master
will be honored.

19 As the water reflects the face,
so the heart reflects the person.

20 •Sheol and •Abaddon are never satisfied, [e]
and people's eyes are never satisfied.

21 Silver is ⌊tested⌋ in a crucible, gold in a smelter,
and a man, by the praise he receives. [f] [g]

22 Though you grind a fool in a mortar
with a pestle along with grain,
you will not separate his foolishness from him.

23 Know well the condition of your flock,
and pay attention to your herds,

24 for wealth is not forever;
not even a crown lasts for all time.

25 When hay is removed and new growth appears
and the grain from the hills is gathered in,

26 lambs will provide your clothing,
and goats, the price of a field;

27 there will be enough goat's milk for your food—
food for your household and nourishment
for your servants. [h]

PROVERBS 28

1 The wicked flee when no one is pursuing ⌊them⌋,
but the righteous are as bold as a lion.

2 When a land is in rebellion, it has many rulers,
but with a discerning
and knowledgeable person, it endures.

3 A destitute leader [i] who oppresses the poor
is like a driving rain that leaves no food.

4   Those who reject the law praise the wicked,
    but those who keep the law battle against them.

5   Evil men do not understand justice,
    but those who seek the LORD understand
        everything.[a]

6   Better a poor man who lives with integrity[b]
    than a rich man who distorts right and wrong.[c][d]

7   A discerning son keeps the law,
    but a companion of gluttons humiliates
        his father.[e]

8   Whoever increases his wealth
        through excessive interest
    collects it for one who is kind to the poor.[f]

9   Anyone who turns his ear away from hearing
        the law—
    even his prayer is detestable.[g]

10 The one who leads the upright into an evil way
    will fall into his own pit,[h]
    but the blameless will inherit what is good.

11 A rich man is wise in his own eyes,
    but a poor man who has discernment sees
        through him.

12 When the righteous triumph, there is great
        rejoicing,[i]
    but when the wicked come to power, people hide
        themselves.[j]

13 The one who conceals his sins will not prosper,
    but whoever confesses and renounces them
        will find mercy.[k]

14 Happy is the one who is always reverent,[l]
    but one who hardens his heart falls into trouble.

15 A wicked ruler over a helpless people
    is like a roaring lion or a charging bear.

16 A leader who lacks understanding is
        very oppressive,
    but one who hates unjust gain prolongs
        his life.[m]

17 A man burdened by blood-guilt[n]
    will be a fugitive until death.
    Let no one help him.

18 The one who lives with integrity will be helped,
    but one who distorts right and wrong[o] will
        suddenly fall.[p]

19 The one who works his land will have plenty
        of food,

NOTES

[a] **28:5** 1 Co 2:15
[b] **28:6** Pr 19:1; 20:7
[c] **28:6** Lit *who twists two ways*
[d] **28:6** Pr 16:8,19; 19:22; Is 5:20
[e] **28:7** Pr 17:25; 29:3; Dt 21:20
[f] **28:8** Pr 13:22; Ec 2:26; Ezk 18:13,17
[g] **28:9** Pr 15:8,29; 21:27
[h] **28:10** Pr 16:29; 26:27; Mt 18:6
[i] **28:12** Lit *glory*
[j] **28:12** Pr 28:28; 29:2
[k] **28:13** Pr 10:6,11; 26:26; Ps 32:3-5
[l] **28:14** 2 Ch 19:7
[m] **28:16** Pr 15:27; 1 Kg 12:1-19; Ps 15:5
[n] **28:17** Lit *the blood of a person*
[o] **28:18** Lit *who is twisted regarding two ways*
[p] **28:18** Pr 2:7; 10:9; 20:7

NOTES

a 28:19 Pr 1:31; 12:11,14; 14:14
b 28:20 Pr 19:2
c 28:21 Pr 24:23
d 28:22 Lit *A man with an evil eye*
e 28:22 Pr 13:11; 20:21; 21:5
f 28:23 Lit *is smooth*
g 28:23 Pr 26:28; 27:6; 29:5
h 28:25 Pr 3:5-6; Ps 37:3-5; Jr 17:7-8
i 28:26 Lit *his heart*
j 28:26 Pr 3:5-7
k 28:27 Lit *who shuts his eyes*
l 28:27 Pr 11:24; 22:16
m 28:28 Pr 28:12; 29:2
n 29:1 Pr 6:14-15
o 29:2 Pr 28:1; Ex 2:23; 1 Ch 29:92
p 29:3 Pr 15:20; 23:24-25; Lk 15:13
q 29:4 The Hb word usually refers to offerings in worship.
r 29:5 Lit *is smooth on*
s 29:5 Pr 26:28; 27:6; 28:23
t 29:6 Pr 12:13; 18:7

but whoever chases fantasies will have his fill of poverty. [a]

20 A faithful man will have many blessings,
but one in a hurry to get rich will not go unpunished. [b]

21 It is not good to show partiality [c]—
yet a man may sin for a piece of bread.

22 A greedy man [d] is in a hurry for wealth;
he doesn't know that poverty will come to him. [e]

23 One who rebukes a person will later find more favor
than one who flatters [f] with his tongue. [g]

24 The one who robs his father or mother and says, "That's no sin,"
is a companion to a man who destroys.

25 A greedy person provokes conflict,
but whoever trusts in the LORD will prosper. [h]

26 The one who trusts in himself [i] is a fool,
but one who walks in wisdom will be safe. [j]

27 The one who gives to the poor will not be in need,
but one who turns his eyes away [k] will receive many curses. [l]

28 When the wicked come to power, people hide,
but when they are destroyed, the righteous flourish. [m]

PROVERBS 29

1 One who becomes stiff-necked after many reprimands
will be broken suddenly—and without a remedy. [n]

2 When the righteous flourish, the people rejoice,
but when the wicked rule, people groan. [o]

3 A man who loves wisdom brings joy to his father,
but one who consorts with prostitutes destroys his wealth. [p]

4 By justice a king brings stability to a land,
but a man ⌊who demands⌋ "contributions" [q] demolishes it.

5 A man who flatters [r] his neighbor
spreads a net for his feet. [s]

6 An evil man is caught by sin, [t]
but the righteous one sings and rejoices.

7 The righteous person knows the rights[a]
    of the poor,
  but the wicked one does not understand
    these concerns.

8 Mockers inflame a city,
  but the wise turn away anger.[b]

9 If a wise man goes to court with a fool,
  there will be ranting and raving
    but no resolution.[c]

10 Bloodthirsty men hate an honest person,
  but the upright care about him.[d]

11 A fool gives full vent to his anger,[e]
  but a wise man holds it in check.[f]

12 If a ruler listens to lies,
  all his servants will be wicked.

13 The poor and the oppressor have this
    in common:[g]
  the LORD gives light to the eyes of both.[h]

14 A king who judges the poor with fairness—
  his throne will be established forever.

15 A rod of correction imparts wisdom,
  but a youth left to himself[i] is a disgrace
    to his mother.[j]

16 When the wicked increase, rebellion increases,
  but the righteous will see their downfall.[k]

17 Discipline your son, and he will give you
    comfort;
  he will also give you delight.

18 Without revelation[l] people run wild,
  but one who keeps the law will be happy.

19 A servant cannot be disciplined by words;
  though he understands, he doesn't respond.

20 Do you see a man who speaks too soon?
  There is more hope for a fool than for him.[m]

21 A slave pampered from his youth
  will become arrogant[n] later on.

22 An angry man stirs up conflict,
  and a hot-tempered man[o] increases rebellion.[p]

23 A person's pride will humble him,
  but a humble spirit will gain honor.[q]

24 To be a thief's partner is to hate oneself;
  he hears the curse but will not testify.[r]

25 The fear of man is a snare,
  but the one who trusts in the LORD
    is protected.[s] [t]

NOTES

[a] **29:7** Lit *justice*
[b] **29:8** Pr 26:21; 29:22
[c] **29:9** Lit *rest*
[d] **29:10** Or *person, and seek the life of the upright*
[e] **29:11** Lit *spirit*
[f] **29:11** Pr 16:32; 25:28
[g] **29:13** Lit *oppressor meet*
[h] **29:13** Pr 22:2
[i] **29:15** Lit *youth sent away*; Jb 39:5; Is 16:2
[j] **29:15** Pr 13:18; 17:25; 22:15
[k] **29:16** Pr 28:28; 29:2
[l] **29:18** Lit *vision*
[m] **29:20** Pr 19:2
[n] **29:21** Hb obscure
[o] **29:22** Lit *a master of rage*
[p] **29:22** Pr 15:18; 26:21; 28:25
[q] **29:23** Pr 11:2; 15:33; 22:4
[r] **29:24** When a call for witnesses was made public, anyone with information who did not submit his testimony was under a curse; Lv 5:1.
[s] **29:25** Lit *raised high*
[t] **29:25** Pr 14:27; 18:10

WORD STUDY

Hebrew word:
lason [lah TSOHN]

HCSB translation:
mocking, scoffing

Focus passage:
Proverbs 29:8

Lason is closely related to the verb *liys* (*to scoff, mock*) and its participle *les* (*scoffer*). *Liys* refers to the act of making slanderous accusations (*scoffing* or *mocking*) that reveal an arrogant attitude toward both human and divine law. The proud *scoff* at the righteous (Ps 119:51), refuse to make restitution for sin (Pr 14:9), and disdain legal justice (Pr 19:28). The *scoffer* (*les*) mocks justice by lying in court (Is 29:20). He does not accept correction (Pr 9:7), lacks wisdom (Pr 14:6), is argumentative (Pr 22:10), and is despised (Pr 24:9). God mocks the *mocker* (Pr 3:34).

a **29:26** Pr 16:15; 19:6
b **29:27** Pr 13:19
c **30:1** Or *The burden*, or *Jakeh from Massa*; Pr 31:1
d **30:1** Hb uncertain. Sometimes emended to *oration: I am weary, God, I am weary, God, and I am exhausted*, or *oration: I am not God, I am not God, that I should prevail.* LXX reads *My son, fear my words and when you have received them repent. The man says these things to the believers in God, and I pause.*
e **30:2** Lit *I am more stupid than a man*
f **30:3** Pr 9:10
g **30:4** Jn 3:13; Eph 4:9-10
h **30:4** Jb 26:8; 38:9
i **30:4** Jb 38:4-5; Ps 93:1; 119:90
j **30:4** Mt 11:27; Rv 19:12-13
k **30:5** Lit *refined*, like metal
l **30:5** Ps 12:6; 18:30
m **30:6** Dt 4:2; 12:32; Rv 22:18
n **30:8** Pr 31:15; Mt 6:11
o **30:9** Dt 6:10-12; 8:11-14
p **30:9** Lit *grabbing*
q **30:13** Lit *and its eyelids lifted up*

26 Many seek a ruler's favor,[a]
but a man receives justice from the LORD.

27 An unjust man is detestable to the righteous,
and one whose way is upright is detestable
to the wicked.[b]

PROVERBS 30
THE WORDS OF AGUR

1 The words of Agur son of Jakeh. The oracle.[c]
The man's oration to Ithiel, to Ithiel and Ucal:[d]

2 I am the least intelligent of men,[e]
and I lack man's ability to understand.

3 I have not gained wisdom,
and I have no knowledge of the Holy One.[f]

4 Who has gone up to heaven and come down?[g]
Who has gathered the wind in His hands?
Who has bound up the waters in a cloak?[h]
Who has established all the ends of the earth?[i]
What is His name, and what is the name
of His Son—
if you know?[j]

5 Every word of God is pure;[k] [l]
He is a shield to those who take refuge in Him.

6 Don't add to His words,[m]
or He will rebuke you, and you will be proved
a liar.

7 Two things I ask of You;
don't deny them to me before I die:

8 Keep falsehood and deceitful words far from me.
Give me neither poverty nor wealth;
feed me with the food I need.[n]

9 Otherwise, I might have too much
and deny You, saying, "Who is the LORD?"[o]
or I might have nothing and steal,
profaning[p] the name of my God.

10 Don't slander a servant to his master,
or he will curse you, and you will become guilty.

11 There is a generation that curses its father
and does not bless its mother.

12 There is a generation that is pure in its own eyes,
yet is not washed from its filth.

13 There is a generation—how haughty its eyes
and pretentious its looks.[q]

14 There is a generation whose teeth are swords,
whose fangs are knives,
devouring the oppressed from the land
and the needy from among mankind.

15 The leech has two daughters: Give, Give.
Three things are never satisfied;
four never say, "Enough!":

16 *Sheol;[a] a barren womb;
earth, which is never satisfied with water;
and fire, which never says, "Enough!"

17 As for the eye that ridicules a father
and despises obedience to a mother,
may ravens of the valley pluck it out
and young vultures eat it.

18 Three things are beyond me;
four I can't understand:

19 the way of an eagle in the sky,
the way of a snake on a rock,
the way of a ship at sea,
and the way of a man with a young woman.

20 This is the way of an adulteress:
she eats and wipes her mouth
and says, "I've done nothing wrong."

21 The earth trembles under three things;
it cannot bear up under four:

22 a servant when he becomes king,
a fool when he is stuffed with food,

23 an unloved woman when she marries,
and a serving girl when she ousts her lady.[b]

24 Four things on earth are small,
yet they are extremely wise:

25 the ants are not a strong people,
yet they store up their food in the summer;[c]

26 hyraxes are not a mighty people,
yet they make their homes in the cliffs;

27 locusts have no king,
yet all of them march in ranks;

28 a lizard[d] can be caught in your hands,
yet it lives in kings' palaces.

29 Three things are stately in their stride,
even four are stately in their walk:

30 a lion, which is mightiest among beasts
and doesn't retreat before anything,

31 a strutting rooster,[e] a goat,
and a king at the head of his army.[f]

a 30:16 Pr 27:20; Hab 2:5
b 30:22-23 Pr 19:10
c 30:25 Pr 6:6-8
d 30:28 Or *spider*
e 30:31 Or *a greyhound*
f 30:31 LXX reads *king haranguing his people*

NOTES

a 31:1 Or *of Lemuel, king of Massa*
b 31:5 Lit *he*
c 31:5 Lit *sons of affliction*
d 31:5 Ps 72:1-2; Is 28:7
e 31:8 Lit *Open your mouth*
f 31:8 Lit *who are mute*
g 31:8 Lit *all the sons of passing away*
h 31:9 Lit *Open your mouth*
i 31:9 Lit *and justice for*
j 31:10 Or *a wife of quality,* or *a wife of good character*
k 31:10 Vv. 10-31 form an •acrostic in Hb.
l 31:10 Pr 12:4; 18:22
m 31:13 Plant from which linen is made

32 If you have been foolish by exalting yourself,
or if you've been scheming, put your hand
over your mouth.

33 For the churning of milk produces butter,
and twisting a nose draws blood,
and stirring up anger produces strife.

PROVERBS 31

THE WORDS OF LEMUEL

1 The words of King Lemuel,
an oracle[a] that his mother taught him:

2 What ⌊should I say⌋, my son?
What, O son of my womb?
What, O son of my vows?

3 Don't spend your energy on women
or your efforts on those who destroy kings.

4 It is not for kings, Lemuel,
it is not for kings to drink wine
or for rulers ⌊to desire⌋ beer.

5 Otherwise, they[b] will drink, forget what is decreed,
and pervert justice for all the oppressed.[c] [d]

6 Give beer to one who is dying,
and wine to one whose life is bitter.

7 Let him drink so that he can forget his poverty
and remember his trouble no more.

8 Speak up[e] for those who have no voice,[f]
for the justice of all who are dispossessed.[g]

9 Speak up,[h] judge righteously,
and defend the cause of[i] the oppressed
and needy.

IN PRAISE OF A CAPABLE WIFE

10 Who can find a capable wife?[j]
She is far more precious than jewels.[k] [l]

11 The heart of her husband trusts in her,
and he will not lack anything good.

12 She rewards him with good, not evil,
all the days of her life.

13 She selects wool and flax[m]
and works with willing hands.

14 She is like the merchant ships,
bringing her food from far away.

15 She rises while it is still night
and provides food for her household
and portions[a] for her servants.[b]

16 She evaluates a field and buys it;
she plants a vineyard with her earnings.[c]

17 She draws on her strength[d]
and reveals that her arms are strong.[e]

18 She sees that her profits are good,
and her lamp never goes out at night.

19 She extends her hands to the spinning staff,
and her hands hold the spindle.[f]

20 Her hands reach[g] out to the poor,
and she extends her hands to the needy.

21 She is not afraid for her household
    when it snows,
for all in her household are doubly clothed.[h]

22 She makes her own bed coverings;
her clothing is fine linen and purple.

23 Her husband is known at the city •gates,
where he sits among the elders of the land.[i]

24 She makes and sells linen garments;
she delivers belts[j] to the merchants.

25 Strength and honor are her clothing,[k]
and she can laugh at the time to come.[l]

26 She opens her mouth with wisdom,
and loving instruction[m] is on her tongue.

27 She watches over the activities
    of her household[n]
and is never idle.[o]

28 Her sons rise up and call her blessed.
Her husband also praises her:

29 "Many women[p] are capable,
but you surpass them all!"[q]

30 Charm is deceptive and beauty is fleeting,
but a woman who •fears the LORD
    will be praised.

31 Give her the reward of her labor,[r]
and let her works praise her at the city •gates.

NOTES

[a] **31:15** Or *tasks*
[b] **31:15** Pr 27:27; 31:27
[c] **31:16** Or *vineyard by her own labors*
[d] **31:17** Lit *She wraps strength around her like a belt*
[e] **31:17** Pr 31:25
[f] **31:19** Pr 31:13
[g] **31:20** Lit *Her hand reaches*
[h] **31:21** LXX, Vg; Hb reads *are dressed in scarlet*
[i] **31:23** Pr 24:7; 31:31
[j] **31:24** Or *sashes*
[k] **31:25** Pr 31:17
[l] **31:25** Pr 31:21
[m] **31:26** Or *and the teaching of kindness*
[n] **31:27** Pr 31:15
[o] **31:27** Lit *and does not eat the bread of idleness*
[p] **31:29** Lit *daughters*
[q] **31:29** Pr 12:4; 31:10
[r] **31:31** Lit *the fruit of her hands*

OT HCSB Bullet Notes™ for Psalms and Proverbs

Among the unique features of the *Holman Christian Standard Bible*® are the HCSB *Bullet Notes*™. These notes explain OT words or terms that are marked with a bullet in the biblical text (for example: •fear of the Lord). Please note that some occurrences of a particular word may be marked with a bullet in the biblical text, while other occurrences of the same word are not marked. For example, if a bullet word occurs two or more times within the same verse, then only its first use has a bullet. Also, words like "everyone", "men", or "people" are marked with bullets only at occurrences that fit the definitions given below.

Abaddon	Either the grave or realm of the dead
acrostic	A device in Hb poetry in which each verse begins with a successive letter of the Hb alphabet
burnt offering(s)	Or *holocaust*, an offering completely burned to ashes; used in connection with worship, seeking God's favor, expiating sin, or averting judgment.
everyone	Lit *sons of man*, or *sons of Adam*
fear(s) God/the LORD	(see "fear of the LORD")
fear of the LORD	No single Eng word conveys every aspect of the word *fear* in this phrase. The meaning includes worshipful submission, reverential awe, and obedient respect to the covenant-keeping God of Israel.
gate(s)	The center for community discussions, political meetings, and trying of court cases
Gittith	Perhaps a musical term, an instrument or tune from Gath, or a song for the grape harvest
Hallelujah!	Lit *Praise Yah!* (a shortened form of *Yahweh*), or *Praise the Lord!*
Higgaion	Perhaps a musical notation
horn	Symbol of power based on the strength of animal horns
Hosts	The military forces consisting of God's angels; sometimes the sun, moon, and stars are included.
human race	Lit *sons of man*, or *sons of Adam*
mankind	Lit *sons of man*, or *sons of Adam*

Maskil	From a Hb word meaning *to be prudent* or *to have insight*; possibly a contemplative, instructive, or wisdom psalm
men	Lit *sons of man*, or *sons of Adam*
Miktam	Perhaps a musical term
Most High	Hb *Elyon*; often used with other names of God, such as Hb *El* (*God*) or Hb *Yahweh* (*Lord*); used to refer to God as the supreme being
people	Lit *sons of man*, or *sons of Adam*
Pit	Either the grave or the realm of the dead
Red Sea	Lit *Sea of Reeds*
sackcloth	Garment made of poor quality material and worn as a sign of grief and mourning
Selah	A Hb word whose meaning is uncertain; various interpretations include: (1) a musical notation, (2) a pause for silence, (3) a signal for worshipers to fall prostrate on the ground, (4) a term for the worshipers to call out, (5) a word meaning "forever."
Sheminith	Hb musical term meaning *instruments* or *on the instrument of eight strings*
Sheol	Either the grave or the realm of the dead
sin offering	In the OT the *sin* (or *purification*) offering is the most important sacrifice for cleansing from impurities. It provided purification from sin and certain forms of ceremonial uncleanness.
song of ascents	Probably the songs pilgrims sang as they traveled the roads going up to worship in Jerusalem; Pss 120–134
testimony	A reference to either the Mosaic law in general or to a specific section of the law, the Ten Commandments, that was written on stone tablets and placed in the ark of the covenant (also called the ark of the testimony)
wormwood	A small shrub used as a medicinal herb, noted for its bitter taste
Yahweh	Or *The Lord*; the personal name of God in Hb